THE GROWTH OF INTERPERSONAL UNDERSTANDING

Developmental and Clinical Analyses

DEVELOPMENTAL PSYCHOLOGY SERIES

SERIES EDITOR

Harry Beilin

Developmental Psychology Program
City University of New York Graduate School
New York, New York

LYNN S. LIBEN. *Deaf Children: Developmental Perspectives*

JONAS LANGER. *The Origins of Logic: Six to Twelve Months*

GILBERTE PIERAUT-LE BONNIEC. *The Development of Modal Reasoning:
Genesis of Necessity and Possibility Notions*

TIFFANY MARTINI FIELD, SUSAN GOLDBERG, DANIEL STERN, and
ANITA MILLER SOSTEK. (Editors). *High-Risk Infants and Children:
Adult and Peer Interactions*

BARRY GHOLSON. *The Cognitive-Developmental Basis of Human Learning:
Studies in Hypothesis Testing*

ROBERT L. SELMAN. *The Growth of Interpersonal Understanding:
Developmental and Clinical Analyses*

In Preparation

HARBEN BOUTOURLINE YOUNG and LUCY RAU FERGUSON.
Puberty to Manhood in Italy and America

THE GROWTH OF INTERPERSONAL UNDERSTANDING

Developmental and Clinical Analyses

Robert L. Selman

Graduate School of Education
Harvard University
Cambridge, Massachusetts
and
Judge Baker Guidance Center
Boston, Massachusetts

ACADEMIC PRESS 1980
A Subsidiary of Harcourt Brace Jovanovich, Publishers
New York   London   Toronto   Sydney   San Francisco

#6424331

BF
723
.S6
S44
1980

ACADEMIC PRESS, INC.
111 Fifth Avenue, New York, New York 10003

United Kingdom Edition published by
ACADEMIC PRESS, INC. (LONDON) LTD.
24/28 Oval Road, London NW1 7DX

Library of Congress Cataloging in Publication Data

Selman, Robert L
    The growth of interpersonal understanding.

    Includes index.
    1. Social perception in children.   2. Interper-
sonal relations.   I. Title.
BF723.S6S44   155.4'13   79-6781
ISBN 0-12-636450-8

PRINTED IN THE UNITED STATES OF AMERICA

80 81 82 83   9 8 7 6 5 4 3 2 1

To My Parents

Contents

3

An Analysis of "Pure" Perspective Taking:
Games and the Delights of Deception   49

II

INTERPERSONAL UNDERSTANDING—
PHASE 1: DESCRIPTIVE MODEL BUILDING

4

Constructing a Model of Interpersonal Understanding   71

5

Four Strands from the Fabric:
A Developmental Description of Four Issues   93

6

Four Domains, Five Stages:
A Summary Portrait of Interpersonal Understanding   131

III
INTERPERSONAL UNDERSTANDING—
PHASE 2: CONSTRUCT VALIDATION

7
A Developmental Analysis of Interpersonal Understanding: The Measures, Their Reliability, and the Design

8
The Development of Interpersonal Understanding: Five Analyses of Validity

IV
INTERPERSONAL UNDERSTANDING—
PHASE 3: APPLICATION

9
A Case Study of Social-Cognitive Development in a Naturalistic Setting
Daniel S. Jaquette

Preface

Recent years have witnessed a dramatic increase in the quality and quantity of research in cognitive development. There is no denying the value, excitement, and gratification of this legitimate and growing fund of basic knowledge generated on behalf of developmental epistemology. However, criticisms of such research are valid in one regard at least. Much developmental–descriptive research is limited—by design, theoretical bias, and circumstance—to hypothetical descriptive results. Particularly in the area of social cognition, the real world beyond the controlled research setting is crying for ways to apply and use basic descriptive information about normal development; conversely, the theoretical and empirical validity of information in the theoretical–academic realm can only be bolstered by the results of practical application. It is on this premise that this book is based. The bulk of the material in this book is basic, theoretically oriented, descriptive research on some fundamental aspects of the development of social cognition; but not stopping there, the book also reports a number of formal and informal exploratory approaches to getting research in social development out of the laboratory and into the lives of children.

The work reported in this book was carried out by the Harvard–Judge Baker Social Reasoning Project, of which the author is director. It was founded in 1973 with the support of a grant from the Spencer Foundation. Based upon the theory that the development of *interpersonal understanding* is founded in part upon stages in the growing understanding of the *coordination of the psychological points of view of self and other* (social perspective taking), this project has initiated a number of developmental and clinical analyses to test the validity of viewing social development in this way. Because the basic and applied work of the project underwent a complex evolution over several years, it is here analyzed in detail. This book emphasizes findings and ideas in four major areas: (*a*) developing conceptions of intrapsychic, friendship, peer-group, and parent–child relationships as a function of developing levels in the child's coordination of social perspectives; (*b*) the interpersonal understanding of both clinical and normal populations of children. in both the calm of interviews and the confusion of naturalistic conditions; (*c*) the social-situational and personality factors that influence developmental maturity of interpersonal understanding and stability or oscillation in use of interpersonal knowledge in real-life situations; and (*d*) a model for training developmental psychologists and other social scientists to undertake research in a clinical context and to acquire the skills necessary for integrating clinical and developmental approaches to healthy as well as psychopathological behavior.

The major themes of the book are introduced in the first chapter, which is followed by four parts. Part I (Chapters 2 and 3) reviews the theoretical and empirical antecedents of a developmental model of interpersonal understanding. Part II (Chapters 4, 5, and 6) describes the first phase of the research: individual work with a large number of subjects over a wide age-range, which yielded a basic descriptive map or picture of stages of development in four major areas of interpersonal conception. Part III (Chapters 7 and 8) presents the *formal* reliability and validity analyses of these stages, which constituted the second major research phase. Part IV (Chapters 9 and 10) reports the still ongoing third research phase: functional explorations of practical application of this basic descriptive information. Many of these explorations are "clinical" in nature, dealing with children whose interpersonal difficulties are so severe as to require special schooling and psychological treatment. This set of clinical analyses looks at how children actually use their interpersonal understanding under real-life conditions and the factors which either impede or promote the usage of an optimal level of interpersonal reasoning. Chapter 11 concludes the book, drawing the major themes together and speaking to future directions for study.

In essence, this book pulls together a body of highly theoretical, detailed work and then goes on to report integration of this developmental research with clinical practicalities. Its tone and focus range from the scholarly to the practical. It is designed for the philosopher, academician, or scholar of theories of development in social cognition and relation to behavior; for researchers in the behavioral and social sciences who wish to consider social and cognitive developmental factors in their work; for advanced students in developmental psychology; and for practitioners, both educators and clinicians, who deal with children on a daily basis. The unifying conviction of this book is that neither formal nor functional analyses of development and behavior stand as well alone as they do together, and its unifying direction is an attempt to indicate ways in which they can do so.

Acknowledgments

A project such as ours requires both intellectual and institutional support. I would like to acknowledge intellectual debts to Freda Rebelsky, who first demonstrated to me the excitement of research in child development, and to Lawrence Kohlberg, who introduced me, years ago, to the general tenets of a theoretical framework that has made work in developmental psychology a personally exciting and profound adventure. No less important, I am indebted to Julius B. Richmond, formerly director of the Judge Baker Guidance Center and professor of child psychiatry and human development, Harvard Medical School, for instilling in me the belief that research in developmental psychology can and should be an integral and enhancing part of any educational or clinical service to children, and for facilitating the opportunity for me to put that belief into practice, to refine theory and research with practical observations. Continued institutional support has come from Donald J. Scherl who has been acting director of the Judge Baker Guidance Center for the last several years. H. Thomas James, director of the Spencer Foundation, provided our project with its initial financial support and has patiently encouraged our work. Support from the National Institute of Mental Health through a Career Development Award, K02-MH00157-02 has facilitated this book's completion.

Support from without must be balanced by support from within. Over the years the educational and counseling staff of the Manville School of the Judge Baker Center and its past and present principals, Lee Saltzberg and David Gilmore, have provided continuous cooperation, support, and suggestions to the project, without which our work could neither have proceeded, nor proceeded so constructively. In the Introduction I present in detail the many and invaluable contributions of the research staff of our project over the last decade (including that of Daniel Jaquette, who authored Chapter 9 of this book, and Gregory Jurkovic, who coauthored one section of Chapter 10). I hope all members of the staff, former and present, are already well aware of my gratitude and admiration for their work. In addition, it is essential to call attention to the assistance we have all had from Nancy Jacobs, my project coordinator of the last 6 years, who has done the work of three people, keeping our project physically organized and psychologically healthy. One sentence cannot begin to express my gratitude to her. Terry Kovich, who has typed the several drafts of this manuscript, has done so with great intelligence, thoughtfulness, and care. Many other people have contributed their time and energy in varying degrees, and I thank them as well.

The author wishes to thank the University of Nebraska Press for granting permission to reprint several sections and figures from the chapter "Stability and Oscillation in Interpersonal Awareness" in the *Twenty-fifth Nebraska Symposium on Motivation,* University of Nebraska Press, Lincoln, Nebraska, 1978, C. Blake Keasey, Volume Editor.

The initial section of Chapter 4 will appear in somewhat modified form in a book on social development edited by David McClelland and to be published by Irvington Publishers, New York, New York.

Part of Chapter 4 is also based on a presentation to a Society for Research in Child Development workshop on the development of friendship, initiated by Steven Asher and John Gottman at the University of Illinois, Champaign–Urbana, and will appear in slightly different form as "The Child as a Friendship Philosopher" in *The Development of Friendship,* Cambridge University Press, New York, New York, S. Asher and J. Gottman, Editors.

Part of Chapter 5 is based on a presentation to the Bank Street–Wheelock Conference on cognitive and affective development, and will appear in a book edited by Evelyn Weber and Edith Shapiro. The publisher of that volume is Lawrence Erlbaum Associates, Hillsdale, New Jersey.

Part of Chapter 10 is a revised and modified version of a paper by Gregory Jurkovic and Robert Selman, "A Cognitive-Developmental Analysis of Intrapsychic Understanding: Implications for the Conceptualization and Treatment of Emotional Disturbance in Children." This chapter appears in a book edited by Robert Selman and Regina Yando and titled *New Directions in Clinical-Developmental Psychology.* The publisher is Jossey Bass, San Francisco, California, 1980.

Anne P. Selman—my editor, severest critic, and biggest booster—has been a true intellectual colleague. To the extent that this book successfully communicates ideas or excites others to do research along the lines articulated, she deserves much credit. Lastly, I wish to acknowledge my gratitude to my sons, Matthew and Jesse, ages 8 and 6, for being so patient with their father. They have made the research in this book real and important to me. I hope some day they will read it with interest.

THE GROWTH OF INTERPERSONAL UNDERSTANDING

Developmental and Clinical Analyses

1

Introduction

This book is a report of several years of theoretical, empirical, and practical work done by the Harvard—Judge Baker Social Reasoning Project.[1] Although conceived years earlier, the project was officially born in the fall of 1973, when, with the support of a 4-year grant from the Spencer Foundation of Chicago, we[2] began a series of interrelated studies designed to explore developmental characteristics of certain social conceptions. The studies and the questions they are designed to answer are an outgrowth of both clinical and theoretical interest in the way the developing child orders and organizes social relations and conceptions.

[1] The Harvard—Judge Baker Social Reasoning Project has been supported by grants from the Spencer Foundation of Chicago, the Foundation for Child Development, and the National Institute of Mental Health. The writing of this book has been supported by a Career Development Award (K02–MH00157–02) to the author from the National Institute of Mental Health.

[2] Throughout this book, the first-person plural is used collectively to refer to the work of a number of Harvard—Judge Baker Social Reasoning Project members over the last 10 years. The author, director of the project, has participated in and overseen all aspects of the research. Especially significant contributions to the work reported here have been made by Steven Brion-Meisels, Elizabeth Bruss-Saunders, Diane Byrne, Ellen Ward Cooney, David Forbes, Carmel Gurucharri, Daniel Jaquette, Gregory Jurkovic, Debra Lavin, and Carolyn Stone. Among their many contributions, I would like to emphasize the

We are extremely fortunate to have as one institutional base for our research the Judge Baker Guidance Center, a child guidance clinic located in Boston and affiliated with the Harvard Medical School. Judge Baker is the third oldest child guidance center in the country, and has provided treatment to troubled children and their families for over 60 years. Operated by the Judge Baker Center is the Manville School,[3] a day school for approximately 60 boys and girls aged 7-15 who have a range of emotional and/or learning difficulties. Access to this school provides us with an unusually complete opportunity to look directly at the nature of social, emotional, and intellectual development. First, it provides our research staff with a clinical sample of preadolescent and adolescent children with whom to try out social-cognitive measures and procedures, and whose performance is subsequently compared with that of public school children of the same age, mental age, and demographic background. Second, this access provides the opportunity for members of our research project to observe a child 6 hours a day, to see how he or she negotiates with peers and older and younger children, and to observe interactions with significant adults such as teachers, counselors, and therapists—in short, the opportunity to gain a full, rich picture of a child's functioning. Third, information about parent-child relationships is available to us, through clinical case conferences and close collaboration with family workers as well as through the developmental history of

---

following in particular: Byrne's collaboration on the delineation of the structural or perspective-taking component of interpersonal understanding, reported in Chapter 2; Brion-Meisels' collaboration on the construction of a two-person strategy game, reported in Chapter 3, and on development of clinical-educational applications, reflected in several of the cases in Chapter 10; Bruss-Saunders' work on developmental descriptions of concepts of parent-child relations, reported in Chapters 4, 5, and 6; Jaquette's collaboration on devising the game described in Chapter 3, on the developmental description of concepts of peer-group relations, reported in Chapters 4, 5, and 6, on the reliability and validity analyses, reported in Chapters 7 and 8, and his work on assessment of naturalistic reasoning, reported in Chapter 9; Cooney's collaboration on developmental descriptions of concepts of persons, reported in Chapters 4, 5, and 6, on the reliability and validity analyses, reported in Chapters 7 and 8, and on exploring the nature of stage transition, as reflected in Chapter 11; Lavin's collaboration in Chapter 3, on the reliability and validity analyses, reported in Chapters 7 and 8, and on assessment of naturalistic reasoning and development of clinical-educational applications, reflected in several of the cases in Chapter 10; Jurkovic's collaboration on looking at interpersonal understanding in psychotherapy, reported in Chapter 10; Stone's collaboration on exploring social influence strategies, reflected in several of the cases in Chapter 10; Forbes' collaboration on certain validity analyses reported in Chapter 8; and Gurucharri's collaboration on analysis of long-term developmental patterns, reported in Chapter 8 and reflected in several of the cases in Chapter 10.

[3] From 1975 until 1978, I was the director of the Manville School, and although now temporarily on leave from that position, I maintain close research, clinical, and educational ties to the school and its functioning, and the Social Reasoning Project continues its activities there.

the child in thorough and extensive clinic records. All are particularly helpful sources of data and information, particularly when one aim of our research project is to assess the validity of measures purporting relevance to children's social competence and functioning.

Our other institutional affiliation provides a different but equally important kind of input and support for our project. The Harvard Graduate School of Education's Laboratory of Human Development not only provides knowledgeable and stimulating colleagues in areas such as developmental psychology, social science, statistics, and anthropology, but a place for reflection, removed from the immediacy, urgency, and frequent crises of a school for 60 very troubled children and adolescents. Furthermore, the doctoral program in Human Development has been a source of dedicated students interested in the integration of skills in social developmental research and clinical–psychoeducational practice who come to work on this project. Their contributions are clearly represented in this report and are crucial to the project.

This book reports project research findings from the last 6 years and describes the framework within which these data have been sought, collected, and interpreted. To explain the questions we are posing and the methods we are using to study the development of social conceptions, it is helpful to go back to experiences, questions, and concerns of a type familiar to most individuals who have had the opportunity to work closely with children in either clinical or educational contexts (cf. Cowan, 1978). For example, a young child of 3 or 4 expresses to a therapist, teacher, or parent the belief that a grandfather who has recently died will be returning for a visit. Is this child necessarily fantasizing or defensively attempting to ward off or deny painful feelings of sadness, abandonment, or guilt associated with the loss of a beloved companion? Or does the response more simply exemplify the 3- or 4-year-old child's naturally immature conceptualization, his or her lack of understanding of the nature of death as an irreversible biological process? Similarly, a 5- or 6-year-old claims that Jennifer is her best friend because Jennifer has the nicest toys. Is this necessarily an indication of a potentially narcissistic or selfish personality? Or may it simply represent the 5-year-old's natural concept of the meaning of friendship? When a 9- or 10-year-old begins to establish a private and secret set of codes with a close peer, is this the manifestation of cliqueishness or simply an example of how a child this age puts into practice his or her newly discovered understandings of how to establish a close and intimate chumship? How to distinguish between children's beliefs that are pathological, selfish, or badly motivated, and those that are simply childish has always been a troublesome problem for thoughtful practitioners who deal with the mental life of children and its relationship to their functioning.

The research in this book is designed to provide one model for, as well as to add empirical data to, the growing body of knowledge about the natural and normal developmental changes in social understanding through which children progress as they grow up. In addition to providing data on normative development, the research I report is also designed in part to examine any differences in developmental patterns that may be found in comparing the social reasoning of children whose social relations are viewed as "age-typical" with that of children such as those who attend the Manville School, whose social relationships and interaction strategies are seen as immature or inappropriate.

Beyond the presentation of data on specific aspects of social–cognitive development, this book deals with several other secondary themes. First, provided on occasion, are some reflections on the process of the research project itself. In a project such as ours, one that is pursued over a number of years and which involves longitudinal follow-up, ideas about both models and methods change at many points: between the times data are collected, as they are analyzed, and even as they are reported. Throughout the life of a project, critical decisions are being made on the basis of practical concerns, what others in the field are finding, saying, or doing, or data gathered in earlier phases. Sometimes, these decisions cut off one approach and lead to another. This book is written with an eye to the explicit presentation of those historical choice points in our own research and the way our decisions have influenced the shape of the project now being reported. In fact, each part (of several chapters) represents a phase in the research process, and at the end of each, descriptions of the choices that presented themselves for the next phase are presented.

Another secondary theme in this book is a result of our project's dual setting, one setting being "practical," a child psychiatric clinic. Interacting with both clinical and academic colleagues rather than with academic colleagues alone tends to introduce subtly different emphases into the design of a research project. One obvious difference in focus is the clinically inspired interest in procedures with relatively immediate practical ramifications. Most assessment or data analysis procedures designed for basic research in child development are not particularly useful as tools for the clinical assessment and diagnosis of individual children. They are usually methods suited to testing theoretical relationships and not strictly speaking clinical or diagnostic tests of individuals. Seldom do they have the breadth to paint a useful or accurate picture of a child. When we began our project, although wary of the dangers involved, we consciously attempted to devise a set of interpersonal understanding interview procedures (not tests) that might eventually bridge in part the gap between the scientific validity of a research tool and clinical worth of a psychological test. Hopefully we could do this without falling between two chairs, that is, not meeting the criteria of either field.

Admittedly, this is an ambitious, even overwhelming goal. Each field has its own distinctive values and ground rules which in certain ways dramatically differ from one another (Santostefano, 1979). Still, the effort has been edifying. The attitude that I hope to convey in this volume is that a psychological measure or method, whether used as a research procedure or a clinical instrument, is only a tool in the hand of its user. Instruments or assessment procedures in psychology are not intrinsically valid or invalid, good or bad. They are used either wisely or foolishly, with reasonable expectations or unrealistically. They are more or less useful, depending on the perspective and needs of the user.

One should always ask why one is using a given procedure. For instance, in the case of our own research, are our interview procedures designed to provide descriptive material on the developmental characteristics of interpersonal conceptions? Are they designed to test theoretical assumptions of a particular developmental model? Is an interview a valid test of a particular *individual's* level of interpersonal understanding? Is it a test of how he or she may reason or use his or her understanding under real-life conditions? Is an assessment of an individual's stage a meaningful way to provide a general assessment of his or her social competence?

This book examines each of the above questions using our particular developmental model of the growth of interpersonal understanding. But these questions represent different phases in the research process, and although at each phase the general model may remain stable, the specific methods used to answer the questions have different implications. Certain phases call for procedures with greater flexibility and characteristics that favor exploration and curiosity. At a later phase, the same basic procedure may need to be standardized and systematically administered. I try to specify, for each phase in the research, why and how a particular method was used.

The remainder of this book is divided into four parts, comprising nine chapters, and one additional concluding chapter. Part I is a description of the theoretical model upon which our analysis of social conceptions stands. In Chapter 2, the first question asked is how social behavior and development can be meaningfully examined with a focus on underlying social–cognitive processes and their development. From this starting point, the concept of developmental levels of social perspective taking (or levels in the coordination of social and psychological perspectives) is introduced and theory and research on this process are selectively reviewed. Here I also try to define social perspective taking by differentiating it from constructs with which it is often confused, for example, role taking or social or person perception. After summarizing some of our earlier research in this area, work that culminated in the formation of the Social Reasoning Project, I consider in Chapter 3 the issue of whether or for what purpose it makes sense to develop a test of perspective-taking levels. This issue is explored in the context of an examination and analysis of two-person strategy games, considering whether social perspective-taking skills are necessary to successful play, or whether simple logical (mathematical) strategies will suffice without the invocation of the social–psychological factors and strategizing that we claim are an essential ingredient of the social perspective-taking process. The aim of this analysis is to define and locate social perspective taking relative to other social and nonsocial cognitive skills and to define what is truly social about the coordination of points of view.

Part II moves forward to the first phase of our current research. In this phase, perspective-taking levels are used in a different way, not as skills to be directly tested but as analytic tools for categorizing developmental differences and changes in reflective interpersonal social conceptions, conceptions in four domains: individuals, friendships, peer-group relations, and parent–child relations. Chapter 4 deals with the constructive phase of measurement: how measures were devised and how a manual for coding interpersonal conceptions expressed in a "clinical interview" by developmental levels was constructed. In Chapter 5, excerpts and examples from the manual provide tangible data which illustrate levels of understanding as they develop in specific issues. Chapter 6 provides a summary of some of the parallels and differences across conceptions in each of the four interpersonal domains we have chosen to study.

Part III describes the second or construct validation phase of our research, a set of studies designed to formally evaluate whether our model generated from the perspective-taking analysis of social interpersonal conceptions in four domains satisfies certain theoretical criteria of stage developmental theory: structured wholeness, invariant developmental sequence, and universality. In Chapter 7, methods, subjects, and reliability findings are described. In Chapter 8, the major validity findings are reported, some conclusions are drawn about social development, and some theoretical suggestions are made for the research needed in the third, or application, phase.

In Part IV, the third phase in our research is described, the application of stage descriptions derived from reflective reasoning in interviews to the analysis of reasoning in other modes—the natural and spontaneous social comments, interactions, and reasoning of both normal and troubled children. Much of our information comes from the observation of the children in the Manville School, children who have difficulties across the range of social relationships, those with peers as well as those with parents or other adult authorities. One approach to this population at this phase could be to start with the assumption that if these children show relatively low levels of interpersonal conceptions in our interviews, we should then try to raise their levels of understanding through some planned intervention, and see if any concomitant behavior change would be observed. However, we feel this would omit a critical intervening step and amount to an unjustified leap of faith. There are few data in the field that provide any clear-cut evidence that a child's reasoning in a reflective interview directly corresponds in level with the same child's reasoning under natural conditions. Therefore we are taking another tack. To shed light on the intervening step and look at naturally expressed and used interpersonal conceptions, we structure already existing aspects of the school program (and programs in "normal" settings as well) to set up situations in which children are encouraged to systematically express and act upon their interpersonal concepts and judgments. At the same time we develop systems for observing and coding their "naturalistic" social reasoning.

In Chapter 9, Daniel Jaquette describes one such effort, the use of the class meeting. For a year, he ran weekly meetings with a class of eight children aged 12 to 14 and in collaboration with other members of our research staff devised a method for the developmental coding of the natural ongoing discussion. (The following year Debra Lavin replicated the class meeting procedure and coding with a younger group of children in the school.) Although only a beginning, this kind of "clinical study" provides some interesting and suggestive data analyses and results and therefore some important leads as to where to go in the area of naturalistic developmental observation of social-cognitive processes and conceptions.

Chapter 10 reports applications of our descriptive system of interpersonal understanding development in a number of different contexts. Returning to the initial problem of ascertaining what children mean when they use certain terms like "trust" or "friendship," or what they understand when adults attempt to ask them to reflect upon their own behavior and feelings, Gregory Jurkovic and I report a "clinical" pilot study of the process of psychotherapy that we undertook. He and I analyzed a year's process therapy notes from his work with several children in the Manville School. We attempted to look at this process from both an "affective" and a "cognitive" perspective, with an emphasis on finding constructs which were understandable to developmental *and* clinical child psychologists. In this chapter I also look at a number of other clinical or exploratory "case studies" which speak to a broad range of ideas we have begun to study in the application phase, particularly in the realm of therapeutic and educational usefulness.

Chapter 11 concludes with two summaries, one practical and one theoretical. In the practical summary, two related issues are discussed. The first, training developmental psychologists in a clinical setting, fills a crucial gap in the experience of the armchair analyst who considers research ideas for the study of child psychopathology. The second, fully integrated research in clinical institutions, can add dimension, perspective, and support to the institution. The theoretical summary is a consideration of some final within-model concerns. Interpersonal understanding is related to personality development by comparing our model with Loevinger's model of ego development. In this chapter, as in the book as a whole, I focus on my goal of a practical theory and a theoretical practice.

Part **I**

BACKGROUND

2

The Foundation:
Social Perspective Taking

A 12-year-old boy, a junior high school student from an intact, middle-class family, suddenly begins getting into arguments and fights at school with peers whom he had regarded as friends when they were all in elementary school together. This situation is sketchy and hypothetical, but not uncommon. In real life, it would evoke a helping response from his environment; his parents, his teachers, and perhaps even his friends would want him to alter his behavior toward others and to feel better. All of them, even the boy himself, would no doubt try first of all to understand his behavior. And they would be likely to bring different perspectives to bear on the attempt to understand; such perspectives differ in at least two ways: in basic beliefs and convictions about behavior (theoretical perspective) and in the distance from which the problem is focused on (contextual perspective, both situational and temporal).

His parents might feel he was experiencing an inner conflict or a personality problem of some kind and seek psychodynamically oriented therapy for him. His teachers might see his problem as stemming from inconsistent expectations and discipline and plan a program for handling him that was essentially one of behavior modification. His pediatrician might see his behavior as a symptom of the physical changes of his age and wait for him to simply outgrow the problems. His guidance counselor might believe that the boy's behavior was a response to the stresses of the new social situation of junior high school and recommend involvement in supervised, group, social activities to ease the social transition. Each of these theoretical perspectives—psychodynamic, social-learning, physical-maturational, and social-psychological—would lead one to interpret or understand the boy's behavior differently. However, it seems unlikely, despite the claims of some passionate proponents of certain views, that his problems could be fully understood or solved by the prescriptions of any one theory.

As theoretical perspective varies, so does contextual perspective. These incidents could be looked at in wider or narrower situational contexts—the children involved, the classroom, the school, the area of the country, or the society at large—or in shorter or longer temporal contexts—the day, week, or year for the child, or his entire earlier development. And it is just as unlikely his difficulties could be understood and solved by looking at only one day and one group of other children as it is they could be solved by looking at only his entire history and the greater society. Several contexts would be relevant and useful just as several theories would be. Furthermore, contexts and theories can interact as well.

The greater the emphasis we put on explanations that are based within the individual, the more diffuse will appear factors of a more sociological nature; the more extensive our analysis of the social system within which this child operates, the less crucial will appear the inner conflicts of this particular child.

I have developed this example at some length for several reasons. The foremost reason is my conviction that because human functioning is so infinitely complex, rich, and multidetermined, it is rarely easily reducible or codable on the basis of one scheme or perspective, no matter how thoroughly studied and conceived the scheme might be. I feel the educator, clinician, and even the parent is best served in dealing with the growing child by an openness to many perspectives, by a large repertoire, a full arsenal. This book reports several years of theoretical and empirical work in developing and applying a model of social cognition and its relation to behavior, which work will, we hope, strengthen and fill in some of the gaps in the repertoire of those who would teach, treat, study, or raise children. And although, as I have just said, no one perspective offers all answers, I believe the descriptive and *practical* insights of work in social-cognitive development go much farther than previously imagined in providing an explanatory framework for certain aspects of social development and behavior.

Having used the anecdote of the socially troubled young adolescent to illustrate the utility and necessity of multiple perspectives, I now

wish to look at it a little differently. I have said one should not cut oneself off from a variety of perspectives. At the same time, it is just as important to specify clearly the theoretical and practical assumptions of the perspective from which you *do* choose to view any given situation, to avoid misinterpretation, confusion, and misunderstanding. This is important in clinical and educational work; it is even more important in research, where typically work is being carried out from only one, very specific perspective. The purpose of this chapter is to define the theoretical and contextual perspectives of our research and to review the most important theoretical and empirical work which constitutes the background for the study and research on which I report in the remainder, and the bulk, of this book.

The General Framework

In this section I deal, somewhat informally and anecdotally, with our theoretical perspective, our area of interest, and the ways in which contextual perspective can and does vary in research, generally and in our own. I also state some of our assumptions and biases and say things in passing about how our approach and our area of interest interrelate.

A DEVELOPMENTAL PERSPECTIVE AND AN INTEREST IN SOCIAL COGNITION

As a way of illustrating a discussion of our theoretical perspective at its most general and fundamental level, let me return once again to the hypothetical anecdote of the last section. First and foremost, we are developmental psychologists, and among the cornerstones of our theoretical perspective is the assumption that human beings develop, grow, and change; that in many important areas these changes are invariant and universal in normal development; and that at any given time, the level of an individual's development along any given line will have real significance for his or her functioning and for the understanding of his or her functioning on the part of other people. One thing that is notably absent in the discussion of this young boy's social difficulties is any mention of his own perceptions of, understanding of, and feelings about this situation and social situations in general. A developmental perspective has at least two important implications for his situation. First, a knowledge of his level of social understanding and development will be useful if not critical to the success of efforts of those who would help him. Attempts to solve the problem which do not take into account where the child "is at," as the term is used both developmentally and colloquially, may well be doomed. Second, and related, it is important, and

will be most accurate in outcome, to try to ascertain the child's own attitudes, opinions, and concepts, as precisely as possible, from *his* or *her* perspective, as close to "from the inside out" as possible.

Our developmental perspective can be further defined as social-cognitive developmental. The theories and research of Jean Piaget and George Herbert Mead play an obvious and important role in all our work. Their and others' work will be taken up in the next section. Here, I will merely state that for us, *social cognition* cannot be reduced, theoretically or practically, to just the simple *application* of cognitive skills (*structure*) to the social sphere (*content*). The development of social conceptions, reasoning, thought—social cognition—is distinct from, though not unrelated to, the development of nonsocial cognition, and this development warrants study. Having so stated, I will devote this section to an informal discussion of our work and our perspective.

Our interest, for nearly 10 years, has been in *social-cognitive bases* of human *social development and behavior,* which become recognizable in the preschool years and which appear to develop relatively rapidly across childhood, preadolescence, and adolescence. Two things are of primary importance to us. First, we wish to develop an approach that can relate differences in social understanding and action among individuals to developmental and hierarchical differences in their social-cognitive construction of social relations and situations, of the relation and coordination of various social perspectives. Second, and closely related, we wish to focus on social development from a perspective which is in part that of the developing child looking out. This is to say, we are interested in the understood conceptual meaning of social relationships from the child's continually developing perspective.

One bias upon which the research in this book is based is that behavior (as physical action of humans) cannot be observed and categorized as *social* in the uniquely human sense without considering the psychological meaning attributed to the behavior by the subject, that is, inherent in the very meaning of the term *social* as used in this book, is the assumption that the specified behavior has some interpersonal meaning *for the participant(s).* Stated somewhat less abstractly, we are seeking to describe how certain underlying social conceptions, looked at developmentally in children, help to give meaning and structure to the observable social behaviors of these developing children. We are less interested in *hypothesizing* temporally antecedent *causes* of social behavior than in *inferring* underlying *bases* of social functioning. The descriptive nature of this approach is seen in the words we use. Rather than make statements that a child acts in certain ways *because* he or she has had previous experiences or reinforcers, etc., we tend to point out that the child interacts or communicates with others in certain ways *as if* he or she had a certain level of (social–cognitive) understanding of the self in relation to the other.

Our interest in developmental differences in the underlying meaning or conceptualization of social actions and interactions leads us to focus on those situations in which different individuals generate outward manifestations that although they are behaviorally similar, may be shown upon closer inspection to be underlain by distinctly different developmental levels of social understanding. As an example, let us consider the following vignette.

Two brothers share bunk beds, a 5-year-old in the top bunk and a 3-year-old in the bottom bunk. One night, after the lights had been turned off, but before the children had received their usual goodnight kisses from their parents, the older brother suggested to the younger that they quietly switch places before the return of the unsuspecting adults. When the parents returned to the bedroom, they found two giggling bodies chortling somewhat hysterically in anticipation as they hid under their covers; the degree of hysteria was quite satisfactorily increased when each child was incorrectly addressed as the other by the "unknowing" parents.

As objective observers, we see the same behavioral reaction in the two children—giggling under the covers with faces hidden from view. However, from the framework that we are adopting, we ask whether this social event has the same meaning for the 3-year-old as for the 5-year-old. Did he understand the social interaction in the same way his older brother did? Probably not. If we adopt the position that humorous reactions are based, in part, on the individual's understanding of a mismatch between actualities and expectations (Zigler, Levine, & Gould, 1967), one can ask what the differences might be between typical 3- and 5-year-olds' actuality–expectation discrepancies. From observations of children of this age and of this particular 3-year-old child, it seems clear that the younger boy generally responded with laughter and amusement when persons or things were simply mislabeled, when *errors* were made. However, the response was elicited whether the labeler was *intentionally* or *unintentionally* in error. For example, he found it just as funny when his father would deliberately call him by his brother's name at the dinner table as he did when they pulled the bedtime switch.

When he was younger, the older brother also found this simple kind of social error or mislabeling very funny, but at this time no longer appeared to take the same pleasure in it. For him, others' benign errors of social misperception or misunderstanding were *really funny* only when they were made *unintentionally*, when someone was really tricked or fooled, when the adult truly did not have access to social information to which the child himself was privy. There would have been great disappointment on the part of the older boy had he suspected, for example, that his parents really *did* know who was under the covers of each bed that night and were not tricked. For the older boy, the crux of the humor lay not only in the errors of actual and attributed labels, in the discrepancy between the reality of who was actually lying under which cover and the verbal assignment of incorrect names by the adult participant; the fun for him was in the trickery itself, the social deception. Whereas for the younger child there was sufficient significance in the understanding of an incongruity between the perspective of the other and the self-observed "reality," for the older child it was the *relation* between the perspective of the *other* (in the case here the parents) and the *self* that is the essential ingredient in the meaningfulness of the interaction.

In time, this trick became a fairly popular game. But by the time the 5-year-old was 7, both boys' reasons for finding it funny and fun had changed. The younger one, now 5, had grown to love the *real* trick. But the 7-year-old now recognized that his parents were not fooled, but only pretending to be taken in in order to go along with the game; and he was thrilled with his own de facto, silent participation in the entire deception. What really tickled him was his own knowledge that he and his brother were attempting deceit, his parents were pretending to be fooled, he knew they were pretending, his brother did not, and he himself was helping the whole thing along by his silence. At this same age, he also had definite suspicions about the veracity of the elaborate Santa Claus routine that went on every year, but he pursued this train of thought privately, sharing it with neither brother nor parents, and ultimately, when all was disclosed, turned out to have genuinely savored seeing all the various perspectives and their relation to each other.

Of course, not all children find this kind of social–cognitive exercise even interesting, much less fun; therefore, many children would be unlikely to so clearly manifest their thinking. Nevertheless, we would maintain that this vignette exemplifies three early, distinct, universal levels in the growth of the child's understanding of the relation or coordination between the self's and others' points of view. This and the further emergence of this kind of understanding represents for us a core aspect of what is basically unique to *human social development,* and is the basis for what interests us in our work. That the child has the potential capacity for knowing and reflecting upon the human ability to look *inward* as well as *back and forth across to others* strikes us as a most powerful and most potentially adaptive of intellectual tools. Because there is evidence that this understanding develops steadily in the years of childhood and adolescence, we have chosen to study its development during this age-period. And to return to the reason for introducing the bunk bed anecdote, we maintain that knowledge of the level of social understanding which *underlies behavior* can be critical to understanding and dealing with that behavior. Many situations are just as uncomplicated and benign as the bedtime switch, but for those which are not, the importance of being able to identify underlying understanding, and to interpret behavior more meaningfully, seems clear.

CONTEXTUAL PERSPECTIVE IN
DEVELOPMENTAL RESEARCH

The vignettes I have used to articulate an area of interest also illustrate strengths and weaknesses in the way we study the development of social understanding. They exemplify the quasi-natural aspects of much of our work. One weakness of this type of research is that it does not tend to produce formally documentable causal connections; in a relatively naturalistic setting, thorough isolation and control of variables is not possible. Conclusions are perhaps less "provable," but sometimes by the same token they are more relevant and useful as well, at least in some contexts. At any rate, we look at differential responses at different ages to events common to the lives of growing children to discover their underlying understanding and to demonstrate that to understand social development requires an examination through the eyes of the involved participants, at their level of conceptualization.

One strength of our approach is that by extrapolation from initial findings, many related research questions are generated. We might continue this brand of research in a boys-in-the-bunk type of case to study whether such a 3-year-old orientation is unique to this situation or general across social contexts; whether most children around this age think this way; whether the 5-year-old obsession with what other people know relative to the self is a rare interest manifested only in this situation or whether one could find evidence for a more pervasive attitude of this type; whether and when other children think at this level. We might assume we could catalogue a wide range of social influencing strategies in children, the form and function of which could in part be understood on the basis of the child's developing levels of understanding of persons and their related perspectives. It might then be useful to see whether some agreement could be obtained on whether an observed shift is rapid and all-encompassing for the individual child (like a pea plant on which one night there are many flowers and the next day many pods), or whether the behavioral manifestations of a shift in underlying understanding are more unevenly emergent (like weeds in a garden that eventually but not immediately overrun the domain, until the whole character of the garden changes).

Of course, how and when one chooses to observe these changes strongly influences whether one sees rapid or erratic developmental changes. This brings us to the issue of context, which I mentioned earlier. In psychological research, contextual perspective varies on at least two dimensions: temporal and situational.

Situational context in our research is important and varies. It can be compared to the lens of a camera, narrowing or broadening its focus, as well as changing what background is chosen. For example, we have studied children's reasoning in individual reflective interviews, where the focus is narrowed to one child and the background limited to the least intrusive. We have also conducted research on groups of children in spontaneous situations in classrooms; here the lens widens its focus to the group and takes in a more complex and full background as well. For us, variations in situational context are carefully chosen and defined and will be discussed when they occur.

Temporal context also varies in our work, and although it seems straightforward enough, a brief discussion of the significance of its variation seems merited. In developmental psychology, observations or samplings across various time spans often provide us with a critical distancing tool. Depending upon what one's comparative frame of reference is, a set of developmental processes can be seen to emerge in either a coherent and orderly fashion, or they can be seen as chaotic and quite disorganized. Many of us are familiar with the experience of driving to the airport through city streets and being struck by the disorder and confusion that surrounds us, only to fly over the same area in a departing plane and marvel at how well things fit into a coherent pattern.

In psychology, a developmental perspective attempts to provide some order by getting off the ground, by looking at the relation of age, time, and the particular developmental process(es) being examined. Like getting into an airplane, developmental approaches use time as a way of getting some distance on individual development and function. How much order is observed will depend, in part, upon how much temporal distance one chooses to get, that is, the length of time over which some developmental process is observed. To pursue the analogy, if height is a distancing tool used by the traffic engineer to observe functional relations in traffic, then time, or age-span, is a distancing tool used by the developmental psychologist in looking at functional relations in development. But one must specify how one is using this tool. Ever increasing height (for example, a satellite view) will not necessarily give ever increasing clarity to the traffic controller; eventually there is a blurring of vision. One must pick a distance appropriate for the problem being looked at. The analogy holds for age-span or time as a tool for seeking coherence in developmental processes as well.

Thus, if a developmental psychologist wants, as we do, to examine how coherently patterns of social conceptions develop in childhood and adolescence, the conclusions drawn will depend in part on whose social conceptions are compared with whose and on how broad an age-span is taken as a means of gaining distance. A comparison of 7- and 8-year-olds' social awareness may yield a picture that looks relatively unpredictable developmentally, but a comparison of the social understanding of the same 7-year-olds with that of 10-year-olds and that of 14-year-olds may yield a much clearer picture, showing that the 7-year-olds are more similar to each other (and consequently more coherent-looking as a group) when contrasted with 10-year-olds and 14-year-olds than when compared to the 8-year-olds. However, information from a comparison of 5- and 50-year-olds may be blurred by the loss of the connecting factors in between.

One responsibility in reporting research such as ours is to make explicit the temporal context within which observations and theorizing are ongoing, to try to specify the "height" at which one is hovering in looking at psychological phenomena. Furthermore, it is also incumbent on the researchers to explain why any given particular context or focus is considered worthwhile, why it has been chosen above alternative or competing distances or approaches. Sometimes the reasons are mundane and practical, a door open and an opportunity for research available. Sometimes there is a recognition of work needed to be done on a particular phenomenon at a particular distance. I try to specify our temporal context and our reasons for choosing it at each given step in our research.

Going back again for a moment to the junior high school student, if we *identify* the situational and temporal contexts of the various views of his troubles, we will see that this clarification helps each of these perspectives, focused at varying distances, add something to our understanding of the child's behavior. Each is made more meaningful when put into a general framework that includes the others. The concept of distance or context is a useful analytic tool that can help us to consider the relation among sometimes competing, sometimes complementary interpretations of behavior. It helps to specify how far back the observer wishes to step in defining the child's problem, relative to some other approach, and to specify how much is to be included. It is well known that what is observed is partially a function of where the observer is standing relative to the action as well as a function of what action there is to observe.

Specifying one's context and frame of reference relative to those of others who may be observing the same problem from a different "observation point" can be critical to amiable communication not only among social science researchers or practitioners coming from different traditions, but among psychologists whose ongoing battles may be due less to differences in opinion of what is observed than to differences in framework within which the observations are interpreted. Observations of phenomena that look coherent, similar, or unitary to one observer may look differential, unrelated, or specific to another largely because of what each means by same or different from a particular level. This kind of argument appears particularly common in the field of developmental psychology, where battle lines are often drawn around how stable or organized some developing capacity is at a particular age in the child's or

adult's life. Lack of significant correlations across various tasks purporting to measure similar skills or abilities of children at similar ages are
often seen as damning the prospects for finding unitary organizational
properties in that area. But whether one finds coherence or disarray,
similarities or differences, is a function not only of what is observed, but
of how it is observed or measured as well, of context as we have been
speaking of it.

In developmental psychology, coherence versus context specificity
arguments often revolve around the question of stages, particularly
cognitive stages. The research presented in this book is about
social–cognitive stages, but it is not as much about whether stages do or
do not exist in children or adults per se as it is about how useful stage
analyses are for understanding differences or similarities in social
development. But usefulness depends upon where one feels most comfortable standing in passing the judgment. To take an example from
practice, for a third-grade teacher, whose children are all about the same
age, stage analyses that order changes over time may explain very little
of the variation in the social behavior observed in the children in the
classroom, and therefore be less than useful. But for the school principal
who must plan programs that have continuity across an age-range of 6 or
8 years they may prove very helpful.

It is interesting to note that parents, who continually collect data on
the development of their children over time, that is, who have a close-in
temporal focus or context, observe rapid change in some areas of functioning but in other areas hardly see it at all. In areas where development appears relatively continuous, for example, physical growth, it is
usually difficult for parents to observe change. It is usually the grand-
parents or distant relatives, who sample this development once or twice
a year, who see physical development most clearly. However, for some
phenomena, other time frames may be more revealing. In areas of conceptual and social development, the repeated sampling and increased
data points of the "parent-qua-researcher," extending over a long period,
appear not to obliterate, but to make even more striking, the changes
observed. Parents often report that their children appear to go through
periods of rapid gain in social understanding followed by long periods of
stability. The parent of one 6-year-old reported that for a long time his
daughter appeared to have no interest in or understanding of the value of
money, that is, the relation of pennies, dimes, nickels, and quarters, even
after she had mastered the basic arithmetic operations necessary. "All of
a sudden," at least to the parent–observer, she showed a powerful interest in the value of money. She seemed to "get the concept" that
money is a medium for exchange, and that the more money one is willing
to abandon, the more of something else one values—for example, bubble
gum, baseball cards, or candy bars—one is likely to obtain from someone
else willing to exchange.

When a new understanding is broken down into component parts, then one sees the complexity of the many requisite skills that must be in place before the child "gets the concept" of something like money. Some skills are typically categorized as *logicomathematical,* for example, the ability to serially coordinate more money and more candy in one-to-one correspondence. Others more appropriately are seen as *motivational,* for example, the identification of some object desired and available in exchange. Still others can be seen as *social* in the sense we are using it here, for example, the understanding that individuals can agree to the exchange of an object of arbitrary value, such as a coin of the realm in the possession of a buyer, for a more directly valued object, such as the bubble gum or candy in the possession of a seller. One can see that the deeper one looks, the more complex even the simple act of putting a nickel on the counter of the candy store becomes. It involves at the least ideas about property rights, the nature and dimensions of monetary values, and contracts between individuals.

To pursue the notion of the usefulness of knowing underlying thinking, suppose one wanted to study the relation between two apparently disparate "developments," for example, an *interest* in the value of money and an *interest* in tricking parents at bedtime. From our view, one might hypothesize that for the child to realize that money has a commonly shared value for many distinct individuals, and therefore acts as medium of exchange that satisfies them all, requires or reflects the same kind of basic understanding of socially coordinated perspectives as was manifest in the child's interest in tricking or pretending to trick his parents. The hypothesis is that both phenomena are in part a function or manifestation of a critical developmental shift in social understanding, a shift toward a more sophisticated understanding of the relations among the wants and needs of individuals.

However, as important and useful as testing this hypothesis might be, it would also be difficult. Our interest in broad underlying bases and the breadth and openness of our methods are well-suited, but there are difficulties imposed by the interference of other factors that impinge on the observed behavior. Clearly, then, great attention must be paid to ways to creatively study the relation and interaction between a wide range of "observable" social interactions and exchanges on the one hand and any "unobservable" underlying, basic levels of social understanding on the other.

OUR INTEREST IN SOCIAL PERSPECTIVE TAKING

Preceding our subsequent research, we constructed a model of social perspective taking; in so doing, we approached several of the many difficult issues that need to be considered. He who has toiled long in a particular garden raising one crop and variations thereof tends to develop a taste and fondness for his produce; so we, who have studied social perspective taking in various ways over time, have come to regard this construct as having a particular, important, and (hopefully) nonidiosyncratic meaning. In any case, it is one that is clearly differentiated from constructs that might look similar to someone who holds a less passionate perspective. The primary aims of the next sections of this chapter are to identify what social perspective taking or coordination is, as well as what it is not; to explore why it is viewed primarily as a social–cognitive process rather than a cognitive process applied to social content; to see how it may relate to cousin constructs like social perception or role taking, as well as to see how it is different from these; to clarify whether and when we see it as a skill, an ability, a conception, a process for gathering social data, or an analytic tool; to touch upon whether it is an understanding of which the child is aware or whether it goes largely unreflected upon; to look at whether it emerges full-blown in childhood, slowly through childhood and adolescence, or throughout the developmental life cycle; to consider whether its development can best be described as qualitative reorganizations of previous levels or a more quantitative and continuous accretion of social knowledge.

These are questions to which we have given much thought and study, and our opinions have been modified on many of them. It may be useful to share not only our present thinking about some of these issues, but the steps we have gone through in arriving at this particular point as well. It makes more sense to let a developmental definition of social perspective taking emerge out of the description of the paths we and others have explored than to present a full-blown definition of a psychological construct divorced from its genetic origins. However, even as I begin, three parameters can be stated that will hopefully take on more meaning as we proceed.

1. Social perspective taking includes a developing understanding of how human points of view are *related* and *coordinated* with one another and not simply what social or psychological information may appear to be like from an alternative individual's perspective as in the construct of role taking.

2. Social perspective taking also involves a developing understanding of the intrinsic psychological characteristics and capacities of individuals, not just the complex coordination of decentered cognitive operations, that is, it has an intrinsically *social* component. Thus while it may be incorporated into a more formal model of decentered thought, for example, Piagetian theory, the social or psychological content is inextricable and equally as important as the logical or operational structure which may in turn be its basis.

3. Because it describes a basic understanding underpinning the self–other relationship as it develops, social perspective taking provides a theoretical infrastructure upon which the child's understanding of a significant number of social and psychological relationships can be organized; social perspective taking can be viewed as an analytic tool for the researcher as well as be seen as a key developing social–cognitive skill or ability in the child.

In presenting a current and working definition of social perspective taking, I will follow this sequence. In the next section, I review the theoretical and empirical approaches that have led to our current developmental definition. In the third section, I review our own work describing social perspective-taking strategies and levels. This leads, in the last section, to a fork in the road, a choice of two research directions. In Chapter 3, we shall report on one foray down the path we have *not* taken.

The Theoretical and Empirical Background: Structural Development and Studies of Social Reasoning

THEORETICAL BACKGROUND

Our theoretical approach is strongly structural–developmental. The term *structural development* refers to a set of assumptions and research methodologies common to a number of theories of cognitive and social development. Although the approach finds its roots in the early interactionist writings of James Mark Baldwin (1906) and George Herbert Mead (1934), the extensive theoretical and empirical work of Jean Piaget (e.g., 1932, 1964) has provided the basic outline of the theory and much of the present impetus for research in this area. The hallmark of such research is an interest in describing an invariant sequence of cognitively based stages, or qualitatively distinct ways of organizing and understanding a certain domain of experience, through which all children pass. In contrast to other approaches, the emphasis is on the structure rather than on the content of thought, on universal patterns of thinking rather than on emotions or behavior.

In our interest in levels of development that satisfy the essential stage criteria of structured wholeness, invariant sequence, and universality, our work is an outgrowth of the Piagetian tradition. Our approach is also clearly Piagetian in its focus on the form of thinking and the relation of expressed thought to underlying cognitive structures rather than on affectivity or individual or group differences.

A particularly incisive, clear, thorough, and influential statement of a Piagetian social–cognitive perspective was published by Lawrence Kohlberg in 1969. In a long theoretical article, he outlined the essentials of a structural–developmental stage model and described in some detail how a Piagetian developmental approach can be applied to the growth of social knowledge and understanding of the social domain. (In this article, Kohlberg also theorized that what he called role taking could be seen in structural–developmental terms and that it played an important role in social cognition. He did not, however, specify or study role-taking [perspective-taking] development. As reported in this chapter, much of our early work, seminal for our later research, can be seen in retrospect as an attempt to do so.)

Our model is also based on the belief that one cannot divorce children's theories of how individuals relate to each other from their theories of the psychological characteristics of individuals; the understanding of selves and the understanding of relations among the perspectives of various selves are interacting conceptions that nourish and enhance each other. In this theoretical assertion, we closely mirror and are strongly influenced by Mead's (1934) postulation that the human capacity to coordinate roles is both the source of a sense of self and the core of social intelligence. For Mead, putting oneself in another's position and the subsequent consideration of one's own actions from that alternative position is the *operation*, uniquely human, that allows for the recognition of the existence of a self. Hence, without social interaction, in Mead's sense, there could not be a psychological self.

For Mead, this growth of self and social understanding goes through a series of "stages," the first of which is characterized as the *play stage*. Here the young child practices (role plays) the *actions* of familiar persons; first the child is the parent, then the child; first the storekeeper, then the buyer; first the good guy, then the bad. This phase is followed by the *game stage*, the more organized social coordination and operations within natural games of greater complexity. For example, as a baseball pitcher the child must *mentally anticipate* the intentions of the first and third basemen and catcher on the child's team and the batter and runners on the other team, as well as act his or her own part. As with play, games are both the product of and the conditions for advances in the ability to coordinate perspectives. But whereas play can take place on the plane of action, games necessarily represent the plane of mental or internal coordination. Through play and games the individual, now perhaps an adolescent, is eventually led, in Mead's view, to a next stage, where there develops a concept of the organized system or community, the "perspective of the *generalized other*." This generalized other represents the abstract, normative, or societal perspective, and requires that an individual gain some conception of social consensus or norms.

According to Mead (1934), the shift from one stage to the next, for example, from the game stage to the generalized other stage, also represents a shift in the reflective understanding of self.

At [the game stage], the individual's self is constituted simply by an organization of the particular attitudes of other individuals toward himself and toward one another in specific social acts in which he participates with them. But at the [generalized other] stage in the full development of the individual's self, that self is constituted not only by an organization of these particular individual attitudes, but also by an organization of the social attitudes of the generalized other or the social group as a whole to which he belongs [p. 158].

When the individual, at the game stage, can put himself into the other's position, he can also differentiate this self-as-actor from the self-as-observer and can carry on an internal conversation. This to Mead is the essence of social intelligence, or of self-reflection. When subsequently the individual can internally carry on the conversation of the group, or society, he is capable of going beyond social reason and self-reflection to social rationality. The self as a "rational being" arises out of the organism's ability to assume the attitude of the group within the cooperative process of society.

EMPIRICAL BACKGROUND

Having briefly described the essentials of the Piagetian and Meadian theoretical traditions from which our work springs, we turn to more recent empirical work. We have already suggested in an anecdotal way some of the benefits and disadvantages which accrue to the use of naturalistic observation of children's social interaction as a means for gaining a picture of the development of the basic characteristics of social understanding. There are two particularly relevant but hopefully only temporary drawbacks. First, it is a particularly expensive method with respect both to the amount of time necessary to gather pertinent data and to the technical equipment necessary. Second, because the study of social understanding involves inference about the social conceptions underlying children's behavior or social discourse, there is always the temptation to get some clarification by stopping the natural flow to ask the child, "What did you mean by that?" Even assuming the child could tell us with this type of interruption, much of the advantage of natural observation would be lost.

Partly as a function of these obstacles, in recent years most developmental psychologists interested in developmental aspects of social cognition have relied on relatively more controllable laboratory methods for their study.[1] One approach has been to use variations on common childhood guessing and strategy games. For example, in 1968, John Flavell, a pioneer in the empirical study of social understanding, published, with a group of colleagues, a monograph of results of imaginative experiments designed to explore the parameters of social-cognitive development and its relation to communication skill development in early and middle childhood (Flavell, Fry, Wright, & Jarvis, 1968). In one of the most familiar social-cognitive measures described in this book, children played a brief game in which they were instructed to try to trick a friend who wants to win some money. In this task, the child is shown two inverted cups, one labeled 5¢ and the other 10¢, with the appropriate coin placed under each. The child is told that a peer is going to enter the room and pick one of the cups to try to win some money, and that the child is to remove the money from one of the cups so as to deceive this second child.

The task requires Child 1 to imagine Child 2's strategy and take the money out of the cup he (1) thinks 2 will choose. The instructions specify for 1 that 2 knows that he (1) will be trying to fool him. Child 1's description and explanation of the relation of his strategy to that of Child 2 are categorized according to levels of social awareness. A score[2] of Level 0 is assigned to children's choices which indicate a lack of realization on the part of the interviewed child that in this particular game an understanding of the other person's motives is relevant and important to one's own choice. The protocols in this category consisted of children who could not or would not attribute a choice to the other child, or to children who could offer no rationale for the choice they felt the other would make.

A child's response is categorized at Level 1 (A) if the child shows awareness that there is a motive behind the opponent's choice but does not indicate awareness that the other participant might also be cognizant of one's own motives or strategies. In fact, although Level 1 reflects the child's attribution to the other child of cognitions related to the game material, it also indicates a *failure* to account for the possibility that

---

[1] Over the last several years a number of excellent reviews of research in social cognition have been published (Chandler, 1976; Flavell, 1977; Kurdek, 1978; Shantz, 1975). In this book I shall not duplicate these efforts, but shall draw upon findings from that literature where necessary or useful to themes or points being made in this volume.

[2] In Flavell's study, four categories, 0, A, B, and C, were used rather than Levels 0, 1, 2, and 3 as used here. We take the liberty of making the transposition of categories to levels in order to better coordinate Flavell's early work with our own developmental model, one which builds in certain ways upon the research perspective put forth in that earlier monograph. Pages 42 to 53 of Flavell's monograph, which describe in greater detail this deceptively simple task and the ramifications of the results, are well worth reading, if not for the numerous leads to further research, then for an historical perspective on some important antecedents of the research described herein.

they are in a situation in which the other child, for strategy's sake, should try to take the self's strategies into account as well.

Level 2 (B) is assigned to the responses of children who indicate an awareness that the *other* child knows that the *subject* knows: (a) One choice has certain advantages (monetary) over the other; (b) this might influence that other child's choice; and (c) this in turn has implications for the choice that the subject is to make. It should be stressed that success at this level implies the child has an understanding of the reciprocal functioning of the social-awareness process; as the child makes a decision on the basis of his attributing thoughts and actions to other, the child also sees that other is capable of similarly attributing thoughts and actions to the self. For example, a child who explains, "She will think I will take the dime box and so she will switch to the nickel, so maybe I better take the money from the nickel box," is classified at Level 2.

Level 3 (C) thinking goes beyond the child's realization that the self must take into consideration that one's opponent can take into consideration the self's motives and strategies. It is a level of understanding at which the child is able to abstractly step outside the dyad and see that each player can simultaneously consider the self's and other's perspectives on each other, a level of abstraction which we now call *mutual perspectivism*. Elsewhere (Selman, 1976b), we have hypothesized that in order to demonstrate an understanding of the mutuality of perspectives, the child must be able to coordinate two relations, a reciprocal social–cognitive operation (I know that my peer can take my perspective) and the inverse of this reciprocal operation (my peer knows that I can take his perspective) simultaneously. When using games such as the one devised by Flavell and his colleagues, this shift to Level 3 or mutual perspectivism is often difficult to differentiate empirically from Level 2. Nevertheless, this hypothesized developmental shift has been recognized as having great significance for the child's concepts of social interaction.

Flavell's results indicate that most youngsters in second through fifth grade use Level 1 reasoning in this task, Level 2 responses begin early but do not predominate until seventh grade (age 12), and Level 3 responses are rare in the elementary grades. Flavell was also aware that level of performance on this task was not necessarily indicative of the child's maximum level of competence, and he developed a five-step model to be used in thinking about the progress from social cognition (competence) through social behavior (performance), beginning with the *existence* of a level of understanding and proceeding through to its *application*. Thus, although few children in the elementary years used Level 3 in his study, they were not necessarily viewed as incapable of its use under different conditions. We shall return time and again to this theme of competence and performance, form and function, for it plays a major theoretical part in our understanding of the validity of social–cognitive developmental analyses of social behavior.

From a contemporary perspective, Flavell's work appears to have provided an important sanction for the continued mining of a then relatively undeveloped field. In addition, Flavell bolstered the validity of doing research as developmental–descriptive naturalists, a role that was not as common in the research atmosphere of the 1950s and 1960s as it is today.

> We were above all interested in trying to glean from our research a detailed but essentially non-causal-analytic picture of a variety of developing subskills within the role-taking and communication domains. The aim was to get a perspective on what sorts of things develop at roughly what ages in the domain, an overview which would, however, be well-fleshed with a lot of concrete developmental data about response to a wide range of domain relevant tasks [Flavell *et al.*, 1968, p. 2].

Finally, his book marked the emergence of relatively easy-to-administer "role-taking" or social–cognitive tasks which facilitated study of the relationships between the processes or skills these tasks operationalized and other aspects of social and cognitive functioning (e.g., Hollos & Cowan, 1973).

Although there have been many empirical studies of social cognition (or role taking) from a developmental perspective since the appearance of Flavell's work, very few if any of the studies have focused on the *coordination of perspectives* in the way Mead conceptualized it. Most of the research (see reviews by Shantz, 1975; Hill & Palmquist, 1978; Chandler, 1976) has gone off in the direction of the other research in the Flavell book, the examination of developmental changes in the child's knowledge about other individual's thoughts, feelings, or motives. What many of them have studied has been essentially the growth of acuity or accuracy in observations, attributions, and understanding of others' subjective perspectives. This work is in some ways closer to the construct *person perception* as developed by various social psychologists, for example, Livesley and Bromley (1973), than it is to our construct *social perspective taking*.

One partial exception is some work based on Piagetian theory, and actually begun earlier than the time of Flavell's report, by Feffer and his colleagues (Feffer, 1959; Feffer & Gourevitch, 1960). Using a social task in which the child is asked to make up a projective story using three cardboard human figures which are placed on a pictureboard depicting one of a number of social scenes, for example, a family setting, these researchers asked children and adults to tell the story from the point of view of each of the characters. Responses were scored on the basis of how well the subject kept in mind the relationship of the characters to each other and thereby insured a consistent story.

From observation of the methods children use to deal with this task, Feffer derived three levels of ability. At the first level, *simple refocusing,* usually in evidence by about age 6, the child is able to change perspective from one actor to another, but the shift results in inconsistency between the original story and the various actors' stories. For example, while telling an initial story about a boy who has come home after a fight, in telling the story from the boy's perspective, a subject might omit this relevant detail. At the second level, Feffer's *consistent elaboration,* the child exhibits a capacity for sequential coordination of perspectives. For example, if in the initial story the child tells his parents about the fight, in the follow-up the father may ask him how the fight got started. The third level, *change of perspective,* emerges at about age 9 or 10 and is characterized by the simultaneous coordination of internal and external perspectives. A story actor is now characterized from an internal perspective when the story is told from his perspective, and from an external view when it is told from that of the other character. For example, after telling his parents about the fight, the parents, according to the subject scored at this level, would show some understanding of the feelings expressed by the child in this story.

Feffer's model is heavily influenced by the Piagetian construct decentration, and while it attempts to code the structure of perspective taking, it essentially ignores the social content upon which the structure operates, a content of the understanding of selves or individuals as spelled out by Mead.

OUR EARLY WORK

In our own early work on perspective taking, we *attempted* to follow Mead's social–conceptual model more closely while still operating *within* a Piagetian structural model of developmental psychology. Previous to our work defining levels of social perspective taking as we now use them, we made two efforts to empirically search for developmental levels in children's perspective-taking ability; these early efforts ultimately led us to look for levels of understanding of the relation *between* social perspectives, a search which we feel was at last closer to the Meadian approach.

Our first early exploration of perspective taking (Selman, 1971a) took place in a study which looked at the relation of perspective taking and moral reasoning, as defined by Kohlberg (1969). Several important ideas and observations, both formal and informal, emerged from the study. First, in assessing moral reasoning, we ran open-ended interviews about subjects' responses to dilemmas. The flexibility of this method provided us with the opportunity to probe reasoning. And although the dilemmas were "moral" dilemmas, subjects spontaneously expressed concepts about human nature, social relations, relations among perspectives, and other social understandings for our perusal, as it were.

The other component of the study, assessing perspective taking, was conducted using several formally coded tasks, one of which was Flavell's 5¢/10¢ game. Our results replicated his. However, despite the originality and importance of the Flavell work, sometimes the most interesting behavior we observed was not susceptible to capture by his scoring system. (In *all* the "perspective-coordination" tasks, including the 5¢/10¢ game, we were struck by observations that one could not garner from a report of research using formal coding, even a report as readable as the Flavell monograph.)

First, one of the most striking observations we made in administering this simple measure was of the attitude of many of the children involved in the procedure. This attitude may best be characterized as one of "assuredness." Regardless of which level the child used, children at each level responded *as if* they had found the key to a puzzle box, and they were sure it was *the right key*. For example, a child scored at Level 2 would typically respond like this:

> He wants the most money so he will take the dime . . . but wait . . . if he knows I know that, then he will take the nickel, because he thinks I will take the dime. *I know!!!* I'll pick the nickel because he will think I will take the dime.

What proved so fascinating about these responses was that the children appeared to be so sure that they had come up with the "right solution." So, for example, as in the case above, the possibility that their opponent might have also considered this strategy as well (a Level 3 analysis) did not appear to occur to them. They had "the answer." Subjects scored at Level 1 did not appear the least bit concerned with the role the self might play in all these strategies or choices that the other player might make; those making use of Level 2 thought it ludicrous to ignore these data.

Another striking observation, less difficult to measure or quantify, was the consistency with which the child would use a certain level of strategizing. While it was sometimes observed that on an initial trial a young subject might use a slightly lower-level strategy, moving up to a next higher level on a subsequent trial, it was also impressive how once a certain level of competence appeared to be gained, the subject continued to invoke that level (Selman, 1971a). These observations, along with the logical character of the developmental levels, levels that appear to have the hierarchical property in which higher levels seem to build upon the lower, led us to suspect that it did in fact make sense to conceptualize the coordination of perspectives and its development in structural terms,

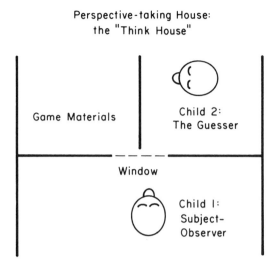

Figure 2.1. Schematic drawing of perspective-taking apparatus.

whereby each higher level is not seen simply as more complex in a quantitative sense, but involves an attempt to provide a qualitative model of the reorganization of the elements of the previous level into new strategies for social interaction.

In another early study (Selman, 1971b), a life-sized, three-room playhouse, called a "think house," was built for assessing perspective-taking ability. From two rooms, only the third room was visible; from the third room, both the other rooms could be seen. Child 1, sitting in that third room, was the subject in the experiment. The first two rooms held Child 2 and the game materials, respectively (see Figure 2.1). The subject was actually an *observer* who had visual access to information unavailable to Child 2, called the "guesser."

Child 1, the subject–observer, whose understanding of perspectives was being assessed, was asked to predict what the guesser would do in a game situation in which it was possible for the subject literally to see that he or she had access to information not available to the guesser. After the subject made his predictions, the experimenter attempted to elicit the reasoning behind the subject's prediction of the other child's response.

The responses (the predictions *and* their justifications) of 60 4-, 5-, and 6-year-olds were categorized into four levels of perspective taking. At Level A, the child acts *as if* he or she fails to differentiate his or her visual view of the immediate configuration from the other's visual view.[3]

---

[3] Flavell and his colleagues (see Flavell, 1977) have done much subsequent work to demonstrate that in the early years spatial and perceptual perspective taking also go through interesting and complex developmental progressions.

At Level B, the child apparently differentiates between self's and other's visual viewpoints but asserts that other's choices (i.e., the contents of another's mind) are unknowable or unguessable, and therefore *refuses* to provide a choice, although he provides a reason for not choosing. At Level C, the child indicates a belief that other's choice is separate or distinct from his or her own but would be the *same* as his would be if he were in the guesser's situation. At Level D, the child indicates that he or she is cognizant that the other child's strategy is *potentially* different from his or her own, even if each decides under similar conditions. We found that use of Levels A and B declined from age 4 to age 6, that use of Level C reached a peak at about age 5, and that Level D began to be used by only some of the 6-year-olds.

Although we found clear age-trends for all levels, Level B, the refusal to guess another's choice, was a particularly puzzling response, because it did not automatically fall into place logically in the developmental sequence. Grappling with the Level B response began to lead us in some of the directions our work has ultimately taken.

One direction our thinking took was to speculate that cognitively more sophisticated children might be the ones to take the philosophical stance that one can never know with complete confidence what someone else is thinking. However, that it was primarily the children aged 4 or 5 who gave this response led us to consider it as intermediary between Levels A and C. In particular, it was the apparent attitude these children expressed in their explanations—the belief that other's responses were not even *potentially* knowable to the self under *any* condition, that is, could not even be guessed at—that led us to see this as a manifestation of an early rather than a later level of social understanding. Furthermore, in other studies it has been found that an older child can also take the position that one person cannot know the thoughts and feelings of another (Selman, 1976a). But with further probing it is often found that the judgments of these older children are made because they believe each individual comes to a particular situation with a unique history of attitudes, feelings, etc., that must be understood before inferences about specific psychological reactions can be readily made. Our 5-year-olds appeared not only to have no such sophistication, but to believe that another person's thoughts and guesses were literally in the other person's head and, not being *visible*, were therefore unknowable.

These interpretations, even as intuitive or logical analyses, would have been impossible without information gleaned from follow-up probes of subjects' reasoning and rationales. Here we find a more formally observed example of the phenomenon we observed informally in the brothers in the bunk beds. Beliefs, attitudes, or behaviors of children at different ages which on the surface appear to be similar to one another prove upon further probing to be based upon very different basic levels of social understanding. Another point, which has become increasingly important in our work, is also illustrated here: that how a child relates one point of view to another cannot be separated, in theory or practice, from that child's theory of human nature, his or her developing assumptions about the nature of persons.

The difficulty we had finding (forcing, perhaps) an ontogenetic niche for the "Level B" responses raises a slightly different theoretical question as well. *Is* "Level B" a level, a universal step in the development of all children's social conceptions, or is it a way station that only some children happen into, a nonuniversal manifestation of some deeper, universal developmental level? It bears mentioning here that before we collected these data, we expected (hypothesized) that responses would most likely fall into what corresponds to what became Levels A, C, and D. "Level B" responses came as an empirical surprise which in retrospect we felt might have been amenable to logical analysis (and perhaps found to be an aspect of Level A) had we had a technique for coding or interpreting responses at a deeper level.

Although it is a modest piece of research, this study provides ample demonstration that even simple developmental models cannot be constructed solely on the basis of an a priori logical system. Empirical effort is critical to the constructive as well as to the verification phase of the research process. In particular, the ambiguity and uncertainty surrounding Level B points up the importance of longitudinal data collection on the same individuals to find out whether a step that "in theory" may or may not logically fit between two other steps is one that in fact all children go through.[4] And conversely, without some theoretical framework, there would be no reason to question the validity of any "level" or even to know how to begin to assess or assign meaning to various responses. Empirical–theoretical interaction is crucial. Furthermore, the data and experiences of this study convinced us that a developmental definition of perspective-taking levels would need to consider the child's conceptions of individuals, the child's beliefs about human beings as social cognizers, as well as his or her understanding of coordination of points of view.

A FURTHER FOCUS ON SOCIAL PERSPECTIVE TAKING

The attempt to integrate level of social perspective coordination and level of social concepts differentiates our definition of perspective taking from many of the constructs in the social–cognitive field. We subscribe to the Meadian assumption that as the growing child, acting as a sub-

---

[4] These data certainly were unavailable in the cross-sectional study we undertook in 1971. How they might best be obtained is an important issue in developmental research, and one that is spoken to in Chapters 4–8.

ject, constructs a model of the coordination between his or her perspective and that of a relevant other, this very constructive activity changes the child's conception of what it means to be a person (i.e., a "self" or an "other"). According to Mead, that persons are uniquely perspective-taking animals is a basic discovery that each child must make on his or her own.

The essential ingredient in this integration is conveyed by Mead's dialectical distinction between the self as a *subject* (Mead called this the "I," or the perspective taker), and the self as *object* (the "Me," or the perspective being taken). It is the integration of these two components that makes perspective taking truly social, and not simply the application of a developing reflexive or recursive thinking ability to some arbitrary social content area.

Let us look for a moment at a study which examines the child's growing ability to apply cognitive operations to social content, but does *not* tap the child's understanding of self and other in coordination. Several years ago, Miller, Kessel, and Flavell (1970) undertook a clever study—"Thinking about people thinking about people thinking about . . . : A study of social-cognitive development." In this study, children at different ages were shown a series of cartoons; in each cartoon, a person was drawn, and above the person's head was the typical cartoon bubble that means the character is thinking about something else, in this case another person. In some of the cartoons, the person in the bubble was shown thinking about a third person, etc. Not surprisingly, Miller *et al.* found that older children demonstrated better comprehension of the more complex (recursive) representations (i.e., the bubbles within bubbles) than did younger children.

Now although this study describes for us the developmental nature of "cognition *about* the social," that is, the logic of recursive thinking ability, applied to a social content area (i.e., people thinking about people thinking, etc.), from the perspective taken here, it was not a study of the basic nature of social cognition, that is, of ontogenetic changes in how children think about the *qualities* of persons that are unique to persons. For example, Miller *et al.* could have just as easily used pigs thinking about pigs or robots thinking about robots in their cartoons to demonstrate the child's growing comprehension of recursive thought.

In sum, we were (and are) convinced that for perspective taking to truly represent an important ingredient in the nature of social-cognitive growth, it must include a developmentally integrated account of changes in understanding of relations *between* persons and changes in concepts of relations *within* persons, for example, relations among feelings, thoughts, actions, etc. Methods needed to be developed that tapped both these aspects.

Thus, by 1972, our work and the work of others had convinced us that a coherent approach to the development of social cognition had to include a thoroughgoing examination of structural shifts in underlying social concepts of human nature and of the human coordination of perspectives. We were furthermore convinced that this development could best be assessed using methods which allowed latitude for probing subjects' reasoning and some free-ranging discussion. And lastly, we were certain the best description of this development would reveal it as one of uniquely *social* cognition, not just one of cognitive structures applied to a social content. Our formal study of these three convictions is described in the next section.

Social Perspective Taking: Our Theory and Research

CONSTRUCTION AND DESCRIPTION OF LEVELS

Our drafting of levels of social perspective taking was in the last analysis a sitting-at-the-desk process, although it was based both on the extensive earlier work (ours and others') described in the previous section and on two large and detailed pools of empirical data. Influenced by the developmental models of Piaget, Mead, Flavell, Kohlberg, and Feffer, we began to look for evidence of levels of social perspective taking in interviews of subjects trying to resolve hypothetical moral dilemmas. We analyzed over 200 lengthy protocols of subjects over a wide age-range. Approximately 100 protocols were of interviews conducted over the preceding 6 years by Kohlberg and his colleagues. The remainder were of interviews we were then conducting to pilot test a group of new moral dilemmas (developed by Kohlberg and myself) prior to their production as curriculum filmstrips. The new dilemmas were written to be particularly appropriate to the common social experiences of children and adolescents.

The choice of moral dilemma discussions as the context for seeking descriptive evidence of perspective-taking levels was not arbitrary. Use of the moral dilemma, from dilemma plots to interview techniques to the development of a theory of moral reasoning and its validation, was pioneered and refined by Lawrence Kohlberg over a period from 1959 to the present. His model is one of the best known and most fully developed descriptive models of an area of social cognition. His theoretical background is Piagetian and Meadian, as is ours.

Kohlberg's model is important in social cognition and generally theoretically compatible with our own work. But there were two other reasons why moral dilemma discussions were an excellent source of data for our purposes. First, as pointed out earlier, there is a strong theoretical and empirical link between social perspective taking and moral reasoning, a link suggested by Mead and Piaget as well as by Kohlberg. According to these theoretical assumptions, the child in a general sense structures and understands his or her social environment through perspective taking, and the child's moral reasoning will depend in part on his or her perspective taking.[5] Such a notion has been empirically supported (Moir, 1974; Selman & Damon, 1975) and findings suggested that one might be able to define an ontogenetic sequence of perspective-taking levels which might structurally resemble the moral stages defined by Kohlberg (1969).

Second, the method and content of the (moral) dilemma are especially well-suited to asking subjects to weigh various points of view and to following up on their responses. Such dilemmas encourage each interviewee to spontaneously elaborate on the interviewee's theory of human relations, his or her beliefs about individuals, motives, and feelings, and his or her strategies for resolving conflict. Precisely this type of information was viewed as essential for gaining an understanding of how perspective coordination might relate to social concepts.

In this phase, we worked back and forth among the hundreds of hours of interviews, our theoretical views, and earlier evidence. We tried to construct the levels such that they both described and were defined by genuine universal development in both the hierarchical sense, in which higher levels are built on lower ones, and the structural or reorganizational sense, in which at each higher level a new operational principle takes command. Out of this process emerged a system of five levels of social perspective taking or coordination, levels that describe changes in an individual's understanding of the interactional character of the relation of self to other at the same time as they describe changes in the child's theory of what constitutes an individual, be it self or other.

A synopsis of one of the dilemmas and some typical probe questions follow:

Holly is an 8-year-old girl who likes to climb trees. She is the best tree climber in the neighborhood. One day while climbing down from a tall tree she falls off the bottom branch but does not hurt herself. Her father sees her fall. He is upset and asks her to promise not to climb trees any more. Holly promises.

Later that day, Holly and her friends meet Sean. Sean's kitten is caught up in a tree and cannot get down. Something has to be done right away or the kitten may fall. Holly is the only one who climbs trees well enough to reach the kitten and get it down, but she remembers her promise to her father.

We concentrated on responses to standard questions that focused on relations among perspectives. Does Sean know why Holly cannot decide

[5] If moral judgment stages refer to the development of progressively more adequate theories about how individuals *should* act, think, and feel with regard to one another, each level of social perspective taking might be seen as referring to the basis for a progressively

whether or not to climb the tree? What will Holly's father think? Will he understand why if she climbs the tree? We also looked at responses to open-ended probes which focused on three aspects: conflicts within the subject's own point of view, the point of view of each character in the dilemma, and the relationships among the various perspectives. In addition, our analysis included the subject's conceptions of persons and ideas about the social nature of human behavior.

A structural description of each level follows. (Examples and excerpts of responses for each level can be found in Selman, 1976a.) Descriptions of concepts at each level are divided into sections on persons and on relations, the former describing a child's notions of how an individual functions psychologically, the individual's understanding of internal complexity, and the latter describing the closely related notions of how these individual perspectives are related, concepts of how viewpoints are mutually understood and coordinated. Each level has two titles, the first (e.g., "Undifferentiated") describing the style of conceptions of persons and the second (e.g., "Egocentric") the style of conceptions of relations.

Level 0: Undifferentiated and Egocentric Perspective Taking (about Ages 3 to 6)[6]

Concepts of Persons: Undifferentiated. At this level, young children do not clearly differentiate physical and psychological characteristics of persons. Feelings and thoughts can be observed and recognized, but the confusion between the subjective–psychological and the objective–physical leads to confusion between acts and feelings or between intentional and unintentional behavior.

Concepts of Relations: Egocentric. Selves and others are clearly differentiated only as physical entities, not psychological entities. Thus subjective perspectives are undifferentiated and that another may interpret the same situation differently is not recognized. Concepts of relations of perspectives are limited by inability to differentiate clearly and by concomitant reduction of differences in perspectives to merely differences in *perceptual* perspectives.

---

more adequate theory about why and how individuals *do* think and act in relation to each other. In this sense, the constructs of moral judgment and perspective taking could be seen as overlapping. Coordinating self's and other's perspectives is involved in a wide range of social interactions most of which are not moral interactions, for example, in the development of basic communication skills. On the other hand, moral judgments are made on the basis of more than just the subject's perspective theory. (However, the way in which one considers other and other's viewpoint could be seen as a necessary part of each person's moral judgment.) (See Selman, 1976a and Selman & Damon, 1975.)

[6] All age-norms are approximate and were obtained from verbal responses to hypothetical dilemmas in reflective interviews.

Level 1: Differentiated and Subjective Perspective Taking
(about Ages 5 to 9)

Concepts of Persons: Differentiated. At Level 1, the key conceptual
advance is the clear differentiation of physical and psychological
characteristics of persons. As a result, intentional and unintentional acts
are differentiated and a new awareness is generated that each person has
a unique subjective covert psychological life. Thought, opinion, or feeling states within an individual, however, are seen as unitary, not mixed.
Concepts of Relations: Subjective. The subjective perspectives of self
and other are clearly differentiated and recognized as potentially different. However, another's subjective state is still thought to be legible
by simple physical observation. Relating of perspectives is conceived of
in one-way, unilateral terms, in terms of the perspective of and impact on
one actor. For example, in this simple one-way conception of relating of
perspectives and interpersonal causality, a gift makes someone happy.
Where there *is* any understanding of two-way reciprocity, it is limited to
the physical—the hit child hits back. Individuals are seen to respond to
action with like action.

Level 2: Self-reflective/Second-person and Reciprocal Perspective
Taking (about Ages 7 to 12)

Concepts of Persons: Self-reflective/Second-person. Key conceptual
advances at Level 2 are the growing child's ability to step mentally outside himself or herself and take a self-reflective or second-person perspective on his or her own thoughts and actions *and* on the realization that
others can do so as well. Persons' thought or feeling states are seen as
potentially multiple, for example, curious, frightened, and happy, but
still as groupings of mutually isolated and sequential or weighted
aspects, for example, mostly curious and happy and a little scared. Both
selves and others are thereby understood to be capable of doing things
(overt actions) they may not want (intend) to do. And persons are
understood to have a dual, layered social orientation: visible appearance,
possibly put on for show, and the *truer* hidden reality.
Concepts of Relations: Reciprocal. Differences among perspectives
are seen relativistically because of the Level 2 child's recognition of the
uniqueness of each person's ordered set of values and purposes. A new
two-way reciprocity is the hallmark of Level 2 concepts of relations. It is
a reciprocity of thoughts and feelings, not merely actions. The child puts
himself or herself in another's shoes and realizes the other will do the
same. In strictly mechanical–logical terms, the child now sees the infinite regress possibility of perspective taking (I know that she knows
that I know that she knows . . . etc.). The child also recognizes that the
outer appearance–inner reality distinction means selves can deceive

others as to their inner states, which places accuracy limits on taking another's inner perspective. In essence, the two-way reciprocity of this level has the practical result of detente, wherein both parties are satisfied, but in relative isolation: two single individuals seeing self and other, but not the relationship system between them.

Level 3: Third-person and Mutual Perspective Taking (about Ages 10 to 15)

Concepts of Persons: Third-person. Persons are seen by the young adolescent thinking at Level 3 as systems of attitudes and values fairly consistent over the long haul, as opposed to randomly changeable assortments of states as at Level 2. The critical conceptual advance is toward ability to take a true third-person perspective, to step outside not only one's own immediate perspective, but outside the self as a system, a totality. There are generated notions of what we might call an "observing ego," such that adolescents do (and perceive other persons to) simultaneously see themselves as both actors and objects, simultaneously acting and reflecting upon the effects of action on themselves, reflecting upon the self in interaction with the self.

Concepts of Relations: Mutual. The third-person perspective permits more than the taking of another's perspective on the self; the truly third-person perspective on relations which is characteristic of Level 3 *simultaneously* includes and coordinates the perspectives of self and other(s), and thus the system or situation and all parties are seen from the third-person or generalized other perspective. Whereas at Level 2, the logic of infinite regress, chaining back and forth, was indeed apparent, its implications were not. At Level 3, the limitations and ultimate futility of attempts to understand interactions on the basis of the infinite regress model become apparent and the third-person perspective of this level allows the adolescent to abstractly step outside an interpersonal interaction and simultaneously and mutually coordinate and consider the perspectives (and their interactions) of self and other(s). Subjects thinking at this level see the need to coordinate reciprocal perspectives, and believe social satisfaction, understanding, or resolution must be mutual and coordinated to be genuine and effective. Relations are viewed more as ongoing systems in which thoughts and experiences are mutually shared.

Level 4: In-depth and Societal–Symbolic Perspective Taking (about Ages 12 to Adult)

Concepts of Persons: In-depth. Two new notions are characteristic of Level 4 conceptions of persons. First, actions, thoughts, motives, or feelings are understood to be psychologically determined, but *not neces-*

sarily self-reflectively understood. In this view, there are more complicated interactions *within* a person that cannot always be comprehended by the "observing ego" of Level 3. Thus, we see, whether or not it is so named, the generation of a notion of the unconscious in individuals. Persons are thereby seen to be capable of doing things not that they "don't want" to do, as at Level 2, but that they don't understand why they don't. Second, there emerges at Level 4 a new notion of personality as a product of traits, beliefs, values, and attitudes, a system with its own developmental history.

Concepts of Relations: Societal-Symbolic. The individual now conceptualizes subjective perspectives of persons toward each other (mutuality) as existing not only on the plane of common expectations or awareness, but also simultaneously at multidimensional or deeper levels of communication. For example, in a dyad, perspectives can be shared at the level of superficial information, of common interests, or of deeper unverbalized feelings and communication. At this level, the adolescent or young adult can abstract multiple mutual (generalized other) perspectives to a societal, conventional, legal, or moral perspective in which all individuals can share. Each self is believed to consider this shared point of view of the generalized other or social system in order to facilitate accurate communication and understanding.

The next section addresses the validity of the system just described.

STUDIES OF VALIDITY

I have argued that a definition of social perspective taking must include two components: a relating–coordinating or structural component (itself including differentiating and relating of perspectives), and a conceptual component that, following Mead, focuses on the intensive qualities of persons or selves. I have also argued that these two components need to be considered jointly; if they are not, there is the danger that the construct will lose its specifically social–developmental quality and be reduced to a cognitive skill or operation applied to a social content area (as in the Miller, Flavell, & Kessel study).

Once levels were constructed which theoretically, logically, and empirically seemed to meet these criteria, as well as those of developmental stages, the next step in the research process seemed clear: to look at the reliability of the coding method and the validity of the system. The theoretical and methodological questions emerging for empirical study, albeit numerous and sweeping, would also appear to be relatively obvious. Is the sequence one through which all children go? Are there critical steps in the developmental sequence that have been overlooked? What evidence is there that each level represents a qualitatively distinct orientation to social understanding? Are there age, social class, or sex differences in the emergence of each level? What is the relation of these levels to other aspects of social–cognitive behavior or reasoning? How pervasive and important an underlying skill or mode of functioning might perspective taking, as defined, prove to be? If its identification can be shown to be reliable in a moral dilemma interview context, can it also then be shown to be reliably identifiable in other contexts? And assuming one might develop a technique for ascertaining the child's highest possible perspective-taking level, what factors determine when and how this will actually be used? Will it be used cooperatively or defensively? Will it be used under conditions of more or less stress or challenge?

We undertook three studies of validity and reliability to address some of these questions.

Study One

In this investigation (Selman & Byrne, 1974), we looked at levels of perspective taking used by young children. The subjects were 40 middle-class children, 10 each (5 boys and 5 girls) at ages 4, 6, 8, and 10. Each subject was presented with two open-ended dilemmas, in filmstrip form, such as the story of Holly and the kitten in the tree.

In interviews averaging 20–25 minutes per dilemma, subjects were asked first to retell the story, to eliminate the possibility that responses were limited by faulty memory. Following clarification of any confusion, the interviewer continued with standard questions and probes regarding various characters' perspectives and understandings. In addition, open-ended discussion and role-playing techniques were used to elicit subjects' use of perspective taking.

Transcripts of subjects' interviews were scored for the highest level of perspective taking clearly exhibited. The correlation between highest level of perspective taking attained in each of the two dilemma interviews was .93. Therefore, to determine a subject's highest level, a clinical assessment was made across both measures to decide if a given level was clearly evident. Perfect agreement on highest level attained between trained scorers was 96%; disagreement by one level was 4%. Differences were resolved upon discussion. Perfect agreement across 20 randomly selected protocols between a trained and an untrained scorer, who used the perspective-taking scoring manual without theoretical or experiential background, was 78%.

Analysis indicated a significant product–moment coefficient of correlation of perspective-taking level to age: r (40) $=$ .80, $p <$ .001. No significant sex differences were found. Table 2.1 presents the percentage of subjects at each perspective-taking level by age.

Both the reliability of our scoring and the strongly age-related

TABLE 2.1
**Percentage of Subjects Reaching a Given Perspective-Taking
Level at Each Chronological Age**

Level	Age 4	Age 6	Age 8	Age 10
0	80	10	0	0
1	20	90	40	20
2	0	0	50	60
3	0	0	10	20
Total	100	100	100	100

emergence of levels of perspective taking supported our contention that social perspective taking was susceptible to structural conceptual definition and description, that our levels as defined were sequential, and that they corresponded to some conceptual–developmental "reality" in children's thinking.

Study Two

This study (Byrne, 1973) differed from the one just reported primarily in the age of the subjects. Fifty-six males, 14 each at ages 10, 13, 16, and adult (22–30) were presented with four perspective-taking dilemmas and given open-ended interviews after each.

The dilemmas used were different from those used with younger children. One example follows:

Dr. Miller just finished his training to be a doctor. He was setting up an office in a new town and wanted to get a lot of patients. He didn't have much money to start out with. He found an office and was trying to decide if he should spend a lot of money to make it fancy, by putting down a fancy rug, buying fancy furniture, and expensive lighting, or if he should keep it plain, with no rug, plain furniture, and plain lamps.

Questions concerning the doctor's thinking about how to attract patients on the basis of office decor were used to elicit perspective taking. Subjects were asked to predict what the doctor would do under various conditions, such as the patients knowing or not knowing that he is a new doctor, or under the condition that the American Medical Association has voted that all doctors should have fancy offices. Other questions required the subject to consider the problem from the point of view of the patients or of society in general. An example of the latter type of question is, "What do you think society thinks about doctors spending money to make their offices fancy to attract people?"

Transcripts of interviews were scored for levels of perspective taking. A scoring system was used which combined modal level with highest level used. Interrater reliability was assessed on ten randomly selected protocols; perfect agreement was 90%, and the 10% disagreement was easily resolved.

Level of perspective taking was significantly correlated with age ($r = .86$). The distribution of subjects by score in each age-group is shown in Table 2.2. As in the first study, our results supported the reliability and validity of our system.

Study Three

In this study, we were able to take advantage of an opportunity rare in psychological research: to work with and analyze substantial amounts of longitudinal data collected over a period of approximately 15 years. (Because this study has not been previously published I report it in more detail than Studies One and Two.) In investigating validity in such a system as ours, longitudinal data are invaluable, but time-consuming and costly to collect. Therefore, the Social Reasoning Project has been fortunate to enjoy a collegial relationship with the Harvard Graduate School of Education's Center for Moral Development and Education.

In 1958, Kohlberg began a study of moral development with a sample of 72 boys aged 10, 13, and 16. Contact was maintained with about 50% of these subjects over a period of 15 years. These subjects were reinterviewed approximately every 3 years. The Center has made available to us the protocols from this study, and because we have been able to adapt our system to the analysis of these data, we have a ready-made if imperfect longitudinal study.

Obviously, there are difficulties involved with taking data collected for one purpose and using them for another. Here, for one thing, the interviews are not specifically designed to elicit responses codable by

TABLE 2.2
Distribution of Subjects by Perspective-Taking Level in Each
Age Group

	Perspective-taking level				
Age (N)	0	1	2	3	4
10 (N = 14)	2	12			
13 (N = 14)	1	7	5	1	
16 (N = 14)			3	8	3
Adult (N = 14)					14

social perspective-taking levels, let alone to provide information gathered under "testing the limits" conditions. Thus we suspect that a perspective-taking analysis of these data might underestimate the individuals' capacity. Also, the youngest subjects in the sample were 10 years old, an age at which many children are already capable of higher level understanding. Furthermore, the design and subject selection may not meet the expectations one might have if one were to design an "ideal sample."

Shortcomings notwithstanding, these data are well-suited to our purposes in many respects. Even if it was not done systematically and deliberately, the interviews focused on a wide range of subjects' social thinking. The 3-year interval used for reinterviewing provides a good distance for looking at patterns of development. The hypothetical interview is a condition which provides minimal stress and maximum consistency for subjects which at this phase in research (theoretical–descriptive) is preferred. Thereby we feel this post hoc analysis, even if it is not *conclusive* evidence of the validity of the ontogenesis of perspective taking, can go a long way toward support of our system.

The present study reports an analysis of interview data from 10 subjects, all of whom were 10 years old at the start of the Kohlberg study and were reinterviewed in at least three of the four subsequent follow-up interviews. All five interviews (initial and four subsequent interviews) were analyzed for level of perspective taking. There were a total of 47 interviews. (Three subjects each missed one of the five interviews during the 15-year period.) Each interview consisted of reasoning about 10 open-ended moral dilemmas, and each interview yielded 20 to 50 pages of transcribed discussion focusing on the way the subject thinks about conflicting sociomoral situations.

All interviews were scored for perspective-taking level without identification of subject, the order of the interview, or the moral stage score. Response to each dilemma in each interview was given a score which indicated the highest perspective-taking level clearly used by the subject. Then each complete interview was assigned a level score which was the highest level used in at least half the dilemmas. For example, if a subject received a score of Level 3 in one interview, the subject had to have evidenced this level in at least 5 of the 10 dilemmas in the interview. A test of reliability consisted of giving a second scorer four "cases" (20 interviews) in random order. The reliability of the measure was determined by two methods. The first was to calculate a percentage of agreement between two raters on the highest evident level of perspective taking, as well as the percentage of disagreement by one level, two levels, etc. The second was to correlate the scores of each scorer. Perfect agreement was 85%; one-level disagreement was 15%. Correlational interjudge reliability was .83.

The data analysis was designed to speak to the following two issues: the relationship between age and perspective-taking level and the claim of invariance of sequence of perspective-taking level. Although the number of longitudinal cases is small (10), certainly limiting definitive statements about invariant sequence of levels, the total number of interviews (47) over five ages is large enough to allow both descriptive and inferential statistical analyses. The association between perspective-taking level and age was significant ($r = .88$, $p < .001$). Table 2.3 presents the perspective-taking score for each subject at each interview. Taking use of Level 3 as an example, this table shows that at age 10 only one (10%) of the subjects has Level 3 as that subject's highest predominant level, at age 16 44% are at Level 3 (the rest have moved on to Level 4), and at age 19 only one subject remains at this level. By age 22 even this subject has reached Level 4; all subjects in the sample have passed beyond Level 3 as their highest predominant level of perspective taking.

A test for the invariant sequence of the perspective-taking levels using the longitudinal data was made by examining the changes in each subject's level which occurred from any given interview at time one (x), to the next interview at time two ($x + 1$). For each subject, four such comparisons were made. The three missing interviews reduce the total comparisons to 35 out of a possible 40.

Table 2.4 illustrates that there were no subjects scored at a lower perspective-taking level at time $x + 1$ than at time x, supporting the claim that the levels define a cumulative ordinal scale. (The data also indicate that no subject jumped two levels over a 3-year interval, which implies growth occurs at moderate speed.)

The results of this longitudinal analysis support the hypothesis that the development of the child's ability to integrate the perspectives of self

TABLE 2.3
Social Perspective-Taking Level Scores for Each Longitudinal Subject at Each of the Five Interviews

Subject	Interview 0 Age 9–10	Interview A Age 12–14	Interview B Age 16–17	Interview C Age 19–20	Interview D Age 22 +
1	2	3	4	4	4
2	2	3	4	4	4
3	2	3	4	4	4
4	2	2	3	3	4
5	2	2	3	4	4
6	2	2	3	x	4
7	2	3	4	4	4
8	3	3	x	4	4
9	2	3	4	4	4
10	2	3	3	4	x

TABLE 2.4
Sequentiality Analysis: Changes in Subjects' Predominant Perspective-Taking Level from Time *x* to Time *x* + 1 (in Percentages and Raw Scores)

	Time *x* + 1		
Time *x*	Level 2	Level 3	Level 4
Level 2	25% (3)	75% (9)	
Level 3		27% (3)	73% (8)
Level 4			100% (12)

and other can be described according to an invariant sequence of levels. The limited number of cases does not allow us to derive probabilities of movement from level to level at specific ages.

Conclusion

The three studies just reported comprised 143 cases in cross-sectional and longitudinal samples. For as far as they went, they provided strong support for the levels of perspective taking as defined. The results speak to both reliability and validity. No subjects were found to regress or to skip levels. Nothing in responses was found which appeared to represent a "new level." Levels appeared to be distinct and to emerge sequentially with increasing age. No sex differences were found. Data were reliably codable.

The empirical evidence, both formal and informal or impressionistic, was enough to support the validity of our model as at the very least a good working model of the development of perspective taking. Nonetheless, further questions of validity, refinement, measurement, and application could certainly have been studied at this point. And at this point in our research a choice had to be made. We had defined perspective-taking levels to our satisfaction in formal skeletal terms and developed assessment methods for looking at subjects' use of these levels in a hypothetical reflective context. One alternative was to continue to address perspective taking per se: to look for other contexts in which to assess it; to work toward a method for "testing" the highest level of which a child is capable; to develop a "pure," context-free, perspective-taking instrument; to develop more extensive age or other demographic norms, etc. Our other alternative was to identify a context or contexts in which perspective taking would seem to have an important, even critical role to play, and look specifically at how some understanding of perspective taking, as already described, might inform us about functioning in these areas. In essence, this alternative meant tentative acceptance of our working model and a further addressing of its validity only indirectly, as we used our system as an analytic tool to suggest or help to define structure in developmental changes in interpersonal understanding.

Having reached this fork in the road, we chose the second alternative. The bulk of our energies, as reported in the rest of this book, have subsequently been directed to use of perspective-taking levels as an analytic tool, which use speaks to their validity only in terms of their utility, when seen as underlying structure, in making sense of children's expressed interpersonal reasoning. Some of the reasons for this choice are explained in greater detail in Chapter 4.

Before commencing our report of the research which followed this decision, we present one exception to it. In Chapter 3 we describe one step down the road not taken, a brief foray into "direct assessment" of perspective taking.

3

An Analysis of
"Pure" Perspective Taking:
Games and the Delights of Deception

In Chapter 2, I put forth the hypothesis that each advanced level of social perspective taking represents a shift, qualitative in nature, in the child's understanding of persons and of the relationship between self's and others' points of view and hence of selves and of others. While a good deal of theoretical and empirical effort has gone into this argument, there are still at least three problems that make the empirical study of "pure" perspective taking a particularly difficult one. First, as Werner (1957) and others have pointed out, qualitative shifts in underlying processes may correspond to continuous and quantitative changes in various surface or behaviorally observable manifestations of these underlying changes. Second, and probably more directly relevant to the problem at hand for us, a model that aspires to deal with the relation between inferred or underlying social–cognitive processes and directly observable manifestations must try to define correspondences between the two without denying the potential role and contribution of other cognitive and perceptual abilities. Third, in positing a sequence of developmental levels, some thought should be given to the relationship between lower and higher levels once the higher levels have been constructed.

For our purposes, it may be most useful to consider these concerns in reverse order, starting with the issue of what happens to lower levels once higher levels have emerged. This problem can be exemplified by the response given by an 11-year-old boy presented with the Flavell 5¢/10¢ problem, with the following modification: He was told that his opponent would be a 5-year-old boy rather than a peer.

This preadolescent, like any good developmental psychologist who knows something about preschoolers, took the money from the 10¢ box. When asked for a reason, he responded, "He will want [to take the box with] the most money." Now if one felt methodologically constrained to end one's inquiry or probing into one's reasoning at this point, and if one felt bound by the criteria for assigning levels discussed earlier, this response would be scored at Level 1 (or A). However, few of us would feel comfortable with this. To complicate matters further, the 11-year-old's response, both the choice and the reason, appear quite appropriate:He is probably correct (perceptive, accurate) in his guess about the likely behavior of the younger child.

So, how shall we interpret his response? Is it to be taken as a regression in reasoning level in the face of a problem that requires only a Level 1 strategy for its resolution? Probably not. It is more likely that this child is making a judgment on the basis of a relatively sophisticated social perception of the likely behavior of 5-year-old children. If we look at the statement, we can see only that the subject is making his prediction on the basis of a concept of persons that is at least Level 1. However, probing shows that the *content* of this particular statement should not be taken for the *structure* of this individual's social–cognitive capacity. In the course of our follow-up questioning of this 11-year-old, he said the 5-year-old would choose the 10¢ box "because he's not thinking that I am thinking about what he may do." Here we see how nested in the fabric of this much higher level of understanding was the initial response, which indicated only a part, an element, of that child's overall structure of understanding.

In this example, what appeared to be a response at a level lower than the subject was capable of turned out to be a higher level response. In some cases, the problem itself only demands or elicits reasoning at a certain level, not beyond. A subject capable of reasoning at Level 4 would neither need nor manifest this level in the 5¢/10¢ game. A subject capable of Level 3 reasoning would neither need nor manifest such understanding in successfully solving problems presented in the "Think House" described in Chapter 2. In such cases, lower-level reasoning does seem to be available to subjects reasoning at higher levels. In the research described in this chapter, we sought a problem which would not limit the levels of reasoning or strategy a subject might use, but which would permit subjects to use the highest levels of which they were capable.

These examples also touch on the second issue above, that of the role of other cognitive and perceptual abilities. The structure of the problem the child is asked to deal with can influence not only the level of the response, but also the skills demanded of the subject. Just as there are few if any completely "development-free" problems, that is, standard situations which elicit *each* subject's *highest* level of social problem solving, neither are there problems which require *only* one social, cognitive, or perceptual skill, purely, without involvement of others. Rather, it may be that most social problems require a certain level of social cognition for adequate resolution, but may not require higher levels, and require varying degrees of other skills as well. In this respect, a developmental model of perspective taking is a formal one that spells out a series of levels of social–cognitive competence within individuals. These levels impinge upon and underlie but do not necessarily dominate the child's social performance in any specified context. One important interest in the research reported in this chapter was in finding a problem in which the role of other abilities would be deliberately limited.

But psychological tests and measures are usually designed to tap performance, not some intangible or hard-to-grasp underlying single competence (which touches on the first issue above, correspondences between underlying skill and action). Therefore anyone who desires to develop a method for assessing developmental levels of social perspective taking or coordination must acknowledge that part of the task is to try to demonstrate these connections.

To recapitulate, any social–cognitive task may have a relatively low ceiling and therefore fail to challenge subjects to use highest levels. Also, responses generated by tasks designed to tap levels of perspective coordination may actually be tapping other social–cognitive functions or processes as well, for example, social perceptions, social attitudes, etc. And there is the risk that the more one strives for a pure measure of perspective taking, unencumbered by other confounds, either internal or external, the less ecological validity findings will have for understanding the functional role of social–cognitive development in social behavior in the real world.

Yet it is hard to abandon entirely the desire to develop a procedure that would elegantly tap developmental differences in social behavior clearly corresponding to level of perspective taking, clearly differentiated from other cognitive and social–cognitive skills, and clearly demonstrative of the qualitative nature of this process. Aware of the pitfalls and the limits on what we could accomplish, we attempted to develop such a problem.

Our search for a "pure perspective-taking task" led us to the strategy games children enjoy playing with each other. Beginning with a trip to the game department of the local toy store, we ultimately found two games which began to approximate some of the requirements detailed above, one of which we were able to modify and use with some success. A brief description and analysis of skills required by each may provide a beginning model of how perspective-taking level functions in relation to other cognitive and social–cognitive skills tapped by these games.

Problems of Task Demands: The Skills of the Game

The first game that attracted our eye was called Fourthought©,[1] which is essentially an elaboration of tick-tack-toe. Advertising copy on the box cover claims inside one will find a "fast-moving game of skill and strategy for two players age 10 through adult . . . mislead your opponent . . . attack and counterattack . . . think one or two moves ahead and hope your opponent doesn't spoil your game plan." The game materials are two sets of 26 marbles, each set of a different color, and a playing board consisting of 64 spaces (8 × 8). In each row there are six or seven spaces with indentations which can hold a marble and one or two flat dead spaces which cannot hold a marble. Play begins when one of the two players places one of his or her marbles into one of the indented spaces on the playing board. Play continues in alternation until one of the players has placed four of his or her marbles in an uninterrupted sequence, either horizontally, vertically, or diagonally, or until all the marbles are used up and the game is drawn. That the board is larger and that there can be no interruptions of the four in a row by either an opponent's piece or one of the dead spaces make this game more challenging than its tick-tack-toe ancestor.

We tried to look first at the skills that the game itself requires or calls forth in a participant and later at the skills an individual possesses and brings to the game. It is often hard to differentiate between these sets of skills. Developmental psychologists generally like to use tasks which potentially elicit responses easily and clearly codable at a range of developmental levels. In this case we were looking for a task that would stimulate perspective-taking activity in subjects. Despite the game developers' claim, our observations and interviews of children and adults playing the game revealed few indications that the players were actually using psychological strategies. Seldom, for example, were they trying to trick an opponent with respect to their own motives or intentions. True, as with the game's more simple relative, tick-tack-toe, to play this game well, one must be able to examine simultaneously the possible and potential strategies of one's opponent *and* one's own present and future

---

[1] Fourthought© is published by Milton Bradley, Springfield, Massachusetts.

moves. However, one does not have to look at the psychology behind these moves. In Fourthought, the process called forth can be more accurately seen as a process of (Piagetian–cognitive) decentration than of social perspective taking. In Fourthought, one could just as well be challenged by a computer or robot with built-in logical contingency plans as by another human. Consideration of psychological contingencies, where the field of battle is between two *social* minds trying to outpsychologize each other, is not overtly elicited or required in this game.

This does not mean that the game does not tacitly require a certain minimal adequacy of social perspective coordination, social logic. For example, young children, between say 5 and 8, play this game as if their opponent and they have no need to pay attention to each other's strategies. This certainly limits the skill of their play. (Perhaps it is partly for this reason that the game developers recommend the game for children aged 10 and over.) However, beyond this, the game itself does not seem to require a conscious psychological perspective-taking attitude.

What then are the skills that Fourthought demands? One skill that can be juxtaposed to the social logic of social perspective taking or coordination is the formal logic of mathematical coordinations. For example, an important ingredient in successful Fourthought play is the understanding that strategies based upon multiple seriation are far more powerful than those based upon single seriation. The strategist who places his or her marbles on the board so that each placement serves multiple purposes, for example, a block on defense and an attack on offense or a two-way attack on offense, stands a better chance of winning than the strategist who plants marbles with only one purpose.

Social and nonsocial (mathematical) *logic* are two skills potentially elicited or required by strategy games. The other two dimensions we looked at are the *perceptual demands* of the task, both *social* and *nonsocial.* Here, nonsocial perceptual demands refer to the weight of rules, limits, parameters, board positions, etc., that need to be "kept in mind" for successful play at any particular moment. For example, in the game of chess, there are a number of what are being called here "perceptual" demands inherent in the game structure. There are a number of different game pieces, each with different value, power, and movements, that must be remembered. In addition, there is always the constant demand to scan the board carefully, to not miss any dangers in the perceptual present, let alone in the logical potential of future moves. In Fourthought, the "factor loading" on the perceptual complexity of pieces and moves is relatively low. Each marble is the same value as the next and there are no "moves" that need to be remembered. Some degree of accurate board scanning is, of course, essential. Nevertheless, nonsocial perception as described is not an especially important factor in this game.

    This leaves social perception as the final factor to be considered of
the skills we are looking at. Social–perceptual skills refer to the degree to
which the game elicits or calls for actions based upon social acuity, that
is, perceptions of how one's opponent tends to play the game from a
psychological perspective. "She is playing so she won't lose," "She
doesn't care if she wins or ties," "He just doesn't want to lose," or "He's
the kind of player that bluffs a lot" are responses indicative of this type
of skill. Fourthought pulled for some degree of social perception but
nowhere nearly as much as a game such as poker, for example.

    Table 3.1 summarizes the way certain games vary in the degree of
these four skills they require, to what degree a particular *task* pulls for
each of the four "dimensions." (This analysis is of course to some extent
an armchair activity, and therefore arbitrary and arguable; it is intended
only as a rough aid in conceptualizing what skills are involved.) Our purpose in using this schematic analysis is to use it to help determine
whether a task is a potentially good one for eliciting the perspective-
taking or coordination factor. Such a task would be one that loaded
relatively high on social logic (perspective taking) while being fairly low
on nonsocial logic and on the perceptual factors, social and nonsocial.

    For example, let us apply this analysis to Fourthought. Even though
the game developers speak of the challenge of this game in terms of
deception or trickery, according to our analysis, there is very little in this
game that demands reflective social perspective-taking activity. In fact,

TABLE 3.1
Schematic Representation of Skill Dimensions of Strategy Games [a]

Game	Skill				Overall difficulty rating
	SL[b]	NL[c]	SP[d]	NP[e]	
Tick-tack-toe	1	2	1	1	5
Fourthought	2	4	2	2	10
Checkers	2	3	1	2	8
Chess	3	5	3	5	16
Poker (Seven card stud)	5	4	3	3	15
5¢/10¢ Game	4	2	2	1	9
Decoy and Defender	5	2	2	1	10

[a] 5 = High amount of this skill demanded
   4 = Moderately high amount of this skill demanded
   3 = Moderate amount of this skill demanded
   2 = Moderately low amount of this skill demanded
   1 = Low amount of this skill demanded
[b] Social logic (perspective taking).
[c] Nonsocial (mathematical) logic.
[d] Social perception (acuity about opponent).
[e] Nonsocial perception (acuity about rules, moves, and perceptual present).

the game requires very little that is social, either in the way of social logic or social perception. The game loads highest (but not as high as chess) on nonsocial logical abilities, and perhaps next on nonsocial perceptual ones. This does not mean it does not require any perspective-taking or social perception for adequate play but that in a relative sense the explicit demands of the task elicit logical thinking skills rather than social ones.

Table 3.1 includes how we judge some other common two-person strategy games require various skills. For example, chess is very high on both nonsocial skills, and relative to these low on both social skills (although still of moderate difficulty in comparison to the other games). This is not because chess does not require *any* social perception or perspective coordination, but because it is heavily weighted toward logical analysis and information scanning procedures and requires relatively less in the way of social skills. Poker (seven card stud), on the other hand, appears to be a game that demands a better balance of the four skills; it requires some understanding of the logic of the cards, including probability theory (nonsocial logic), but it also requires the ability to remember what cards have already been drawn (nonsocial perception). Accurate assessment of what kind of risk taker one's opponent is and some immediate assessment of how one's opponent is likely to respond to the way the self plays the game are necessary (social perception). And one *must* be able to use social perspective coordination to know what one's opponent will do as well (social logic).

As the astute reader may discern, the dichotomies used are not clean and neat; the world does not divide that cleanly into perception and conception, nor does reality necessarily divide cleanly into the social and the nonsocial (cf. Broughton, 1978). Nevertheless, despite its limitations, this kind of analysis seems worthwhile because it provides a way to look at tasks to determine whether and to what extent they would be likely to elicit the kind of social behavior (game play) which is interpretable according to the underlying perspective taking. Using this scheme, we sought a game high on social logic (perspective taking) and relatively low on the other skills.

Development of a Task: Decoy and Defender

We did find a game, Evade©, commercially available,[2] that seemed to have built directly into its structure an emphasis on reflective considera-tion of the coordination of psychological expectations as a key element in play. At the same time it did not seem to require much in the way of the

---

[2] Evade© is published by the 3M Company, Saint Paul, Minnesota (1971).

other three skills in our scheme. Evade is played by two players on a 36-square checkerboard (6 × 6). Each player has six tokens lined up across the six back spaces of the board, the *goal line*. Two of these tokens are designated as *flag carriers*, the other four as *defenders*. In the commercial version of Evade, flag carriers are identified by placing a magnetic metal disc underneath the flag carriers, tokens otherwise undistinguishable from the others. Neither player knows the whereabouts of the opponent's flag carriers, and each is required to remember where his or her own flag carriers are. The object of the game is to be the first to get one of one's own flag carriers to the opponent's goal line.

Evade is packaged and advertised as an adult game; our interest was in adapting it and developing a method that would yield responses and behavior in children that could be categorized according to the perspective-taking levels. Therefore, starting with the standard adult version, we set out to make adjustments in the game rules such that it would be appropriate for children as young as 5 or 6, responses could be parsimoniously explained in terms of perspective-taking levels, and other task demands would be minimized. Through several cycles of pilot work with children of various ages, we evolved "Decoy and Defender." It is a two-person competitive game intended as an informal assessment or demonstration procedure for observing and interpreting the child's manifest social perspective-taking behavior and reasoning in developmental terms.

In Decoy and Defender, the object of the game and the playing board are the same as in Evade. Each player also has six tokens. However, they are modified to stand up so that the player to whom the tokens belong can *see* rather than have to remember which two the player has designated as flag carriers and which four remain defenders, but the opponent cannot. We made this adjustment to limit the amount of nonsocial perceptual skill required.

As in most board games, players alternate moves, and are allowed to move one token one space per turn, either straight ahead or laterally. Diagonal and backward moves are not allowed. The basic defensive move is the *freeze*. A freeze occurs when a player moves one of his pieces, either a flag carrier or a defender, into a square already occupied by an opponent's piece. Once a freeze is made, both players' pieces are removed from the playing board for the remainder of the game, but neither player is told what type tokens have been frozen. To prevent freezing of all 12 tokens, and thereby to insure a game resolution and increase the chances for continued perspective-taking strategy, we adopted a rule limiting each player to only two freezes.

We felt Decoy and Defender, as described, came closer to meeting two criteria for tapping perspective taking. First, the structure of the game should call forth or elicit a *perspective-taking attitude* in each of the players. In making this statement I realize that it refers most appropriately to the responses of the cognitively mature player rather than to the play of the child. Adults who play this game realize that there is a need to reflectively consider the coordination of psychological (not just logical) points of view, or what we are calling here taking a *social* perspective-taking attitude. In addition, they recognize that the object or content of these coordinations is the understanding of the social–psychological operations of the opponent. Decoy and Defender is a game in which the successful player or winner, ideally speaking, deceives the opponent with respect to the self's strategizing, and at the same time is not deceived by the opponent's strategy. As distinct from the thinking involved in Fourthought or from reflective thinking per se, social perspective taking by definition requires that both the structure of thought and the object or content of thought be social or psychological in nature. So does the game of Decoy and Defender; therefore it should elicit behavior representative of underlying perspective-taking processes. (For further illustration of how successful play of Decoy and Defender involves social perspective taking, please note Level 3 strategies as described in the "Method and Scoring" section of this chapter, page 60.)

Second, the game should be designed so as not to require or elicit to any great extent the other factors described in our four-factor model. Unlike Fourthought, for example, there is no inherently logical strategy (e.g., multiple seriation) to the game of Decoy and Defender other than the logic of using and manipulating social perspectives. In addition, there are few rules to learn or remember and fewer needs to scan and store information from one move to the next; the information is readily available at any given point in the play by a quick scan of the board. Of course, the game is not devoid of these other factors; such a situation would be impossible to achieve. Decisions whether to play defensively or offensively, for example, whether it is best to try to freeze the opponent's flag carriers before making an attack on his goal line, rest upon strategizing that does not require perspective taking per se. Nevertheless, even this kind of strategizing requires a perspective-taking attitude for its implementation.

Method and Scoring

Obviously, it is interesting to developmental psychologists to understand whether young children approach this game with or without a perspective-taking attitude, and if such an attitude is present, how it may be manifested. If we are correct that the game of Decoy and Defender is structured so as to elicit primarily perspective-taking related strategies or aspects of behavior, then it follows that the levels that have so far been defined should be able to order that observed behavior, particularly if comparisons are made of the observed behaviors of children at different ages.

To approach this problem, members of our research staff observed and interviewed two samples of children. The first (pilot) sample consisted of 30 children aged 5 to 13 who were observed playing the game with peers and with staff members. From our work with this group, a set of strategies that children at different ages appeared to use in order to successfully play this game was identified, and a method devised which would allow us to code the observed strategies reliably in a subsequent sample.

Our activity with these two groups of children can be viewed as an experiment, but it may be more accurate to think of it as a *research demonstration*. It is a useful game for adults to play to get a feel for what the perspective-taking process is like. In essence, it brings what is usually an "unconscious" process into reflection. The game demonstrates that a certain orientation is necessary when both the content and structure of the game revolves around the human capacity to consider the human capacity to take self and other's point of view together. By adulthood this understanding is often taken for granted. Thus, our aim in administering this procedure to children at different ages was not to find whether or at what age perspective-taking abilities were manifested on yet another task, but to experientially demonstrate that a developmental perspective-taking model is a useful way to order *observed* differences in strategy *behavior* in children who are likely to vary in social experience (as expressed by chronological age differences). To do this we found with our first group it was necessary to devise a method that consisted of both direct observation and subsequent interviewing in which the child was asked to *reflect upon* the game experience (which was observed by the adult experimenter). (The second phase of this two-phase method is called the *post-game wrap-up*.)

Before continuing with details of procedure with the second group, the developmental aspect of strategies observed in the first group will be described.

As noted, a strategy was defined on the basis of *both* the subjects' moves as observed during the game *and* the accompanying explanations (or lack thereof) provided by the subjects upon reflection in the post-game wrap-up. These strategies are described as offensive or defensive at each level.

LEVEL 0 STRATEGIES

Offensive Strategy. The child begins immediately with a flag carrier and moves it directly toward the opponent's goal line in what we characterized as the *rush for glory* approach. In reasoning, the child does not give any clear-cut indication that if one person wins the other must lose; both players can win if and when they reach the other side. The child likens the game to a race and speed of movement is seen as the determining factor in winning. One wins when one gets to the other side.

Defensive Strategy. A "nondefense" strategy is evident; no attempt is made to block or freeze the opponent's tokens. The player acts as if the other player's moves are independent of his own and irrelevant, as if the object of the game were a footrace from one end of the field to the other. Reasoning is the same as on offense, above.

LEVEL 1 STRATEGIES

Offensive Strategy. The child acts in ways that imply a concern that the other players will try to hinder the player's attempt to reach the opponent's goal line. For example, the child takes one of his *defender* pieces and moves it toward the opponent's goal line, announcing in a loud clear voice some variant of "I'll move this *flag carrier* up to win." We called this an example of the *overt decoy* strategy. The subject acts as if he or she is cognizant that the opponent is concerned with the self's moves and strategies, but the subject does not act as if he or she is aware that the other player may be able to judge that the self's *actions* may differ from the self's *words* (intent). The subject acts as if the other person will assume that what the self says he or she is doing is in correspondence with that which the self actually does. For instance, in follow-up of the example given above, the child is either unable to articulate a reflective statement about why he or she verbally announced an incorrect move, or the child simply expresses the assertion that the opponent would believe what he or she said to be true without any further elaboration or reflection.

Defensive Strategy. The player acts as if he or she is cognizant of the attempt by the player's opponent to win and acts to "block the first piece" the opponent begins to move toward the self's goal line. The player is able to articulate that both self and other want to win and that therefore the opponent is trying to move his or her flag up as quickly as possible, that is, to get across first. Speed is still the strategy of choice for the self and other's strategies are assumed to be the same. No mention is made of the possibility that other will be attempting to deceive the self.

LEVEL 2 STRATEGIES

Offensive Strategy. The child acts in ways that imply a greater concern with tacit deceptions, fakes, and judicious use of defenders. For example, without saying anything, a player moves a defender (rather than a flag carrier) assertively forward, as if to score, in effect trying to decoy the opponent or lure the opponent into a false freeze. This was the *covert decoy* or *single fake* strategy. The player is able to articulate that he or she is trying to act in ways that will mislead the opponent without the opponent being aware that the self is aware that the opponent is being misled. In effect the child acknowledges that other is trying to figure out the self's motives, so the self can put forth signs that lead other to incorrectly assess these self-motives. The child rejects the suggestion to verbalize a false move out loud as being ineffective or silly. ("The other guy will see through that.")

Defensive Strategy. In play the subject appears to be "selective" in the use of blocks or freezes. The subject lets some pieces go past his or her line of defense and freezes others. The child is able to articulate that the opponent may be trying to fake or trick the self and that the first of the opponent's players to move toward the self's goal line may or may not be a flag carrier. This type of reasoning suggests the player is aware that the opponent is considering the self's strategy making, that other is trying to "fake out" the self.

LEVEL 3 STRATEGIES

It is not surprising to find that with age and development, strategies become more intricate, complex, and contingent. What makes this game challenging is not the complexity of the mathematical logic demanded but of the social logic, balancing and weighing alternatives on the basis of what you think your opponent thinks; what you think your opponent thinks you think, etc. Nonetheless, the game of Decoy and Defender, although more challenging than the 5¢/10¢ game, has only so many potential moves and countermoves. Thus we stopped describing strategies at Level 3; and at Level 3 the higher level development in the intricacy of strategy making was less readily inferred from the direct observation of game playing actions alone and more readily inferred from the subject's reflective reasoning about his or her actions.

Offensive Strategy A. The player assertively and without hesitation moves a flag carrier straightforwardly toward the opponent's goal line. If the opponent moves a defender toward the piece, the player shows no actions that suggest caution or retreat or evasive action, but moves in a way that puts the onus on the defender to decide whether the defender wants to use one of his or her freezes on this piece. The reasoning given that is coded at Level 3 is some variation of an explantion we call the *double fake*. By this the subject acknowledges that he wants the opposition to think that the self is trying to fake a rush to glory to lure a false freeze on the part of the opponent: a double fake. If the opponent is convinced that the self is faking, the opponent may actually let a winning flag carrier through the defense.

Offensive Strategy B. In an action called the *false flee*, the offensive player moves up a decoy in the same manner as the subject who, using the double fake, moved up a flag carrier, or in the same manner that the player using the single fake (Level 2) also moved up a decoy. However, the difference between this strategy and the one at Level 2 is that in this case, the player makes moves contingent upon the reactions of the opponent. If, for example, the opponent makes moves that would tentatively indicate an attack, either a block or a freeze, the initiator of the offense then moves his decoy in a manner that implies an attempt to *evade* the defender. The player is able to articulate that he is attempting to convince the opponent that his decoy is a flag carrier, and that by taking evasive action, that is, "wasting some of the self's moves," deception will appear more convincing. In addition, subjects at this level are able to see that by causing one's opponent to use up his or her freezes injudiciously, one's chances of winning are increased because such a state leaves an opponent essentially defenseless when a flag carrier finally moves toward the opponent's goal line.

We did not observe any readily identifiable defensive strategies at Level 3, perhaps because good defense is implied or included in such sophisticated offensive strategies.

To recapitulate, using a combination of behavioral observation and follow-up reflective interviews, we identified eight distinct strategies. These strategies were categorized as either offensive or defensive in function and conceptually linked to the first four perspective-taking levels.

This accomplished, the Decoy and Defender game was then administered to 24 target children in a new sample. Three boys and three girls from each of four grades (1, 3, 5, 7) were selected from a suburban New England area school for observation and reflective interviewing. Each target child was asked to choose a classmate with whom he or she would enjoy learning how to play a new game. In a quiet room, the Decoy and Defender rules were explained to the subject and his or her companion–opponent, and each player participated in a practice game with the experimenter while the other player observed. For both practice trials the experimenter used a Level 2 offensive strategy. The target child first observed the experimenter play the first trial with his or her opponent; then the child played the game against the experimenter.

After each trial, the children were asked the following questions to ascertain how well the basic game rules were understood:

1. What kind of moves can each player make? Can you move backward?

2. Can (your opponent) see which of your pieces is a defender and which is a flag carrier?
3. How do you freeze (your opponent's) piece? What happens to a piece when it is frozen?
4. How may freezes are you allowed?

In both trials rule clarifications were made when necessary. As would be expected, the younger children had more difficulty with rules per se, but children at all ages appeared able to grasp and maintain these rules after these two trials.

The third and fourth games were played between the two children. Sitting between both players so that she could observe the moves of each, the experimenter made note of the sequence of moves made by the target child, paying particular attention to points at which switches from offensive to defensive (or the reverse) strategies seemed to occur. Each of the subject's behavioral sequences which appeared planful was noted by the experimenter on a code sheet for subsequent discussion.

Following the third trial (the first child–child game, from which data were drawn), the experimenter told each child that she was interested in better understanding how each child had tried to win the game. Beginning with the target child, the interviewer then spent 10 or 15 minutes privately with each child, ostensibly because to talk in front of the other child might give away strategies for the fourth and final game.

In the interview with the target child, the experimenter drew upon her observations of the play, described each of the strategies she was able to observe, and using the game board as a tool to describe the observed moves, asked the child to comment on or explain them. Following this interview the child was asked to spell out what he or she thought was the best strategy for winning. Following the interview, the second child was also queried with respect to play but in a less systematic way. A second game followed, after which both children were interviewed together as to what they liked or disliked about the game, and whether they had learned anything from playing.

Results and Discussion

Behavior described to the subject by the experimenter, followed by the subject's reflections upon this behavior, were coded as a single unit in accordance with the previously described system. If, in the interview, the subject demonstrated the use and understanding of more than one strategy, each was coded. Table 3.2 shows the number and kind of offensive and defensive strategies coded for children at each grade level.

Most subjects were observed to use and were able to identify both an

TABLE 3.2
Number, Social Perspective-Taking Level, and Kind of Strategies at Each Grade Level

	Level of social perspective taking								Total number of strategies generated by subjects
	0		1		2		3		
Grade	Offense	Defense	Offense	Defense	Offense	Defense	Offense A	Offense B	
1	4	2	2	1	—	—	—	—	9
3	1	2	4	5	1	—	—	—	13
5	—	1	4	3	4	3	2	—	17
7	—	—	—	—	3	5	6	3	17

offensive and a defensive strategy. Exceptions were three first graders who did not seem to use and were unable to reflectively acknowledge a defensive plan. Because the size of the sample (24) is relatively small in comparison to the number of categories to which children's strategies can be assigned (even with multiple scores), to look statistically at the relation between level of strategy and subjects' grade level, the data were merged as in Table 3.3. A significant positive association was found between grade and level of strategy.

Four results of this demonstration study merit some emphasis and attention. First, the levels of social perspective taking helped us make sense of our observations, and the age trends for the emergence of strategies representative of each perspective-taking level are similar to those reported in the previous studies, presented in Chapter 2.

Second (which refers back to the third issue raised at the beginning of this chapter), although it is not surprising to note that the older children used socially more complex strategies than did the younger children, it is not immediately clear how to understand the ways these older subjects used lower level strategies. On the one hand, no seventh grader used a Level 0 or 1 strategy. On the other hand, the older children did use strategies at more than one level, and they tended to use more strategies during the game than did the younger children (see Table 3.2).

TABLE 3.3
Summed Numbers of Strategies by Social Perspective-Taking Level and Grade [a]

	Social perspective-taking level	
Grade	0 and 1	2 and 3
1 and 3	21	1
5 and 7	8	26

[a] $\chi^2 = 24.96$; $p < .01$.

The fifth and seventh graders used a total of 34 observed and reflected-upon strategies as compared to 22 for the first and third graders. What then is the relation between higher and lower levels in the child's repertoire? On the one hand, higher strategies do not appear to be simply additive in the sense that with maturity, the child simply quantitatively accumulates more strategies, for we see that few of the strategies used by the younger children are also used by the older ones. Nor, on the other hand, do the older children appear to reject outright all lower strategies once they construct higher level ones. For example, many of the older children used strategies at a number of levels. Logically and developmentally, these strategies appear to be hierarchically related to one another in the sense that higher level strategies build upon and reorganize the elements inherent in prior approaches. While no seventh grader used the rush to glory strategy in the naive way it was used by several of the first graders, these older children were cognizant of this approach and made use of it as part of their more complex and socially sophisticated approaches.

Third, to understand the emergence of levels within this hierarchical model requires techniques and methods that include or tap into both behavioral and cognitive–reflective components of social functioning. Without the former we cannot be sure which strategies children will actually use in social interaction (as opposed to which they tell us they would use). Without the latter, how can we be sure we understand the meaning behind these strategies as they are observed? Can the 12-year-old's double fake be distinguished from the 5-year-old's rush to glory without some understanding of the child's conceptions? Not much better than the boys-in-the-bunks' behavior can be seen as anything but identical without knowing how the situation is understood. Here, we can hark back to the first issue we raised at the chapter's start. At least in the context of strategy games, subjects seem to be willing and able to connect their actions to their reasoning for us.

And finally, to touch upon the second issue we originally raised, we felt that although an assessment of "pure" perspective taking is probably impossible by definition for a truly *social*–cognitive skill, we did succeed in creating a real situation which elicited relatively high amounts of perspective taking and lower amounts of other skills.

Conclusion

In this chapter, I have briefly addressed the issue of "pure" perspective-taking assessment and reported one empirical venture into the area. This venture was introduced as one step down a road we have chosen not to take, that of further work on perspective taking per se. As a solo step, we felt it was intriguing and productive and provided a starting point for further research using both action and reasoning as clues to the meaning of social behavior. At this point, however, I leave "pure" perspective taking and by way of a brief recapitulation of the major issues in Part I (Chapters 2 and 3) take the reader back to the road we have followed, that of using perspective taking as an analytical tool in various interpersonal contexts.

In Chapter 2, I discussed context and perspective in psychological research. Following a description of our own general developmental social–cognitive perspective, I reviewed the theoretical and empirical antecedents of the work reported in this book. I then reported our early efforts in exploring perspective taking which led to the definition, description, and initial validation of a system of five levels of perspective taking or coordination, defined as including an understanding of both the coordination of the perspective of self and other *and* the nature of man as a perspective-taking animal. Each level involves a greater understanding of the relation of self and other and its complexity. The levels are sequential and not simply additive, but hierarchical.

In Chapter 2, several other issues were raised which will continue to be addressed throughout the book: the relation of surface behavior or reasoning to underlying conceptual structures, the relation of reasoning in a reflective hypothetical context to reasoning in other contexts, the importance of looking at an individual's social–cognitive development, and the relation of one's behavior to social reasoning, to name a few. In Chapter 2 and in this chapter, our initial validity studies and our digression into perspective-taking assessment broach methodological concerns which are also refrains in our work: criteria of validity, interpretation of reasoning, contexts of subjects' responses, and correspondences among areas and types of responses.

Before closing this chapter and moving on to the description of using perspective-taking levels as tools in ordering the development of interpersonal understanding, I want to discuss three major issues that are raised by our view of social development and the direction we choose to take. I call these the problems of age, inference, and distance. They are closely intertwined.

The Problem of Age. The problem of age is really the question of when in the child's social development each level of social understanding is achieved and manifests itself in such a way as to truly influence or significantly shape social behavior. Ways to try to assess such a question and other opinions on the subject vary as widely as they do in any general discussion of when children (or chimpanzees for that matter) "have" certain concepts or cognitive capacities (Flavell & Wohlwill, 1969), whether one is asking when the first clear sign emerges or when a conceptual level gains enough strength to appear to influence a broad range of behavior.

In addition to these still open questions is a related issue. It is interesting that Mead, whose theorizing forms a cornerstone of much of the research in this book, resisted the temptation to attach age norms to his developmental stages of self and social conceptions. Social interactionists who have followed in this tradition (Blumer, 1969; Turner, 1970) also appear to avoid scrupulously the assignment of ages to Meadian-type stages. The explanation for this is undoubtedly a deeply felt commitment of his followers to Mead's assumption that social meaning arises predominantly from the social or interactional contexts in which an individual finds himself or herself, and not from chronological, time-released, cognitive capacities within each individual. Developmental psychologists, on the other hand, are usually committed to making some statement about the correspondences between social–cognitive competence and age and generally believe in the importance of the individual developmental component in social relations. Few developmental psychologists believe social skills are totally dependent on the nature of the interactional context, and although much debate and empirical energy is focused upon *when* children can do something, it is generally agreed that reasonable estimates *can* be made.

Some midground between the stands of psychologist and social interactionist would seem to provide a potential resolution of the issue of age and of individual developmental ability versus social context as the source of social meaning. In the case of perspective taking we do assign some very general age-trends, at least on the basis of the various experimental measures used to date. It appears that the subjective level (Level 1) emerges in the late preschool and early elementary school years, that the self-reflective level (Level 2) appears in the early elementary grades and middle childhood, that the mutual level (Level 3) is largely a preadolescent phenomenon, and that the in-depth level (Level 4) is a conceptual discovery of adolescence and young adulthood. In conjunction with this description of children in general, it is also important to avoid the error of assuming that a particular child has a certain competence based upon his performance on a one-shot psychological test. We believe strongly in the importance of level of perspective taking, but as a result of that, we believe equally strongly in the importance of careful assessment. We want to keep a loose model of perspective taking in mind as a framework that can help to order observation of and make generalizations about children across a wide age-range as well as to look at a specific time or place in the child's life in relation to a specific skill. We also "compromise," as it were, in our notion of the relative importance of individual competence and social contexts; both are important, and neither can explain social relations alone, as the work reported later in the book begins to establish.

The Problem of Inference. I have noted that one distinction between behavioral and social–cognitive models of social development is the degree to which the explanations of data are based upon categories that describe the subject's observable actions versus those that describe the subject's inferred "invisible" understanding. In this chapter, we even tried to find direct action-reasoning connections in strategy games. However, one way to view perspective taking is as a very basic form of social understanding that underlies other social understandings and behaviors. This does not mean that perspective taking is viewed as a hypothetical construct or an abstraction, for example, the way Loevinger (1976) discusses ego development. A more apt analogy is to the way some psycholinguists discuss the underlying principles and rules of grammar and syntax as "deep structures" which influence the surface characteristics of everyday speech. In Chapters 2 and 3, I have discussed methods in which we attempt to directly infer perspective taking levels from a range of psychological tasks. However, if our own emerging view of perspective taking as a "deep structure" is somewhat analogous to deep language structures, that is, as a level of social understanding that may underlie other, less structural layers of social comprehension such as moral judgment, social conceptions, etc., this implies, in turn, certain questions about the relevance and usefulness of energy investment into a search for a "pure" or context-free measure of this phenomenon. But if the measurement of perspective taking per se is no longer our aim, we are forced, at least temporarily, back to further inferential descriptive work, as the next part of the book describes.

The Problem of Distance. The first section of Chapter 2 began on a relativistic note by stressing that how one sees social development depends, in part, upon not only the theoretical perspective but also the contextual framework or distance from which one chooses to view a specified developmental process or problem. What is gained in vista or scope by looking at a general process across a wide range often corresponds to what is lost in specificity of detail. We have painted a picture of perspective-taking development as a basic and universal social-cognitive process. Therefore although it explains much of the variation in social behavior across a broad age-range, it may have less explanatory power within a more narrow spectrum of ages or shorter measurement intervals. However, it still certainly seems important to look at the behavioral ramifications of an individual child's or various age-groups' discovery of subjectivity, self-reflection, and mutuality of perspectives,

and then to go on to what this model can say about, for example, differences in the social natures of children who may be at the *same*
perspective-taking level. These are serious questions, and must be
studied if research in social cognition is to have relevance beyond its own
construct validation.

The rest of the book falls into three more sections corresponding to
the three phases of our extension or application of social perspective-
taking levels to interpersonal understanding.

Part II : Phase 1: Descriptive Model Building
Part III: Phase 2: Construct Validation
Part IV : Phase 3: Application

INTERPERSONAL UNDERSTANDING— PHASE 1: DESCRIPTIVE MODEL BUILDING

4

Constructing a Model of
Interpersonal Understanding

In Part I (Chapters 2 and 3), I reviewed the background of our research, described levels of perspective taking or perspective coordination, reported our decision to pursue use of these levels as analytic tools rather than skills or abilities in and of themselves, and reported one final piece of research. Parts II, III, and IV (Chapters 4-10) are devoted to the three phases of the principal body of our contemporary research on interpersonal understanding: descriptive model building, construct or internal validation, and application to other modes of social functioning.

The subject of this part (II) is the first phase, the goal of which is to use a structural analysis to describe developmental patterns in relevant areas of reflective interpersonal reasoning. In this chapter (4), I describe how, on the basis of extensive clinical interviewing, we outlined a five-step sequence of interpersonal conceptions in four domains: individuals, friendships, peer groups, and parent–child relations. In Chapter 5, I present detailed in-depth illustrations of these domains. In Chapter 6, I give more general pictures of each.

Part III, Chapters 7 and 8, is devoted to the second, or construct validation phase, in which we formally evaluated the degree to which these levels of developing reasoning satisfy certain essential criteria of cognitive developmental stage theory: structured wholeness, invariant sequence, and cross-cultural generality.

In Part IV, the third phase of this research process is described. These developmental descriptions, derived from the analysis of *reflective reasoning*, are applied to *spontaneous* social comments and social interactions in natural interaction with one another. In Chapter 9, children's groups are the focus, and in Chapter 10, a range of case studies is considered.

More specifically, the purpose of this chapter is to provide a rationale for the way in which our particular model was defined and developed, and to describe in greater detail than is usually the case in this field the nature of the research process during this first, critical, constructive phase. One question I consider is how particular domains and issues within each domain are identified for study. I also discuss some of the general characteristics of a structural or "stage" analysis and whether our model fits within this general set of guidelines and parameters. I also try to convey how the perspective-taking model, which at this point is "in our head," interacts with the data that are collected, the child's responses, from which is inferred what is "in the child's head," to yield a working developmental model of interpersonal conceptions. Then in Chapter 5, to illustrate this process, I take *one issue from each* of the four domains in our system and describe how the responses of our subjects were coded and categorized at each of the five (perspective-taking) levels. Space does not permit complete, five-level description of all 22 issues; our intention is that the presentation of these four strands, one from each domain, permit the reader to extrapolate to the design of the entire cloth and to evaluate both the system itself and the inferential process used for its construction.[1] Finally, Chapter 6 ends Part II with a slight shift in focus, away from the formal model we use to frame the "reality" of children's growing interpersonal concepts and toward an overview picture, less focused on models and more focused on the empirical growth of interpersonal concepts in childhood and adolescence. However, by waiting until the end of the section to provide an "overview description" of children's understanding of social relations, I mean to stress the belief that empirical pictures are indeed colored by the frame within which they are presented; the more explicitly the relation of the frame to the picture is stated, the more clearly and honestly the work can be evaluated.

---

[1] An Interpersonal Conception Manual, constructed in Phase 1 and used in the conduct of research in the other phases, consisting of the complete stage-by-issue gridwork of the developmental analysis of interpersonal concepts is available from the author at the Social Reasoning Project. In the manual, scoring procedures and methods are also discussed in greater detail than in this volume.

The Child's Search for Order and Stability: Developmental Aspects of the Growth of Interpersonal Understanding [2]

Conventional wisdom points to our era as one of rapidly changing social values. These changes, we are told, are taking place in many contexts: political, societal, family, and individual. Much recent attention has centered on flux in adult social values and institutions. Traditional values, mores, and institutionally associated norms and prescriptions are breaking down. Change and ambivalence in adult attitudes toward careers, marriage, adult relationships in general, and having and raising children have emerged, in part, from the individual's ability to make choices about events that were previously seen as givens in life. For example, it is often observed that having children in contemporary urban society is not the financial necessity it once was in a rural agricultural society and has, in fact, come to be viewed as a major investment of time, money, and responsibility. Family planning is based less on chance and more on choice. Taken to their logical conclusions, these changing action choices, and the associated beliefs about and attitudes toward basic social relationships, may well bring about real alterations in the nature of relationships themselves, for example, between husband and wife, or between parents and children.

Furthermore, the repercussions of new social patterns, such as the entry of many more women into the labor force, are not only economic. These patterns also stimulate redefinition of relationships between the sexes. Such sweeping social changes touch every life, they challenge and influence each individual's conceptualization of intimate, personal relationships, not only consciously but also at more unreflective levels, not only across male–female boundaries but across lines of intimacy in adult life in general. In addition to the search for emotional support through new definitions of intimacy and friendship in adult dyadic relationships, there has emerged for some an emphasis on the value of nonfamilial group life and group support systems. A particularly interesting contemporary manifestation of this movement is the widespread formation of mutual-help groups, composed of people who either presently share or have previously experienced common problems and concerns, often with strong psychological components. Single parents, parents of handicapped children, widows and widowers, those recently discharged from mental institutions, or people with any one of a number of medical disabilities in common have discovered that by sharing their common

[2] This section and the next will appear in a somewhat modified form in a book on social development edited by David McClelland, to be published by Irvington Publishers, New York, New York.

problems they can form a group with the power to support individual members in self-initiated practice.

These changing attitudes toward friendship, intimacy, parenting, and family, peer, and group social relations are complemented by changing values, individually directed inward toward the meaning of psychological development within the self. Concerns for self-actualization, concerns for understanding internal relations among conflicting emotions or between one's behavior and one's feelings, and a move toward increased self-reflection are concurrent manifestations of the search in adult life for new values, for a new social and psychological order.

If the new social order with its changing social relations and values poses a baffling set of options for adults, it would seem to follow that the corresponding options for growing children must be equally baffling. How do children come to know and understand such a quixotic social reality? First, how might changing, often conflicting and ambivalent, contemporary adult attitudes toward parenting affect the child's developing understanding of the nature of parent–child relationships? Second, how might the recent adult emphasis on personal insight and consciousness raising inform children's conceptions of the individual and of the self's potential? Third, to what extent might this rapidly changing social order impinge on the quality of friendship and peer-group relationships children establish, maintain, and develop for themselves during their childhood, preadolescent, and adolescent years? Social scientists from many disciplines are trying to answer these questions and, above all, the question of whether there is any order to the way children develop social understanding and values in a society, whether fluctuating or stable.

Many psychologists would view the task of answering as the documentation of the effects of a changing social order, and in essence, a changing social reality, on the impressionable beliefs and attitudes of children. There is, however, reason to claim that there is order and structure to the way children think about social relations as they grow up which operates despite social change. It has stimulated the research efforts of a group of social–developmental psychologists whose historical roots can be traced back through Jean Piaget (1932) to James Mark Baldwin (1906) and George Herbert Mead (1934). Developmentalists in this tradition would not deny causal relationships between the adult social order and the child's developing social attitudes. But the implicit model of social development as only a one-way street, from the top down, so to speak, does not fit the developmental approach to the acquisition of basic social understanding in children. This approach begins with the hypothesis that the development of social concepts can be organized into a series of universal and invariant developmental stages, or modes of organization, by which the child progressively structures social experience as he or she experiences it.

Table 4.1 presents a summary review of some relevant major research efforts to describe formally the development of various aspects of social judgment and knowledge from this developmental perspective. Included are the principal investigators, their areas of study, the age-ranges of their subjects, the types of data collection and data analysis used, and any applications of their work in educational or clinical settings.

Kohlberg's efforts represent the earliest spadework in a parcel of the cognitive–developmental garden that Piaget himself left relatively fallow after his earliest period of research, marked by the completion of *The Moral Judgment of the Child* (1932). Kohlberg and the other researchers identified in Table 4.1 do not represent every stage-developmental analysis of every social category of experience, nor do they necessarily agree with each other on all points of theoretical contention. However, I have referenced these particular works for three reasons. First, all of them focus on structural change in the development of knowledge, concept, or judgment about various moral or social *relationships* (e.g., fairness between persons and relations of self and other, self and self, self and societal norms, and self and faith or God) rather than social *objects* (person perception, concepts of birth, etc.). Second, with few exceptions, most of these studies provide some longitudinal data, follow-up of the reasoning of the same individual, which allows the

TABLE 4.1
Stage Oriented Developmental Descriptions of Social Knowledge

Investigator	Domain	Age-range	Data collection methods	Data analysis[a]	Educational programs
Kohlberg, L. (1969)	Moral judgment	10–adult	Hypothetical dilemmas and interviews	CS, L, CC, JA, D	Yes
Turiel, E. (1975)	Mores and social conventions	10–adult	Hypothetical dilemmas and interviews	L, CS	No
Selman, R. (1976a and b)	Perspective taking, interpersonal understanding	5–young adult	Hypothetical dilemmas and interviews	CS, L, JA, D	Yes
Damon, W. (1977)	Friendship, authority, social convention, positive justice	3–12	Hypothetical dilemmas and interviews	CS, L, JA, D	No
Broughton, J. (1977)	Self, mind/body	10–adult	Interview	CS	No
Furth, H. (1977)	Occupational roles	5–11	Interview	CS	No
Fowler, J. (1976)	Faith	4–adult	Interview	CS	No

[a] Key: L = longitudinal; CS = cross-sectional; CC = cross-cultural; JA = judgment-action; D = demographic norms.

making of inferences about the validity of the developmental sequence posited. Third, the researchers provide a qualitative descriptive analysis of the categories under examination, rather than simply a direct reduction of the description of the experiences to someone else's stage system, for example, Piaget's cognitive model.

In general, these researchers have attempted to expand, modify, or correct their own approaches rather than take them as dogmatic givens. Furthermore, each considers the relevance to his research of four basic or first-order developmental assumptions: that there is (a) a qualitative difference among stages; (b) an invariance of developmental sequence through these stages; (c) a structured wholeness across stage systems; and (d) a hierarchical integration among stages. A brief explanation of these first-order assumptions is essential to an informed understanding of this developmental approach. But first, it is central to a sympathetic understanding of structural developmental models (and to their practical or educational implications) to realize that these first-order assumptions apply in varying degrees to two inextricably related, but theoretically separable, phenomena: the formal description of the development of social conceptions and the way these social concepts are actually used by people. Concern for the organization of social concepts themselves refers to the way issues, such as trust in friendship or loyalty in a group, develop and logically relate to one another at any given developmental stage. Concern for an understanding of the way individuals actually use these concepts is important both as a guide to their behavioral choices and as a way to think about how people capable of different levels of understanding view their own relationships. A major aim of this book is to clarify this dichotomy, spelling out in greater detail the distinction between the *formal, structural* analysis, or the description of social concept development, and the *functional* analysis, or the study of actual social conceptual usage. For now, we move to a survey of these first-order assumptions and the way developmentalists have studied their applicability.

Stage-Developmental Structures:
Four First-Order Concerns

QUALITATIVE DIFFERENCES

Stage analyses of social understanding imply qualitative differences in the way social reality is organized. These differences are viewed as qualitative because they represent and require when going from one stage to the next a fundamental restructuring in the way an individual views social relations, not simply a quantitative addition of new social data. For example, to understand that the value of friendship is based in part on similarity of *psychological* interests (a reciprocal orientation) represents a qualitative shift from a prior friendship value orientation based on the attractiveness of the toys or material possessions of the potential friend (a physical–material orientation) or on a friend as a person who does principally what the other person wants (a one-way orientation). Although in the temporal sense, this natural developmental shift from a physicalistic or a one-way orientation to a reciprocal and psychological one may occur slowly and gradually, fluctuating widely in the process, the shift is still basically a qualitative reorganization, resulting in a new paradigm or world view, as opposed to a quantitative increment in knowledge. The qualitative reorganization is seen to come about in part by taking old elements (or concepts) and putting them together in new and unique ways to form new concepts or structures.

INVARIANT SEQUENCE

Stage analyses organize modes of interpersonal or social understanding in an invariant sequence. While environmental and/or physiological factors are believed to be capable of altering the rate of progression from stage to stage, they cannot alter the sequence. In the previously discussed friendship example, it would be logically impossible or "unnatural" from the standpoint of this developmental theory for a child to first "construct" or arrive at a psychologically reciprocal orientation toward others only to have that "develop" into a one-way relationship perspective. This is not to say that a child who has developed an understanding of the importance of psychological reciprocity for friendship relations might not regress or act in a one-way fashion. It is only to stress that the conception of the one-way orientation naturally develops, and must be developed, prior to the conception of the reciprocal orientation, that the reciprocal orientation is actually constructed in hierarchical fashion out of inconsistencies that the child becomes aware of and the conceptual conflict experienced when implementing a one-way orientation and observing its effects.

STRUCTURED WHOLENESS

Each stage of social understanding represents a structured whole across a range of concepts. A given response represents not merely factors specific to that situation, but an underlying logic, which characterizes thought at that stage across a variety of social processes. For example, Stage 2 responses in Kohlberg's descriptive system appear to have an underlying structure similar to that level in other systems within the social-cognitive "family," for example, Damon's, Broughton's, Selman's, etc. While differences among domains of social cognition are recognized, according to this developmental theory, the similarities among conceptions in each domain ought to be based on specifiable underlying social–cognitive organizations or structures.

However, it must be stressed that this structured wholeness principle refers primarily to the underlying logic of parallel conceptual systems, that is, *to the formal analysis*. Whether a child consistently *uses* a particular level of reasoning across most social contacts and interactions still remains a challenging and critical empirical question for this approach. In fact, little research exists that speaks to the issue of variation in the stage or level of conception individuals actually use across a range of real-life social experiences and problems.

HIERARCHICAL INTEGRATIONS

Stage analyses of social understanding are hierarchical integrations. Stages form, in order, increasingly comprehensive structures, which are used to organize views of and interactions in social life. Research has not yet clarified the exact nature of the relation between higher and lower social–conceptual forms. Some researchers appear to suggest that lower stages are rejected once higher levels are attained (Turiel, 1969); others claim that they are available when the individual, perhaps for reasons of personal stress, is incapable of using higher level solutions (Werner, 1964). The quality of access among developmental levels and the function served by lower stages once the child develops a higher-level awareness are important issues to study. Social psychologists interested in the relation between social understanding and social–psychological factors such as peer pressure, as well as clinical psychologists who might focus on the role emotional factors such as anxiety or personal traits play in the social thinking of disturbed or healthy individuals, need to have a better sense of the fluidity of conceptual use and the availability of lower stages once higher levels of construction have been developed.

More directly, the hierarchical model as I see it implies that children who are capable of more advanced forms of social conception and reasoning will, on occasion, suggest solutions to social problems using conceptions available from lower stages, but that some ceiling does exist at any given time for the growing child. For example, in one of our hypothetical peer-group interview measures, children are asked to "figure out" what has gone wrong with a street hockey team. Some, whose responses were scored at Stage 1, are capable only of seeing the problem as one of individual skill or material problems such as "lousy players," "not enough practice," or "not enough people." Responses coded as Stage 2 can point out problems of bilateral cooperation such as "not enough teamwork" or "they argue when they should be friendly." Coded at Stage 3 are those responses that show a concern with achieving a sense of solidarity, such as "The team has to work together as a unit." The stages are viewed as hierarchical insofar as those who give reasons coded as Stage 3 may also list such problems as "lousy players" or "not enough teamwork" in addition to "working together as a unit." However, regardless of how much "teamwork" or "togetherness" is actually needed, children who have only attained Stage 1 reasoning will be unable to conceptualize these higher level alternatives. On the other hand, if the problem at hand only called for solutions generated at Stage or Level 2, we would not expect children capable of higher-level reasoning to necessarily exhibit their highest ability.

SUMMARY OF STAGE DEVELOPMENT

From this theoretical perspective, then, the child is not a passive recipient of what society (parents, educators, clergy, etc.) transmits; the young child comes to social experience with a set of immature but continually developing cognitive structures, which provide the means for the reinterpretation (assimilation) of social experience at a level that makes sense for the child. At the same time, relevant social experiences that do not quite make sense to the child at a particular level provide the elements for the child to change his or her own organizational structure (to accommodate) to one that is more advanced cognitively. The child is enabled thereby to interpret greater complexities of social organization.

For example, our own study indicates it is natural or "normal" for young children (ages 3 to 6) to tend to believe they can have only one friend at a time, even as they tell us that they have "millions of friends." This apparent contradiction can be maintained because children at this age tend to interpret the concept of a friend as "the child with whom I am actually playing at the moment." Developmental research indicates that this "momentary playmate" orientation toward friendship is eventually replaced by the belief that one can be a friend with more than one person at a time, or that someone can be a friend even if that person is not the one being played with at the moment. According to the stage-developmental model, this new social understanding develops out of the interaction of children's earlier belief systems with their actual experiences in relating to peers, the observation of a discrepancy between the initial belief and social or empirical actuality. The new concept is viewed by developmentalists as more adequate, for two reasons. First, it describes a new reality for the child, a new attitude that the child constructs out of the seeds of the earlier attitude. Second, being an integration of previously unrelated concepts into new related ones, it is an understanding which is *qualitatively* more advanced than the earlier concept. Of course, if the reality of the social world were such that actual friendships were not kept beyond the immediate period of social gratification by more mature members of society, then such new concepts might not be expected to develop or be maintained by the child in that society. But even given that they are, the child must go through the earlier level of understanding before the later level can be discovered. In this sense the sequence of conceptual development may be seen as invariant and hierarchical.

THE USE OF THE TERMS *LEVEL* AND *STAGE*

Recently there has been discussion within social–cognitive developmental circles about when it is appropriate to use the term *stage* to represent a descriptively analyzed mode of thinking and when it would be more appropriate to use the term *level* (cf. Cowan, 1978; Damon, 1977). It would appear the term *stage* is viewed as a construct implying stronger claims of formal characteristics. For example, it seems that the criterion of *structured wholeness* must be demonstrated across many contexts or modes of functioning for stages, but levels only require a developmental *sequence* in the path of thinking about a delimited area of social events or relations. Another implication of some stage–cognitive models is that they are actually hybrids: of cognitive and personality development (cf. Loevinger's model of ego development) or of cognitive sophistication and prescriptive action choices (cf. Kohlberg's model of moral development). In these models, stage shifts, as noted previously, represent transformation not only in conception but in personality structure, attitude, belief, or action structure.

While I do not believe that our analyses of interpersonal understanding are necessarily representative of transformational action choices or directly descriptive of personality changes, I plan to use the term *stage* in this book to describe our work for three reasons. First, our analysis is of developmental change in systems of thought that have both a *structural* (or operative) component which I call perspective taking or perspective coordination and a *content* (or operated-on) component which is interpersonal concepts or issues. Second, I believe the developmental shifts in understanding represented by the model are predominantly qualitative, that is, are paradigm shifts, rather than an additive accumulation of social knowledge that would represent a valid but different model. Third, I believe the construct of "structured wholeness" needs to be understood or worked through in the context of the distinction between formal and functional models, and that the criteria for structured wholeness differ for each—the criteria in the former model being primarily logical or analytical and those in the latter empirical and observational.

Hereafter, I will use the term *level* to refer to developmental aspects of perspective taking to represent their relatively *formal* nature, and stages to refer to codevelopments in our system of interpersonal concepts to represent their relatively *content*-laden nature. I will also use the term *level* to refer to ontogenetic changes in any particular issue (e.g., conflict resolution) within an interpersonal domain (e.g., friendship). This distinction will become more evident as we proceed.

THEORETICAL MECHANISMS OF DEVELOPMENT

What are the *mechanisms* of development from the theoretical perspective I have just reviewed? Movement from stage to stage is thought to occur through the basic mechanism of conceptual conflict, as I have suggested. Conceptual conflict can be seen in a child's awareness of "external" evidence that conflicts with his or her personal or "internal" understanding of social reality or in a child's sudden awareness of conflicts, inconsistencies, or inadequacies in his or her internal system of beliefs or values.

An example of internal–external conflict might be the case of the young child, who normally thinks that people who fight are not friends, who observes fights between two older children who remain friends or observes parents showing affection to one another after a heated argument. The young child can ignore the external data, or can begin to change (redefine) his or her concept of friendship and other relationships to fit the observed evidence. A child will be more likely to ignore data when his or her own personal social–cognitive structures are so immature that the new evidence is too far advanced or complex to be assimilated. Systematic exposure to slightly more advanced evidence or reasoning that is difficult to ignore, yet not too advanced to be assimilated by present modes of thinking, creates a developmental environment that is theoretically optimal (Rest, 1974; Turiel, 1969).

An anecdote may provide an example of how conflicts between internally held but primarily unexamined beliefs, may also yield the seeds of social–conceptual development. A 3-year-old, concerned over the issue of death, learns that when people grow up and get old they eventually die. He announces that he will stop eating because, by his logic, he "knows" that eating three good meals a day will make him grow bigger and taller and growing bigger is seen as the cause for "growing up" and therefore dying. The consciousness of internal cognitive conflict emerges when he is reminded of something else he "knows," that if he doesn't eat, he may not grow big, but that he will probably become sick and most likely reach the same endpoint he is assiduously trying to avoid. The child arrives at a "crisis" of conceptual conflict, and his resolution, satisfactory but transitional, is announced with great relief. "I will continue to eat but I will not let myself get bigger and taller." In cases like this the child will actually work through for many months the inner contradictions inherent in his concepts, but the insight itself has brought to reflection a

new relation between ideas that existed before only in unrelated juxtaposition.

Construction of a Social-Cognitive Map
of Interpersonal Understanding

How then does an investigator interested in exploring the development of social concepts, understanding, awareness, or judgment choose
to map out the social world and pick an area to study? One factor might
be expected to be the perceived importance or relevance of the domain
for understanding the social encounters in every day life. Certainly very
common social experiences, such as the child's relations to adult
authorities such as parents or teachers, might be viewed as relevant domains, whereas the study of less common social relations or experiences,
such as relations with royalty or career diplomats, might seem rather
esoteric and irrelevant. Another factor to consider is how children
themselves naturally construct their own categories of social experience.
What are the domains of social experience as they see them? What
categories remain separate throughout development and which become
differentiated with development? (See Turiel's [1978] attempt to understand how children naturally come to understand the differences between morals and manners, for example.)

Our choice of domains for social-cognitive mappings and soundings
was strongly influenced by a number of factors, some theoretically
oriented, others more pragmatically weighted. Our choices were influenced by a desire to understand theoretically how children understand
the nature of transactions, exchanges, and relations *between* individuals
with differing roles and perspectives, and the nature of the experience of
conflicting or alternative perspectives *within* the same individual.
However, our selection of domains was also pragmatically influenced by,
for example, questions and concerns expressed in the various frames of
reference used in the field of mental health in understanding social
behavior and relations. Clinical perspectives are heavily oriented toward
certain kinds of dynamics and relations. The nature of intrapsychic
dynamics—for example, the nature of ambivalent feelings, self-awareness, personality, and personality change—is one such group of
dynamics, as are the nature of the parent-child relation, the quality of
friendships, and peer relations. These are, not coincidentally, just the
relations I have noted are in particular flux in contemporary society.
Thus, a collective theoretical, practical, and societal impetus specifically
led our focus to conceptions in these four domains—persons, friendship,
peer group, and parents and children—domains which are felt to be both
critical to healthy development and intrinsically related to one another.

Having identified a set of domains, we proceeded through three steps in the detailed construction of a developmental-social-cognitive map, a map which can allow the specification in some detail of normal growth in the way children think about their interpersonal world.

STEP A: PILOT EXPLORATORY WORK[3]

This step had two goals: to develop a set of issues within each domain and to develop meaningful interviews to be used in Step b of this phase. We followed a recommendation made by Flavell (1974) and began by *predefining* a set of issues for each domain that seemed to represent from an adult perspective the differentiating or unique features that needed to be considered (Selman & Jaquette, 1978) and which also had occurred in informal discussions with children concerning the various domains. It was hoped these issues would represent the basic and common concerns of our subjects in understanding each of the domains.

We were then ready to proceed with concurrently refining our set of issues and developing meaningful interviews and questions. As we began to collect pilot information, we kept our "target categories," or issues, loosely defined and flexible, but maintained them as rough guidelines to devise a first approximation of the kinds of questions which might best be asked of subjects and of the areas that were of consistent importance and interest to children. While it might well be foolish to assume that one can begin to interview subjects across wide age-ranges with no framework at all, the other extreme, a too rigidly defined, preformed, and prefabricated system, would cut off researchers from many issues and trains of thought that might emerge as critical to the subjects themselves.

In reshaping this conceptual starting point by its trial application to the real-world substance of children's and adolescents' thoughts and ideas, we used many sources: observation of a wide range of subjects, open interviews and conversations with children and adults, naturalistic eavesdropping on the peer conversations of children and adolescents in school, conversations with parents of often defensive and hard-to-interview teenagers and preteens, projective techniques, drawings, informal and formal therapy sessions, and class discussions. As we did so, a common or "culturally universal" core of concerns across ages began to emerge—the issues which comprise the final list. (See Table 4.2.)

To be sure, seldom was a fifth grader heard to claim that his street gang "lacked cohesiveness" (Peer-Group Issue 2) or a third grader to ask

---

[3] This section and the next two sections will appear in a somewhat modified form in a book on the development of friendship edited by Steven Asher and John Gottman, entitled *The Development of Friendship*, to be published by Cambridge University Press, New York, New York.

TABLE 4.2
Issues of Interpersonal Understanding Related to Concepts of the Individual, Close Friendships, Peer-Group Organizations, and Parent–Child Relations

Individual	Friendship	Peer group	Parent–child relations
1. *Subjectivity:* covert properties of persons (thoughts, feelings, motives); conflicts between thoughts or feelings within the person	1. *Formation:* why (motives) and how (mechanisms) friendships are made; the ideal friend	1. *Formation:* why (motives) and how (mechanisms) groups are formed; the ideal member	1. *Formation:* motives for having children and why children need parents
2. *Self-awareness:* awareness of the self's ability to observe its own thoughts and actions	2. *Closeness:* types of friendship, ideal friendship, intimacy	2. *Cohesion–loyalty:* group unity	2. *Love and emotional ties:* between parents and children
3. *Personality:* stable or predictive character traits (a shy person, etc.)	3. *Trust:* doing things for friends; reciprocity	3. *Conformity:* range and rationale	3. *Obedience:* why children do as their parents tell them
4. *Personality change:* how and why people change (growing up, etc.)	4. *Jealousy:* feelings about intrusions into new or established friendships	4. *Rules–norms:* types of rules, and reasons for them	4. *Punishment:* the function of punishment from the parent's and the child's perspective
	5. *Conflict resolution:* how friends resolve problems	5. *Decision-making:* setting goals, resolving problems, working together	5. *Conflict resolution:* optimal ways for parents and children to resolve their differences
	6. *Termination:* how friendships break up	6. *Leadership:* qualities, and function to the group	
		7. *Termination:* why groups break up or members are excluded	

her friends for better ways to "resolve conflicts" (Friendship Issue 5). These are researchers' terms for ideas the subjects in the pilot work spontaneously expressed in their own rich and often colloquial language, concerns about how to "get team spirit" going in a faltering group or ways close friends could "get it back together," "make up," or "stop hassling each other." The developmentalist's issues really are generated, then, from the ongoing and reciprocal interaction between "academic" conceptual analysis and the common "everyday" parlance and naive psychology (Heider, 1958) of the subjects themselves.

Although we used many sources and media to probe and reshape this initial approximation, the most frequently used and easily replicable method in this step and throughout our research is, as we mentioned, the open-ended interview, and in particular, one in which we ask the individual to resolve a series of hypothetical interpersonal dilemmas, here each focused on one of the four domains. For each of the domains under study, we produced two commonplace and familiar dilemmas depicted by preadolescent or adolescent actors on 6- to 8-minute sound filmstrips, each most appropriate in content and theme for children aged either 7 to 11 or 11 and over.

For instance, to study developmental changes in friendship concepts, we presented, in either filmstrip or verbal form, a dilemma in which a character near the subject's age has been asked by a newcomer in town to go to a special event at a time which, unfortunately, conflicts with a previous engagement with a long-time chum. In the preadolescent form of this dilemma, the heroine, Kathy, has been asked by the new girl to go to the ice skating show with her the next afternoon. This conflicts with a previous date with Debby, her best friend, to plan a puppet show. To complicate matters, the filmstrip makes explicit that Debby, the old friend, does not like the new girl. In the adolescent version, the structure of the situation is similar, but the content is different: The old friend has a personal problem about which she needs the heroine's advice. This change is an important accommodation to naturally occurring developmental differences in social concerns from early childhood to adolescence.

In Phase 1, whether in Step a or b, we were not highly concerned with traditional methodological issues such as whether the sex of the story protagonist matches that of the subject or whether the subject actually likes movies or puppet plays. This is because in the initial phase of the research, our purpose, more like that of the developmental philosopher than the developmental psychologist, was to elicit a compendium of as many natural concepts from children and adults of different ages as possible. "Testing" a particular child, assigning that child to a particular developmental level, or getting sex or age norms in friendship concepts elicited under reflective interview conditions is premature if the initial descriptive groundwork, the social–cognitive mappings of conceptions, is not fairly well established. What *was* important to obtaining a thorough library of responses was to sample empirically the reasoning of individuals who varied as widely as possible in experience and upbringing.

At the end of Step a, we had tried out a useful spectrum of issues and questions about those issues in interviews with over 50 male and female subjects of various ages and backgrounds and in less formal contacts with many other subjects. We had learned which issues we should plan to pursue and which lines of questioning we should expect to be profitable and to yield enough information of the right kind for interviewers to feel they were getting a reasonably good picture of conceptions in a given domain. (Table 4.2 lists the issues in each domain in their final refined form.)

Reflecting the developmentalist's methodological and theoretical bias, one final criterion for the selection of issues and interview questions was that they should provide responses which can be easily categorized according to some cognitive or structural developmental system; that is, these issues and questions should yield responses which are capable of being reliably ordered in a hierarchical sequence of stages.

These interpersonal issues, as already mentioned, also reflect the concern among clinical and social psychologists with how children relate to and organize their interactions within themselves and with their parents, friends, and peers. Furthermore, as it happened, an intense and often untapped interest in these issues was demonstrated by the children in our pool of pilot interviewees, for example, interest in what it means to be a good parent or friend or in how one best wends one's way into a clique or group.

We also, as we refined our issues, were influenced by our interest in comparing in some detail the interpersonal understanding of children in general with that of children who have difficulty in their social relationships and self perceptions. We hope such a comparison across specific issues will generate some understanding of how interpersonal concepts help to determine both specific social behaviors and the more general ways that children relate to the social world.

And we should also note that whereas the issues or processes obviously are "adult" categories, the assumption is that children have experiences with the kinds of processes which the issues and domains reflect and therefore construct their own increasingly differentiated and integrated conceptions of these categories. Although at lower levels or younger ages these categories may not be differentiated in the child's mind, nevertheless, the categories are applicable to their interactions and hence to their understanding.

Domains, issues, dilemmas, and questions in hand, we were ready for the next step of Phase 1.

STEP B: FORMAL DATA COLLECTION

In this step, we collected data for the analysis and manual construction of Step c. Following the general tenets of the Piagetian *methode clinique* (1926), we interviewed as broad a range of subjects as we could using a series of semistructured questions which permitted following up and probing of subjects' ideas. At this phase, the dilemma–interview procedure was not viewed as an *assessment of an individual's* thinking or ability, but as an *eliciting interview*, a means of gaining increasingly complete descriptive information about what concepts exist in the domain, a stimulus to thinking on the part of both interviewer and interviewee, such that together they could explore as thoroughly as possible each social relationship under examination.

Following pilot findings and experiences from Step a, for each dilemma interview, each of the preidentified issues was used as the basis for a series of intensive semistructured questions about the dilemma and about the subject's beliefs and experiences around the issue that together lasted up to 40 minutes per interview (on a whole domain of four to seven issues) and generated up to 25 pages of transcript from some older subjects. For each issue we used an initial probe question related directly to some aspect of the dilemma. The response to this standard question normally required follow-up probes for clarification of meaning. This discussion of the hypothetical story was followed by an inquiry into the child's general understanding of the issue under examination. This, in turn, was followed by an exploration of the subject's application of the issue to his or her own personal experience.

For example, to explore children's thinking about the issue of *conflict resolution* in the friendship domain, we began with the following reference back to the hypothetical dilemma. Suppose Kathy goes to the ice show with the new girl. If Debby (the old friend) and Kathy have a big argument over this problem, how would they work things out so they stay close friends? A follow-up probe to test the subject's limits of friendship concepts, that is, to ask the subject to consider an alternative underpinned by higher-level reasoning, might be used to follow up the initial response, for example, "Could their friendship become better or stronger if they have an argument over Kathy's going to the ice show with the new girl?" General discussion of the *nature of conflicts* between friends was then explored with a set of questions such as these three: (*a*) What kinds of things do good friends sometimes fight about?; (*b*) What's a good way to settle arguments between friends?; and (*c*) Can good friends have arguments and still be friends? Finally, to tap the reasoning children use when they consider their *own personal experience* with disagreements and fights between friends, we asked the interviewee whether he or she would be willing to share with us any personal experience of this type that he or she felt was important to his or her understanding of this issue.

During this phase of the research it was not unusual for an individual to participate as a subject in an interview for more than one of the domains. However, manuals describing the developmental aspects of concepts in each domain were constructed independently; that is, data were not organized by *subject* but by *domain.*

The subject pools used for descriptive responses during Step b are as follows:

Individuals Manual	$N = 91$
	age-range 3 to 34
Close Friendship Manual	$N = 93$
	age-range 3 to 34
Peer-Group Relations Manual	$N = 103$
	age-range 4 to 41
Parent–Child Relations Manual	$N = 118$
	age-range 5 to 18

Approximately two-thirds of the children in the samples interviewed for the domains other than parent–child conceptions came from families in which at least one parent had a professional level occupation. The other one-third were from predominantly nonprofessional working-class backgrounds. Twenty percent of the subjects were from minority groups. Forty-one subjects in the parent–child relations pool were drawn from the same pool used for the other domains; the other 77 subjects were children between 5 and 18 drawn from the subjects in an independent study of families seen as potentially at risk due to limited economic resources. While it might be expected that this type of sampling variation would bias normative comparison across domains, it was not expected at this phase to impede greatly the descriptive process. Where it may have had some effect, as we shall see, was in failing to provide a pool that would produce data sufficient for distinguishing Stage 3 and 4 conceptions in the parent–child domain (Bruss-Saunders, 1979).

After completing interviews in each domain, we proceeded to Step c, the descriptive analysis and manual construction.

STEP C: DESCRIPTIVE ANALYSIS AND CONSTRUCTION OF INTERPERSONAL CONCEPTS MANUALS

The last step in this initial phase was to develop a detailed description of levels of concept for each issue, which resulted in the construction of an issue-by-stage manual for each domain. The transcribed interviews of the subjects described in Step b were used as the raw material for this process. First, each interview was analyzed as a whole to evaluate the highest level of perspective taking or perspective coordination manifested by the subject in the interview in accordance with the previously developed procedure. (See Chapter 2.) We then began to look at how a subject, capable of a given level of perspective taking, actually conceptualized each issue in each domain. When a particular concept, explanation, rationale, solution, or analysis seemed to be reported with some regularity (for example, if it were mentioned in more than five protocols), we analyzed what level of perspective taking seemed to be logically necessary for a subject to generate such a social concept.

A concrete example of this process may be helpful. On the basis of an overall rating of an entire interview about friendship relations, a subject shows the capacity for using Level 3 perspective taking, whereby the self is understood to be able to step outside a dyadic interaction and view self and other from a third-person perspective. In rereading the subject's interview and looking specifically for concepts dealing with the issue of conflict resolution, we found the subject to say, "I think fights are an important part of close friendship. Nobody is perfect, and you're bound to get a close friend angry at you once in a while. If you don't work it out things build up and pretty soon the whole relationship is blown. In fact sometimes if you have a real fight and find out you're still friends, then you've got something that is stronger."

The above concept seems, theoretically, to rest strongly on the idea that friendship is a relationship, a system made up of two people in interaction over time. This idea appears to manifest, semantically, a conception of conflict resolution based upon the structure of Level 3 perspective coordination.

Of course, another subject may manifest Level 3 perspective taking somewhere in the course of an interview and not use or express concepts of conflict resolution that appear to represent this Level 3 structure. According to the model that guides our work, each perspective-taking level is logically necessary but not sufficient for the manifestation of a structurally parallel social concept about any specific issue (Selman, 1976b).[4]

---

[4] Although the topic will be considered in greater detail in Part IV, it should be stated that the relation between structures and concepts being considered here under the methodological conditions of a reflective interview does not imply that levels of conception or social–cognitive structures are not manifested either earlier or later in time (age) under less verbally constrained modes of social functioning (cf. Selman & Jaquette, 1978). Verbal discussion under interview conditions is but one medium that allows us to look at concepts as they develop. Once this is done, we can begin to look at the same concepts as they are used under other conditions or in other modes of expression. However, at this phase, it is important that we use the same method (reflective interviews) to look for both perspective-taking level and conceptions of interpersonal understanding. Otherwise methodological factors would provide unnecessary interference to the structural analysis.

A central observation in our descriptive work was that the empirical analysis of the protocols indicated that there were often not just one but multiple concepts manifest about a given issue at a given level. For example, other subjects' responses to questions about conflict resolution were coded at Level 3 if they suggested a conflict between friends might be due to a personality conflict between them or a personality conflict within one of the two individuals. Not only do these concepts seem to be based on Level 3 understanding, but they point out how concepts about issues in one domain interrelate with concepts about issues in another, in this case concepts about the issue *personality* in the domain of intra-psychic relations (individuals) and concepts about the issue *conflict resolution* in the friendship domain. When a subject says "a friendship must be based upon dependability," he or she is clearly saying something about his or her concept of individuals as well as of friendship relations.

Thus the procedure of using the (deeper) levels of perspective taking as analytical tools or organizing principles and moving to the (relatively more surface) concepts of intrapsychic, friendship, peer-group, and

TABLE 4.3
Flow Chart of Phase 1 (Descriptive Phase)
Step c (Descriptive Analysis)
Case: Friendship Domain

Step	Process
1	Protocols of friendship interviews transcribed
2	Each protocol given overall perspective-taking score
3	Each protocol broken down into responses about various issues, for example, conflict resolution, intimacy and closeness, etc.
4	Spectrum (across subjects) of responses about each issue analyzed for level: all responses assigned to "library" on level-by-issue basis: this is the *level*-by-issue manual
5	For each issue, aspects or themes emerge (from responses) which characterize each level
6	Stages of friendship concepts described: *stage*-by-issue manual of friendship concepts assembled: at each stage various aspects in each issue characterize the given stage of concept of friendship

Note: Both *level* and *stage* refer to modes or styles of social reasoning (developmental, logically coherent, etc.), which correspond to given levels of perspective taking. In this description, thinking of a certain type about a specific *issue* is designated as being at a certain *level;* thinking of that type, when consistent in an individual across all issues in a given *domain,* is designated as being at a certain *stage.* We use *stages* to refer to the more complete concepts in domains and *levels* for both the underlying perspective taking and the less complete concepts or responses about issues.

parent–child relations, as well as moving back and forth among these social domains, provided a means of assigning levels to the various empirical conceptual responses obtained.

A library of these responses at each level for each issue was then developed. These responses varied in length from a sentence or two to over 20 lines of transcribed discussion. This library of *level*-by-issue categorized responses became the raw material for the construction of an interview manual for each domain. Through the process, each issue at each level was characterized by a set of one or more social concepts reflected in responses which we called aspects or themes. (Those we have identified cannot be seen as an exhaustive and complete set of aspects, but as a descriptive beginning or foundation.) This procedure, repeated for each of the issues at each level, yielded a level-by-issue-by-theme description for concepts about issues in the friendship, individuals, peer-group, and parent–child domains with a variable number of themes (or aspects) at each level for each issue. (See Table 4.3 for a summary of the procedure.)

The process of constructing such a detailed descriptive map was greatly facilitated by having responses to the same questions from subjects at different ages and by using a technique that probed responses which on the surface sounded similar ("A good friend is someone who is close to you"), but whose underlying meanings are developmentally quite different ("That means he lives down the street" at age 5 versus "That means that you share a lot of the same values" at age 15).

This concludes the description of the process of Phase 1. The next two chapters present our developmental model of interpersonal understanding in greater detail.

5

Four Strands from the Fabric:
A Developmental Description
of Four Issues

To further explain and illustrate our analytic process and our model of interpersonal understanding, I shall draw in this chapter from the four manuals and summarize in some detail the developing themes which we have observed to emerge at five levels for one selected issue from each of the four domains. (For a complete discussion of *all* issues in each domain, the reader is referred to the manuals on each domain.) The issues I have chosen are:

1. *Self-awareness* in the *individual* concepts domain
2. *Conflict resolution* in the *friendship* concepts domain
3. *Leadership* in the *peer-group* concepts domain
4. *Punishment* in the *parent–child* concepts domain

In making this presentation I shall also describe one of the dilemmas used for facilitating the discussion between subject and interviewer about each domain.

Concepts of Individuals: The Human Capacity
for Self-Awareness[1]

The child's developing concepts about individuals have frequently been elicited in individual interviews following presentation of this dilemma:

> Eight-year-old Tom is trying to decide what to buy his friend Mike for his birthday party. By chance, he meets Mike on the street and learns that Mike is extremely upset because his dog, Pepper, has been lost for 2 weeks. In fact, Mike is so upset that he tells Tom, "I miss Pepper so much I never want to look at another dog again." Tom goes off, only to pass a store with a sale on puppies; only two are left and these will soon be gone.

The dilemma, then, is whether to buy the puppy for Mike, and how this will affect Mike, psychologically.

As is typical in our structural–developmental research, the interview using this dilemma[2] covers a range of related issues basic to the child's developing concepts of psychological processes within individuals. Each issue has a basic orienting question followed by a series of relatively standard probe questions designed to elicit further explanation and clarification of the child's reasoning. For example, to explore the issue of self-awareness we start with a general question such as, "Mike said he never wants to see another puppy again. Why did he say that?" Depending, in part, on the child's initial level of response, the experienced interviewer might choose from a range of "stage-related" follow-up questions such as: "Can someone say something and not mean it?", "Is it possible that Mike doesn't know how he feels?", "Can you ever fool yourself into thinking you feel one way when you really feel another?", and so on. In addition to providing the stimuli for the child's discussion of issues raised in the dilemma, these questions act as a springboard for further probing of the child's general understanding of the issues. Following are the descriptions of concepts at each level.

---

[1] This section will appear in a somewhat modified form in a book to be edited by Evelyn Weber and Edith Shapiro, and to be published by Lawrence Erlbaum Associates, Hillsdale, New Jersey.

[2] A second filmstrip (or story) using older actors is oriented toward older children; in it a boy (or girl) finally wins a Ping-Pong game against an older child who has defeated him (or her) many times in the past and then he (or she) finds out that the older opponent may have "thrown the game." The erstwhile winner claims that he (she) did not really care about winning anyway; the interviewer probes the child's speculations about the validity of that statement, using questions similar in structure to those used for the Lost Puppy Dilemma.

LEVEL 0: PHYSICALISTIC CONCEPTS
OF SELF–AWARENESS[3]

There are two aspects of children's responses that characterize the earliest reflective concept of self-awareness. First, when asked questions about the inner self, the child does not appear to view the nature of inner or psychological experience as different from the material nature of outer experience. Second, although very young children can articulate a sense of being aware of a self, the nature of the self itself seems to have a quasi-physical quality.

WHERE DOES THE RAIN COME FROM?
I think from the clouds.
HOW DO YOU KNOW THAT? DID ANYONE TELL YOU THAT?
I just told myself. That's how I knew.
WHAT DO YOU MEAN YOU TOLD YOURSELF?
My words told me.
WHEN YOU THINK, WHERE DO YOU THINK?
In my mouth.
HOW DO YOU THINK?
My words tell me.

(3) [Numbers in parentheses give age of subject.]

This sense of self-communication as one part of the body telling another part of the body something appears equivalent in a syncretic sense to the child's notion of thinking.

I am the boss of myself.
HOW DO YOU KNOW?
My mouth told my arm and my arm does what my mouth tells it to do.

(3)

These excerpts point out the need to be cautious in interpreting self-aware-sounding statements of young children at too high a level when the conception of the psychological self may be still undifferentiated from that of the physical self. Similarly, when the young child apparently uses evaluative language to describe himself or herself (e.g., "I'm a good boy"), this does not necessarily mean that he or she is evaluating the motives or personality underlying his or her actions, but may simply mean the child is reporting directly the actions themselves. The self-label "good boy (girl)" may, in effect, be undifferentiated from the evaluative statement, "I did something good," that is, may be a simple report of a value attached to a specific act rather than a truly self-

[3] We are using the term *level* to refer to developmental aspects of perspective taking and of individual issues in domains, and *stage* to refer to developmental aspects of reflective interpersonal concepts. See also note on Table 4.3.

reflective statement that points to inner experiences, states, or attitudes. To the young child (using Level 0 concepts), persons, including the self, are viewed as either all good or all bad. Furthermore, this evaluation appears to shift as easily as do the specific actions of the person being evaluated.

LEVEL 1: AWARENESS OF DISTINCTION BETWEEN ACTIONS AND INTENTIONS

There are three interesting aspects to the quality of thinking about conceptions of self-awareness coded as Level 1. First, young children do not realize that people can hide their inner or "true" feelings. Of course, young children do know how to lie, that is, they are well aware they can hide *facts* from or deny their actions to others. For example, the child who eats a forbidden cookie is capable, at quite an early age, of denying the reality of the situation and being aware that he or she is doing so. Despite this, however, we have drawn the inference from our interviews that the young child does not seem cognizant that one can *purposefully* misrepresent one's *inner* experiences, that is, one's thoughts, feelings, or motives to either another or to the self. The following interview provides some insight into this immature form of understanding.

MIKE SAYS HE NEVER WANTS TO SEE ANOTHER PUPPY AGAIN. WHY DID HE SAY THAT?
Because he lost his dog Pepper.
DID HE MEAN WHAT HE SAID?
Yes.
HOW DO YOU KNOW?
Because he said it.
CAN HE SAY IT AND NOT MEAN IT?
He could be lying.
WHY WOULD HE DO THAT?
I don't know. His dog may not be lost.
COULD HE THINK HE DIDN'T WANT A DOG BUT REALLY WANTED ONE?
Nope.
WHY NOT?
Because he said he wanted one.
IS IT POSSIBLE THAT MIKE DOESN'T REALLY KNOW HOW HE FEELS?
He said he was sad.

(9)

When the interviewer first asks the child whether Mike meant what he said, in the interviewer's mind the question is whether Mike was being true to himself, that is, in touch with his own feelings. The first thing the interviewed child responds, "He meant what he said because he said it," is fairly typical of young children's analyses of inner experience. People do not seem to be credited with the ability to purposefully distort inward-looking observations. When the child is asked "Can he say it and not mean it?," the response "He could be lying" is an indication of his confusion, for although he seems to know that objective actions can be distorted in their presentation to others, he does not seem aware that the same principle can apply to subjective feelings. This question may become more understandable when the child has a better sense of self-awareness; but for now, although the child indicates he is aware of Mike's depressed subjective state, he responds to a question about self-deception ("Can he say it and not mean it?") as if it were a question of the factuality of Mike's comment that he feels sad because his dog is lost, and he responds in kind ("He could be lying; his dog may not be lost").[4]

A second and related aspect of self-awareness concepts interpreted as Level 1 is that although now covert attitudes (intentions) and their overt representations (actions) are seen as separate, children using this level still seem to believe that a person's overt actions "must" eventually belie that person's inner attitude, that if one is a careful observer of another's outside, one can begin to make a good guess about how that person feels inside.

> HOW DOES MIKE FEEL INSIDE?
> Sad.
> HOW DO YOU KNOW?
> Because of the way he looks.
> COULD HE LOOK SAD AND BE HAPPY INSIDE?
> He could but you would be able to tell if you watched him long enough, he'd show you he was happy.

> (8)

While there is validity to this assertion—we do know something of inner feeling from observation—when the child's thinking appears to be limited to this Sherlock-Holmesian, keenness-of-material-observation concept, the child's responses are coded at Level 1.

Third, the young child's conception of "fooling oneself" or the "awareness of unawareness" is qualitatively different from that of older children and adults. Because Level 1 perspective taking is not yet truly a self-reflective perspective on the self's inner life, the young child seems to view "fooling oneself" as changing one's subjective beliefs, feelings, or motives rather than *being unaware* of feelings, etc.

> WHAT DOES IT MEAN TO FOOL THE SELF?
> You do something and then you disagree with it. You find out you didn't want to do it.

> (8:5)

---

[4] It is important to stress that it may be more accurate to state that the child reinterprets or understands the question at a lower level rather than assert that the child "does not understand the question at all."

According to Level 1 theorizing, one does not fool oneself in the sense of being actively self-deceptive; one simply discovers there has been a shift in one's subjective concerns. One may have been wrong about what one thought one wanted originally, but now one knows.

LEVEL 2: THE EMERGENCE OF AN INTROSPECTIVE SELF AND THE SECOND-PERSON PERSPECTIVE

Concepts coded as Level 2 incorporate the further understanding that the individual can take a clear perspective on the inner life that was distinguished from outer experiences at the previous stage. In social perspective-taking terms, the self is now seen as able to put itself in the place of a second person and look back toward the self's inner states. At least four manifestations of this important developmental shift are the consequences for the child's understanding of the nature of self-awareness.

First, the ability to take a second-person social perspective allows the child to rethink the relative importance of outer appearance and inner reality. Whereas at Level 1 the child responds as if he or she believes that the inner can be ascertained from the outer (and in a sense this is a valid insight maintained through life), at Level 2 the child favors the theory that inner experience is reality and outer actions are only an appearance or one manifestation of that reality. In other words, there appears to develop an articulated sense of the *priority* of inner experience (how one "really feels" about social events or interactions) over outer appearance.

HOW IS IT YOU CAN HIDE THE WAY YOU FEEL?
If he felt real sad and stuff, you put a smile on your face and you go with everyone else and try to be regular, but sometimes you can really be sad.
IS THERE A KIND OF INSIDE AND OUTSIDE TO A PERSON?
Yes.
WHAT WOULD THAT MEAN?
If there was a brother and a sister, like the brother always says I can't stand you, but really inside, he really likes her.
REALLY DEEP INSIDE. WHAT IS THAT INSIDE, CAN YOU DESCRIBE IT?
Yah, I guess so, really what you really feel about something.

(10:11)

Second, Level 2 perspective taking marks the emergence of a working belief in the self's ability to constantly monitor the self's thoughts and actions. How does the shift manifest itself in beliefs about the ways in which the self can fool the self? How is it different from the Level 1 "changing one's opinion?" The following interview excerpts may give us some ideas.

IS IT POSSIBLE, TO FOOL YOURSELF?
Yes, sometimes.
HOW CAN YOU FOOL YOURSELF?
You can say to yourself, I didn't really care and keep on saying you didn't care, and when someone brings up the subject, you say I didn't really care and sometimes it works and you don't really care about it.
DO YOU THINK DEEP DOWN INSIDE YOU THINK YOU REALLY DON'T CARE, OR DO YOU THINK YOU ACTUALLY DO CARE, DEEP DOWN INSIDE?
You really care.
WHEN YOU SAY THAT, CAN YOU TRY TO FOOL YOURSELF INSIDE?
No.
WHY NOT?
If you are really upset about something, you don't really forget about it that easy.
WHY NOT, WHY IS IT HARD TO FORGET ABOUT THINGS THAT UPSET YOU?
It is hard, you are thinking about that thing most of the time. So it is real hard to forget about it.
SO YOU THOUGHT IT ISN'T POSSIBLE TO FOOL YOURSELF?
No.

(12:4)

COULD JERRY FOOL HIMSELF INTO THINKING THAT HE DIDN'T CARE ABOUT THE GAME?
Yes.
HOW IS THAT POSSIBLE TO FOOL YOURSELF?
If you really talk about it and talk about it and you think you do.
WHY DOES TALKING ABOUT IT MAKE YOU THINK YOU DO?
Well, if you think about it, you think it is not really true, but if you really talk about it a lot and you start getting tired of talking, you don't think it anymore.

(8:2)

While at the previous level, self-deception was seen to occur due to external events or forces, at Level 2 we repeatedly see a new theme; through mechanistic force of habit, or by repetition, a belief can be changed by the self's effort.

There is another way that "fooling the self" is apparently understood in a Level 2 framework—in the manner of "forgetting." By forgetting, the average 10-year-old usually means that the "observing ego" has had a lapse in vigilance, or is attending to other matters at the time and cannot be bothered to review the particular issue at hand.

CAN YOU THINK OUTSIDE YOU KNOW HOW YOU FEEL, BUT YOUR INSIDE FEELS A DIFFERENT WAY?
Yes.
HOW IS THAT POSSIBLE?
Because you fool yourself.
YOU THINK YOU CAN FOOL YOURSELF?
Yah.
HOW CAN YOU FOOL YOURSELF?
By forgetting something.

HOW CAN YOU FORGET SOMETHING?
You don't remember it.

(8:9)

WHAT'S THE DIFFERENCE BETWEEN FOOLING YOURSELF AND FOOLING
SOME ONE ELSE?
When you fool yourself, you kind of don't know that you fooled yourself
sometimes, but when you are fooling another person, you know that you are doing
it.
WHY IS IT YOU DON'T KNOW YOU ARE FOOLING YOURSELF WHEN YOU ARE
FOOLING YOURSELF, HOW IS THAT POSSIBLE? DOESN'T YOUR MIND ALWAYS
KNOW WHAT IS GOING ON?
Yah, but sometimes you forget you are thinking about a different thing when you
are fooling yourself. And you are thinking you are not fooling yourself.

(9:2)

Although this form of self-deception is still somewhat passive in
nature, it is seen, apparently, as being under the self's control to a
greater extent; to restore the state of accurate awareness, all that is
needed is to reattend to or refocus on the particular problem at hand.

Third, at Level 2 the child becomes reflectively aware that the individual, the self included, can consciously and often deceptively put on
a facade which is meant to mislead other individuals with respect to
what she or he believes is "really" going on internally. The idea of *front-
ing* or putting on an appearance is understood by the child as a useful
way for people to cover up their inner feelings, for example, to save the
self from embarrassment or ridicule.

SUPPOSE THAT JERRY FINDS OUT KEITH LET HIM WIN AND HE SAYS
TO KEITH "I NEVER REALLY CARED ABOUT PING-PONG ANYWAY." WHY
WOULD HE SAY SOMETHING LIKE THAT?
Because he wants to make it like he didn't really care if he lost or not, it doesn't
matter to him.
WHY WOULD HE TRY TO DO THAT?
To cover up his feelings.
WHAT KIND OF FEELINGS IS HE COVERING UP?
Sad ones.

(13:6)

DO YOU THINK THERE IS A DIFFERENCE BETWEEN FOOLING YOURSELF
AND FOOLING SOMEBODY ELSE?
Yes.
WHAT IS THE DIFFERENCE?
It is easier to fool them because they don't have your mind.

(12:3)

A fourth aspect identified as related to the development of a conception of self-reflective, Level 2 self-awareness is the child's belief that one
can gain an inner strength by having confidence in one's own abilities.

This new belief demonstrates how the structure of a self-awareness concept can be related to the content of self-esteem. Inner awareness itself is now seen as a tool to be used as a confidence builder. Simply put, there is a newly minted belief that knowing you can do it helps you do it.

DO YOU THINK THERE ARE ANY OTHER REASONS THAT KEITH MIGHT HAVE HAD FOR LETTING JERRY WIN?
Well, because he didn't want him to go off and start being a poor sport about it.
HOW WOULD LETTING JERRY WIN STOP HIM FROM BEING A POOR SPORT?
Because it would make him think that Jerry did it by himself and so he is improving in playing Ping-Pong, so he will start playing a lot.
WHY WOULD HE START PLAYING A LOT IF HE THOUGHT HE WON THE GAME?
Because if he won the game he would think he would start getting better and start playing Ping-Pong more.
DO YOU THINK HE MIGHT BE TRYING TO BUILD UP JERRY'S CONFIDENCE?
Yah, he lets him win so he can make him think, "I am really better now, I can play better and sometimes win with Keith . . . ."
WHAT DOES CONFIDENCE MEAN, WHAT DOES HAVING CONFIDENCE IN YOURSELF MEAN?
To know that you can really do something good.
BUT HOW WOULD HE FEEL IF HE FOUND OUT THAT KEITH LET HIM WIN?
I would just forget it, because I would think he was doing it just to encourage you to make you think that you can play better.
HOW DOES LETTING THEM WIN ENCOURAGE THEM?
It makes them think that they can play better, say I can play better now and I can go and play all kinds of Ping-Pong games.

(8:2)

IF JERRY WINS BUT FINDS OUT THAT KEITH LET HIM WIN, HOW IS JERRY GOING TO FEEL?
I don't think he will feel too good. He wanted to win by himself.
WHY IS IT BETTER TO WIN BY YOURSELF?
That means that you did it by yourself and the other person did not let you win, you have confidence in yourself.
WHAT DOES THAT MEAN, TO HAVE CONFIDENCE IN YOURSELF?
It means you think you can do things by yourself.
WHY WOULD IT HELP TO HAVE CONFIDENCE?
If you have confidence in yourself, then you can do more things better.
WHICH IS BETTER, CONFIDENCE IN YOURSELF OR SOMEONE ELSE HAVING CONFIDENCE IN YOU?
I think you having confidence in yourself is better.
WHY?
Because when someone else has confidence in you it means they trust you. When you have confidence in yourself it means that you trust yourself and you can do other things like that.
HOW DOES A PERSON BUILD CONFIDENCE IN HIMSELF?
He keeps on thinking that he can do things, trying to build confidence.

(9:4)

Although the emergence of this attitude plays a major role in the social development of the preadolescent child, still, as within any developmental construction, the Level 2 orientation has both new strengths and remaining limitations. For example, in the two excerpts above, the interviewer is interested in eliciting the child's understanding of the concept of self-confidence. Rather than directly asking the child what self-confidence is, the interviewer uses the concept in the context of the particular dilemma and observes how the child interprets it. The emerging Level 2 idea of self-confidence as a mode of behavioral control is an example of how at this stage, in contrast to the previous one, the psychological aspect of self is seen by the child to have greater control over action. However, concepts of self-awareness coded as Level 2 still tend to be focused on a self composed of relatively concrete actions. One gains strength or self-confidence by knowing and being assured of one's physical capabilities; to think one can *do* something is an action orientation. At higher levels, self-confidence will be understood as an awareness that the self can *be* something or someone; higher level thinking implies an additional understanding of feeling good about the self as a psychological whole.

LEVEL 3: CONCEPTS OF THE SELF AS OBSERVED AND OBSERVER, AND TAKING A THIRD-PERSON PERSPECTIVE

George Herbert Mead (1934) strongly believed that a mature concept of self emerges from the child's (cognitive) capacity to take the perspective of another on one's own actions (our Level 2); out of this "self-as-*action*" ideology there then emerges a "self-as-*entity*" phase which requires a second-order ability to observe the self simultaneously as observer and as observed. In Mead's terms, there emerges a concept of *mind*, or what we call a third-person perspective on the self, which is the hallmark of Level 3.

Three aspects emerge at this level: the concept of the mind as the observer of a self-aware self, the idea of fooling the self through an act of will, and the notion that thoughts and feelings can emerge even when opposed by "will" or "mind." They are perhaps best discussed together.

We know from earlier examples that young children can use the word *mind* (e.g., the 4-year-old who says his mind told his legs to move); however, the Level 3 *concept* of mind, as the observer of the self-as-entity, represents the young adolescent's cognizance that one can take a reflective perspective (mind) on a self-reflecting self. In this sense, the Level 2 conception of subjective duality (the inner or true versus the outer or apparent—"She says she doesn't want a puppy, but really she does; she is hiding how she feels") is transformed at Level 3 into a deeper, more dynamic and simultaneous understanding of the relation between self-as-subject and self-as-object (she is trying to think about how she really feels); depth is added to duality.

IS IT POSSIBLE TO HIDE YOUR FEELINGS FROM YOURSELF?
Yes, you just don't tell it to anybody. You put it out of your mind.
IS IT POSSIBLE TO REALLY SUCCEED IN HIDING IT FROM YOURSELF?
Yah, you just put it out of your mind and you don't want to know about it.
DO YOU THEN NOT KNOW ABOUT IT, OR INSIDE, DO YOU STILL KNOW ABOUT IT?
You still know about it, but you don't think about it or talk about it.

(12:10)

WHAT IF YOU FORGOT ABOUT SOMETHING, IS THAT FOOLING YOURSELF?
Yes, that might be fooling yourself but now it is sort of like a mixture.
WHAT WOULD IT BE A MIXTURE OF?
It might be sort of forgetfulness and trying to put it out of your mind.
IS THERE A DIFFERENCE BETWEEN FORGETTING SOMETHING AND PUT-TING IT OUT OF YOUR MIND?
Yes.
WHAT?
When you forget something you can forget something like your keys or something like that, but you can't put keys out of your mind or put it in your mind.

(12:11)

These quotes also illustrate that at Level 3, mind is seen as serving a dual role, not only as an *organ* where mental processes are located (Broughton, 1978) but also as a *monitor* who decides which thoughts get into the domain of awareness and which are kept out.

DO YOU THINK JERRY COULD FOOL HIMSELF INTO THINKING THAT HE DIDN'T CARE ABOUT IT?
Yah, he could do that.
HOW?
It is playing and doing it and doing it and saying I don't care, I am not going to play and finally you just wouldn't want to play anymore.
HOW IS IT WHEN YOU REPEAT SOMETHING OVER AND OVER, THAT THAT SOMETIMES MAKES IT RIGHT?
You see all the points, I am not going to play, I'm not going to lose anymore and those points kind of take over your brain.
IS THERE A DIFFERENCE IN FOOLING YOURSELF AND FOOLING ANOTHER PERSON?
Oh yah, there is a big difference. I don't think that I could fool myself really. What do you mean fooling myself?
SOME KIDS THINK THAT FORGETTING ABOUT SOMETHING IS FOOLING THEMSELVES.
If I did something wrong, I really can't forget about it, because of time. I can't make myself forget, I will always remember it. The point about not playing just takes over your mind. You are just thinking I don't want to play because I am—I

don't want to lose and then you just think up points, I can just say I don't like playing Ping-Pong, I am not going to win because I don't like it and you brainwash
yourself into not liking it. You could keep on telling yourself, I don't want to play
this, I don't have to play the game, and from them, you could keep on saying that
and it would just take over your brain, just the part of playing Ping-Pong and you
just wouldn't want to play anymore.
CAN YOU EXPLAIN TAKING OVER YOUR BRAIN?
So that would be fooling yourself, wouldn't it? I had a whole different idea of fooling myself.

(13:9)

Here, mind as "monitor" or "will" can control consciousness ("It is doing it and doing it [and it will] kind of take over your brain") but not completely ("If I did something wrong, I can't make myself forget").
Sometimes, feelings and behavior are not controlled by the mind.

WHY WOULD HE SAY SOMETHING THAT HE DIDN'T MEAN?
It just comes right out, you can't help it.
WHY CAN'T YOU HELP IT? THAT IS KIND OF INTERESTING.
There are a lot of things, if you get real upset or something you just come right out,
you don't mean to say it, but you just say it.

(13:4)

At Level 3, the child rejects the passive explanation ("I just forgot")
in light of a more active model of human experience: "You keep on telling
yourself, I don't want to play this . . . you could keep on saying that and
it would just take over your brain." The child who talks about a mixture
seems to be going through a transition, one which takes into consideration the earlier stage explanation, but which also includes the higher
level explanation as well. "It is sort of like a mixture . . . it might be sort
of forgetfulness and trying to put it out of your mind." Brainwashing is
almost literal, forcefully washing the thought from the brain. However,
at Level 3, no matter how long one is not aware of inner experience, self-
reflection always appears to be seen as potentially available "if one tries
hard enough," "thinks about it long enough," or "pays more attention."
This is a matter of will.

Perhaps this is the most striking difference between Level 2 and
Level 3 conceptions of self-reflection—a shift in viewing the self from
passive observer (a keeper of secrets, a hider of ideas, a forgetter of
unpleasant feelings) to an active psychological manipulator of inner life
(a forceful remover of painful ideas). What appears new and striking at
Level 3 is a belief in the observing ego—that is, the self-aware self—as an
active agent. This concept of active agency strikes us as a development
in the child's own theory critical for a child's feeling of having some control over his own thoughts and feelings, even if it is not perfect. For the

Level 3 child, the mind (or ego) is now seen as playing an active moderating role between inner feelings and outer actions.

LEVEL 4: THE DISCOVERY OF TRUE SELF-DECEPTION AND THE UNCONSCIOUS AS A NATURAL EXPLANATORY CONCEPT

The critical realization of Level 4 is that no matter how vigilant the conscious mind is, no matter how hard the mind works, there are still internal experiences not readily available to conscious awareness. At Level 3, this was seen, but ascribed to an unarticulated failure of will. At this level, an adolescent sees that individuals can and do have thoughts, feelings, and motivations which are resistant to self-analysis by even the most introspectively functioning mind. Not until well into adolescence are the two aspects to this discovery articulated. First, there is the discovery of the concept of the *unconscious* and of unconscious psychological *causes* of behavior, that is, that below inner reality there may be an even deeper reality, and this affects feelings and behavior. Second, there is a natural conceptualization of the existence of unconscious *processes*—the focus here being on the child's own growing natural theory of psychic phenomena such as coping and defending as autonomic processes. The development of the concept-in-theory of the unconscious emerges out of a need to explain observed aspects of social behavior and experience that previous conceptions of intrapsychic phenomena were inadequately structured to explain.

However, it is not necessary for the adolescent to use psychological terminology to demonstrate that he or she holds a reflective awareness of these psychological processes. As the following interview demonstrates, an awareness that persons can behave on the basis of motives or needs of which they themselves are not aware, and that no purposive act of "conscious effort" or "will" can yield a total understanding of certain of the self's actions to analysis by the self's mind, can be expressed without ever using the word *unconscious*.

IF MIKE SAYS HE NEVER WANTS TO SEE ANOTHER PUPPY AGAIN, WHY DOES HE SAY THAT?
Because he doesn't think that any puppy could take the place of Pepper.
DOES HE REALLY MEAN THAT, THAT HE NEVER WANTS TO SEE ANOTHER PUPPY AGAIN?
No.
CAN YOU SAY SOMETHING AND NOT MEAN IT?
That is something right off the top of his head, like when you are really upset, you might say get out of here I never want to see you again. But you are really going to see them tomorrow and you are not going to be mad at them.

SO MIKE MAYBE DOESN'T KNOW HOW HE FEELS?
He is just talking out of emotions. He may think that at that instant he doesn't
want to see another puppy, but he will get over the initial loss.
IF MIKE THINKS ABOUT WHAT HE SAID, WILL HE REALIZE THAT HE REALLY
WOULD LIKE ANOTHER DOG?
Maybe, but maybe not. He might not be aware of his deeper feelings.
HOW IS THAT POSSIBLE?
He may not want to admit to himself that another dog could take Pepper's place.
He might feel at some level that would be unloyal to Pepper to just go out and
replace the dog. He may feel guilty about it. He doesn't want to face these feel-
ings, so he says, no new dog.
IS HE AWARE OF THIS?
Probably not.

(16)

The adolescent develops a more advanced practical understanding of
psychological functioning; he or she doesn't necessarily construct a formal psychological theory.

Concepts of Friendship: The Resolution of Discord
and Conflict between Two Individuals

In exploring our subjects' ideas of friendship, we used the dilemma
summarized earlier, in which the young protagonist must choose between a date with her old friend and one with a new friend. As with other
dilemmas, questions and probes are first close to the story, then more
general, and then touch upon subjects' personal experiences.

Conflict resolution, the issue discussed here, is not a process limited
to the friendship relationship. It is a process, however, that plays a
critical part in the maintenance of friendship and, depending upon how it
is manifest, can play a progressive or regressive role in the development
of the relationship itself. Within the domain of friendship, the issue of
conflict resolution refers to children's and adults' ideas about how persons maintain friendships in the face of difficult situations, methods or
procedures for rectifying discord and disagreement within a friendship,
and notions of the kinds of conflicts that are seen as natural and expect-
able in a friendship.

As noted earlier, questions asked include the following:

1. What kinds of things do good friends sometimes fight or disagree about?
2. What are some good ways to settle fights, arguments, or disagreements with
   a friend?
3. Can friends have arguments and still be friends?

Following are the descriptions of concepts at each level.

LEVEL 0: MOMENTARY FRIENDSHIPS AND PHYSICAL SOLUTIONS TO CONFLICTS

At Level 0 children's suggestions for solutions to conflict between friends appear to be both momentary and physicalistic. Two consistent aspects or themes have been identified: conflict resolution through noninteraction and conflict resolution through direct physical intervention. In the former case, the child's reasoning about conflicts appears to be made without any reflective consideration of the psychological effects (feelings, motives, attitudes) of a given strategy upon *either* party. Two mechanisms are often articulated for dealing with conflict within this theme. The first is to simply suggest that one of the involved parties move to another activity ("Go play with another toy"). The second is to suggest a physical separation for a time ("Go away from her and come back later when you're not fighting"). It should be noted that despite the first impression given by such responses, young children coded at Level 0 do *not*, when their reasoning is probed, seem to see resolution through separation as a time to cool off and reflect on the problem (a Level 2 concept), but as a primitive "out of sight–out of mind" solution. They believe that if two people do not interact physically, they cannot be in any conflict. Furthermore, conflict does not seem to be a disagreement of perspectives, but a case of one party not getting to *do* what it is (or act in the way) he or she wants because of some action on the part of the other party.

The second theme or aspect often mentioned as an alternative method for conflict resolution to physical withdrawal is physical force, or as one 5-year-old girl blithely said when asked what to do when two friends argue, "Punch her out."

LEVEL 1: ONE-WAY FRIENDSHIP AND UNRELATED SOLUTIONS TO CONFLICTS

Level 1 reasoning is reflected in responses that indicate a new understanding that the subjective or psychological effects of conflict are as important as the physical effects. However, the principle appears to apply only with respect to one of the individuals involved. Rather than viewing conflicts as between two subjective perspectives, children whose concepts are scored at this level appear to view conflicts as essentially a problem that is *felt* by one party and *caused* by the actions of the other. It is for this reason that we term these children's understanding of conflicts *one-way* or *unilateral;* their resolutions are also one-way.

Essentially, the child seems to be saying that what is important is to reduce the *psychological* effects of the conflict on the identified recipient by having the other party reverse the effects of the conflict-producing *activity*. Three strategies or themes for achieving this goal emerge at this stage. The first is negation of the problem action, thereby appeasing the offended friend's feelings ("Stop the fight and give him back what you took or take back what you called him"). A second and related suggestion is the performance of positive action that will return a person who is experiencing psychological discomfort back to a state of comfort or psychological calm ("Give him something nice that will make him feel better").

What is significant by omission in the suggestions of children whose responses are coded as Level 1 is any concern (or awareness) that the actor performing the rectifying actions needs to coordinate his or her action (objectivity) and intention (subjectivity). It is not so much a question of a child's not feeling it important to match words and actions, that is, to "mean it"; it seems more a case of a child's exerting so much effort coordinating the *feelings* of one actor with the *actions* of the other that he or she does not have the conceptual "energy" to think at the same time of coordinating the feelings and actions *within* each actor.[5]

A third aspect of this level orientation is manifest in the tacit assumption that conflicts arise out of the negative actions of *one* of the two parties. The cause and locus of conflict is believed to be one actor's transgressions, not a coordinated mutual disagreement. Being focused on one individual as the cause of the other's discomfort, the subject also appears to assume that the seeds of resolution are also entirely in that party's hands.

HOW DO TWO FRIENDS MAKE UP IF THEY HAVE HAD A FIGHT?
Around our way the guy who started it just says he's sorry.
IS THAT ENOUGH?
Yup.

(8:3)

There are of course cases when in fact one person "started it." However, when the child can *only* conceive of a disagreement as started by *one* person, even when it in fact arises from honest disagreement, we feel this

[5] The foregoing analysis raises the issue of how much the child's social–conceptual immaturity can be seen as a function of relative immaturity of information-processing skills, that is, limits in ability to perform multiple psychological or cognitive operations at the same time. However, although "information-processing" capacities (cf. Stein, 1974) can explain or account for certain interpersonal or social problem-solving skills in the developing child, they cannot entirely account for the development and form the child's "theory of interpersonal concepts" takes. For example, a 7-year-old's belief that a good friendship is a one-way friendship cannot simply be a function of the maturity of his information-processing capacity. According to the developmental approach, critical interaction occurs between cognitive capacities (operations) and social experiences or realities (content) to generate the themes, aspects, and strategies we code in a developmental system.

represents a particular *social-cognitive* limitation that is typical of Level 1 conceptualizations.

LEVEL 2: BILATERAL FRIENDSHIPS AND COOPERATIVE SOLUTIONS TO CONFLICTS

Advances in understanding coded as Level 2 reflect the subject's cognizance that both parties participate psychologically in a conflict, and so both parties must engage actively in its resolution. One aspect of this level of understanding is, therefore, that a satisfactory resolution of a conflict between friends requires an appeal to each person's sensibilities, each person's judgment.

HOW DO YOU SOLVE PROBLEMS WHEN FRIENDS DISAGREE?
Somebody wants to play one game and the other wants to play another game and you can settle it, but first we will play your game and then we will play my game.
WHY DOES THAT MAKE THINGS BETTER?
Then each person gets to do what they want.

(14:3)

CAN A PERSON STOP A FIGHT?
No. You've got to get both of them to agree.

(12:3)

The limitation of this belief appears to be in the child's assumption that each party can be satisfied independently of the other. Still lacking is a sense of truly *mutual* problem solving. This Level 2 belief that everything is fine as long as each is happy regardless of whether or not they come to a mutual consensus, indicates that the conflict is still not seen to originate within the relationship itself. Rather, some external circumstance or event is seen to be the cause of the disagreement and hence, its removal is the source of resolution.

A second aspect, an advance over concepts coded at the previous stage, is the child's belief that it is no longer sufficient to simply "take back one's words" and the realization that in recanting, one must "*mean* what he or she says," that is, must be sincere in his or her apologies rather than simply going through the motions.

HOW DO FIGHTS GET STARTED?
You will be playing and somebody will start to tease you or call you a name.
HOW DO YOU PATCH THINGS UP?
You make her take it back—you make sure she means it or you let her have it.

(10:1)

These excerpts also exemplify structural correspondences across domains. Recall that in the issue of self-awareness (domain of individuals),

Level 2 was characterized by a distinction in the child's mind between the *appearance* of outer manifestations (e.g., words) and the *truth* or reality of inner beliefs (e.g., feelings). For example, with this conception now in hand, the child is able to grasp not only that one should "mean it," but also a third aspect, that conflicts can arise when one party, in a moment of anger, says or does something he may not really mean. This is a more sympathetic interpretation of conflicts and their resolution.

> CAN YOU BE FRIENDS WITH SOMEONE EVEN IF YOU HAVE FIGHTS?
> Yes. If you have a fight and say I hate you and you brat, I hate you, I hate you, and if they really meant it, then it wouldn't be good, but if they didn't really mean it, and they really meant it at the time, except they didn't really mean it, then that's okay.
> IF YOU HAVE THAT KIND OF FIGHT, HOW CAN YOU MAKE IT BETTER?
> Well, if you say something and don't really mean it, then you have to mean it when you take it back.
>
> (8:6)

Another aspect or strategy for resolving actual or potential conflicts which appears to require Level 2 perspective-taking understanding is the awareness that *psychological* space between "warring factions" often needs to be provided if conflicts are to be resolved peacefully and positively.

> IF YOU ARE HAVING TROUBLE WITH YOUR FRIEND, WHAT DO YOU DO?
> Sometimes you got to get away for a while. Calm down a bit so you won't be so angry. Then get back and try to talk it out.
>
> (14:1)

The kind of "getting away" described by children coded as Level 2 is quite different from the "forgetting as denial" suggested by younger children coded as Level 0. In the latter case "out-of-sight" appeared to be equated with "out-of-mind." Here we infer that out-of-sight is seen as a way for mind to recollect its thoughts and feelings.

A fifth aspect or strategy, based upon what appears to be a reciprocal understanding of perspectives, is to appeal directly to the other's perspective, that is, to get the friend's okay.

> SUPPOSE YOU WANT TO GO WITH THE NEW FRIEND AND YOU KNOW THE OLD FRIEND WILL BE ANGRY?
> You go up and ask your old friend if it is okay with him. You try to get him to see why you want to go.
>
> (12:6)

Here, getting the friend's okay really means presenting one's own point of view so as to convince the friend to change his or her point of view. As such, this is an important new strategy for conflict resolution.

However, in these last two cases, as with all the resolutions offered that are coded as Level 2, the reflective actions taken do not really rest on *mutual* agreement or coordination. There is an understanding that each party requires satisfaction, but not that each may care about or need to attend to the other's sense of how well the issue is resolved.

LEVEL 3: STABILITY OF FRIENDSHIPS AND MUTUAL SOLUTIONS TO CONFLICTS

The core reorientation at Level 3 is the understanding that certain friendship conflicts reside within the relationship itself, in the interaction between the parties, rather than in external annoyances to each party individually. We will discuss five new aspects.

First, individuals whose responses are coded as Level 3 indicate a belief that resolutions cannot be arrived at solely through détente: *each side must feel that both he or she and the other are truly satisfied with the resolution and would be satisfied if in the other's place.*

> If you just settle up after a fight that is no good. You gotta really feel that you'd be happy the way things went if you were in your friend's shoes. You can just settle up with someone who is not a friend, but that's not what friendship is really about.
>
> (15:6)

> Alan and I had a problem, which movie to go to. So we try to decide but if one person gives in just for the other and is not really happy about what to do that's no good either. You both have to really agree.
>
> (14:8)

A second aspect is recognition that friendship conflicts may be due to conflicts of personality and a resolution made might be personality change.

> She doesn't like the new girl.
> WHY?
> Well, one is a show-off and the other is very shy.
> COULD THEY EVER BE FRIENDS?
> Well, only if one of them changed their personality. Shy people don't usually like show-offs.
>
> (13:8)

A third aspect is recognition that conflicts of a certain type may actually strengthen a relationship rather than weaken it. Subjects at Level 3 see true friendship as continuing through thick and thin. A fourth and related aspect or strategy is that conflicts should be "talked out" or "worked out." Because one locus of conflict is seen as *between* persons, this "working through" is understood to be a more difficult process than the expedient types of resolutions generally suggested as adequate at Level 2. Because the working through is seen as a commitment by both parties, there is the awareness at Level 3 that through this mutuality, conflict resolution may strengthen friendship bonds.

IF YOU HAVE PROBLEMS WITH FRIENDS, WHAT IS THE BEST WAY TO WORK THEM OUT? IF YOU HAVE AN ARGUMENT?
Usually we get into fights sometimes, he comes down my house and steals my bike out of the garage, or I steal his bike to pick at him or get at his nerves, usually I just call him up and tell him I am sorry, it always happens like that and then we just make up.
SO A PERSON USUALLY SAYS IT IS THEIR FAULT?
Sometimes they do. Sometimes it was their fault and you agree, and sometimes it was your fault and you agree. Sometimes it is easier to do that with a friend. They understand. Every friendship, you always fight and everything, about something.
SO IS PART OF A DEEP FRIENDSHIP GOING THROUGH THESE FIGHTS?
Yah, I guess so.
IT SOUNDS CONTRADICTORY, A FRIEND IS SOMEONE YOU CAN HAVE FIGHTS WITH, WHY IS THAT?
Because you show that you really like the kid and that you are friends. If you didn't have a fight with the kid, it means you do this, I do that. You all work together and things like that. Everybody disagrees with everybody about something. No one is perfect with each other.

(14:1)

The fifth aspect of conflict resolution we identified at Level 3 is a distinction made between superficial conflict and deeper bonds. At Level 2 inner feelings and outer appearances are distinguished. At Level 3 there is a further recognition of the dichotomy between the immediate inner reaction during a period of conflict and the longer term affective relation that transcends these immediate feelings. The *bond itself* is seen as a source of healing, a means of conflict resolution between close friends.

Like you have known your friend so long and you loved her so much, and then all of a sudden you are so mad at her you say, I could just kill you, and you still like each other, because you have known each other for years and you have always been friends and you know in your mind you are going to be friends in a few seconds anyway.

(12:9)

The emphases of Level 3, then, appear to be on *active* interpersonal communication and sharing, and on verbal or mental rather than physical-action resolutions.

LEVEL 4: AUTONOMOUS INTERDEPENDENCE AND
SYMBOLIC ACTION AS A RESOLUTION TO CONFLICTS

If Level 3 understanding can be characterized as an interpersonal orientation based on a close-knit mutuality, Level 4 can be seen as a partial rejection of that mutuality when it precludes autonomous growth and development. At first, what we hear from subjects is the rejection of a perceived overdependence or overbonding in Level 3 relations. This move, in moderation, can be viewed as independence, but in its extreme is a counter-dependent position.

> Then you come to the place where you almost depend on the other person and you're not an individual anymore. If you tell—like if she knows everything about you if you depend so much on the other person, I think it is egotistical.
>
> (16—advanced placement student)

This independence, based on an understanding but partial rejection of mutuality, is itself subsequently tempered by the belief that total independence is as futile as total dependence.

> No man is an island. I'm not saying you got to fuse with a friend and lose your identity all together. I'm just saying you got to rely on other people to some extent, so it might as well be a close friend who you trust and who you're in vibes with. WHAT DO YOU MEAN, IN VIBES WITH?
> Well, someone who understands you and you understand them without always having to say things all the time.
>
> (24)

The idea of nonverbal communication, the idea of taking actions as *symbolic of the (repair of the) relationship* is one critical aspect of conflict resolution at Level 4.

> WHAT IS THE BEST WAY FOR ARGUMENTS TO BE SETTLED BETWEEN GOOD FRIENDS?
> Well, you could talk it out, but it usually fades itself out. It usually takes care of itself. You don't have to explain everything. You do certain things and each of you knows what it means. But if not, then talk it out.
>
> (16)

The other particular aspect we identified in the reasoning of subjects coded at this level is the understanding that intrapsychic conflicts, that is, conflicts *within* a person, can be a factor in conflicts *between* that person and a friend.

> Sometimes when a person's got problems of his own, he finds himself starting fights with all his friends. The best thing you can do is try to be understanding but don't get stepped on either.
>
> (27)

> You have to get yourself together if you expect to get along with others. A lot of relationships break up because one of the people are not really happy with himself. Of course, a good relationship like a good friendship is a good way for a person to find himself . . . if he doesn't do things to alienate his friend first.
>
> (31)

One good way to straighten things out between friends is to understand how the problem may relate to problems the person has in general. For example, lots of people have problems with authority. If they start to see the friendship as an authority relation, there might be trouble. But to solve it they have to sort out their own feelings.

(34)

The first excerpt also demonstrates the balance between independence and dependence. Help, commit, but keep a sense of self, keep some distance.

A third mode suggested for resolving conflicts between persons who are seen as capable of having everdeepening relations and commitments to one another is to "keep the lines of communication open," to rely on established channels.

Friends are always having to deal with each other's problems, hurt feelings, slights, things like that. The only way to maintain the friendship is by keeping open lines of communication.

(34)

By this, the subjects seem to mean (a) keeping in touch with one's own deeper feelings; (b) keeping in touch with the more personal and sensitive concerns of the friend; and (c) establishing a mode or operating procedure for communicating these feelings back and forth with one another over time.

Concepts of Peer Groups: The Role and Function of Leadership

The domain of peer-group relations presents some special problems and difficulties to a conceptual–developmental analysis.[6] For example, many younger children have little familiarity with the vocabulary or experience of group life among peers, making interviewing a sometimes abstruse and difficult interaction. Before reading or showing a filmstrip dilemma about peer groups, we found it useful to familarize the child with the term *group* as well as different examples of groups by reading or paraphrasing the following introduction.

I want to show you [read you] a filmstrip [story] about two street hockey clubs called the Jets and the Cougars. Have you ever heard of clubs before?____What do you know about them?____ Clubs are a group of kids that get together almost every day to plan what they would like to do. Sometimes they have meetings, elect leaders, wear uniforms, or even have secret passwords so only members can get

---

[6] Acknowledgment is made to Daniel Jaquette for collaboration on analyzing this domain.

in. Sometimes clubs hold their meetings in special clubhouses, but other times they just meet in the woods or over at one member's house. When new members join many clubs have initiations which are kind of like tests a member has to go through before being let in. But clubs are only one kind of group that kids are part of. Can you think of other groups kids might have?_____ There are the Girl and Boy Scouts, Indian Guides, teams that play sports, musical groups, your classroom, and just the regular neighborhood group of kids. All these different groups are alike in one way: they are all made up of lots of kids that get together to do things together.

We then showed a filmstrip or told a story about groups and their functions. The following story was aimed primarily at children in the 4- – 12-year age-range.

The Jets and the Cougars were two street hockey clubs that got together every week for a game of street hockey. In street hockey you try to get a little ball into a net or goal that is guarded by one player called the *goalie*. But you have to watch out because the other team is trying to get the ball in your goal and if they do it more times than your team does, they win the game. When the Jets and the Cougars got together to play, the Jets won every single game. In fact, the Jets were a much better club. They had uniforms, better players, they worked better together, and they had better spirit. The Cougars weren't too good. They tried hard, but they just couldn't seem to work very well together. One of their big problems was that they didn't have a very good goalie. Scott was playing goalie for the Cougars now, but almost every time the Jets took a shot against him they would score. During a time-out the Cougars got together and agreed that they had to get a better goalie if they were to have any chance at all against the Jets. But who could they get? They talked about it among themselves until Scott remembered a friend of his, Mike, who had just got over a broken ankle. Mike had been on a team before and was very good, so the Cougars went off to ask him to join their team. But the Jets overheard the Cougars talking about Mike and they thought he might want to join a winning team. So the Jets ran over to Mike's house, just as Mike was saying he would really like to join a team. The Jets tried to get him on their team by offering him a uniform, a trip to a real ice hockey game, and a chance to be cocaptain. The Cougars tried to get Mike on their team by telling him that he could really help their team, that Scott, his good friend, was on their team, and that he would be a great player on the Cougars, but only average on the Jets.
Mike agrees with some of the reasons for both teams, but can't decide which team to join.

As with other domains, follow-up questions were directed toward the elicitation of concepts across a number of issues. To tap leadership conceptions, the issue we will follow, the following questions were asked:

1. Do you think the Cougars need a captain or leader? Why?
2. Does having a leader help a group? How?
3. Can a club have more than one leader? How is that possible?
4. What sort of person makes a good leader?

Included then in the issue of leadership are the functions of leadership in a group, the qualities of a good leader, and the possible positive or negative consequences of having a leader for the group. Following are the descriptions of conceptions at each level.

LEVEL 0: PHYSICALISTIC CONNECTIONS IN GROUPS AND PHYSICAL POWER IN LEADERS

At Level 0, leadership appears to be seen as undifferentiated physical power over others. The child seems to believe that the leader is supposed to tell followers what to do and the followers are supposed to do it. There appears to be no understanding of the group functions of leadership nor of the group's conscious moderation of the leader's actions on the basis of whether the followers want that kind of leader. The principal aspect we identified was a leader's physical power over a group.

WHAT KIND OF LEADER SHOULD A GROUP HAVE?
There should be more than one leader, like two leaders.
WHY TWO?
Because if there is a whole bunch of people and one person for a leader, that's no good, but a whole bunch of people and two leaders then that's better. Because if one person wouldn't have a loud enough voice, but if both persons said the same thing at the same time, they would all hear.

(6:2)

Here being a leader means the physical capability of controlling others ("having a loud enough voice").

LEVEL 1: UNILATERAL GROUP RELATIONS AND AUTHORITARIAN LEADERSHIP

There are two aspects which appear to characterize leadership concepts coded as Level 1. First, the leader is seen to have a specific function as the one who is the most skilled and knowledgeable. Second, leadership is seen as a series of unilateral authoritarian relationships.

Focusing on the former aspect, the child seems to understand that leaders perform a definite function for the group in helping to successfully perform collaborative activities. The leader is seen to be at the top of a pyramid of specific knowledge about group activities which is transmitted downward. The resulting concept of group leadership appears to be the firm belief that the leader must be the best, know the most about the group's activities, and transmit the knowledge in a *one-way* fashion downward.

SUPPOSE YOU WERE MIKE AND WERE ELECTED LEADER OF THE JETS. WHAT WOULD YOU DO TO MAKE THE CLUB BETTER?
I would teach them to do tricks with the ball, like teach them to hit the ball way up

in the air and then when it had landed it could land right in the net. I would teach
them a lot of tricks.
WHAT KIND OF THINGS SHOULD A LEADER FIRST DO FOR HIS CLUB?
Give them time and make sure they do the right thing and help them.
WHY IS HELPING THEM IMPORTANT?
If they don't get help, they could fall down and hurt themselves.

(6:0)

On the positive side, the child believes the leader helps other members
improve their individual skills ("teach them to do tricks"). However, the
child does not appear to understand the possibilities for cooperative in-
terchange of information. The leader knows best. Significantly, the
leader does not yet act as an organizer or coordinator for the various interests present in the group.

The latter aspect is similar to that described in Piaget's hete-
ronomous stage of unilateral respect, where there is absolute defer-
ence to authorities. However, detailed interviewing indicates that
what appears to be an unchanging power structure is actually seen as a
series of absolute authorities. The limitation is that as long as the child
is capable only of Level 1 understanding, he or she can conceive of
disposing of one unilateral leader but does *not* appear to have the
social–cognitive capabilities to conceive of changing the structure of
leadership from its basic unilateral nature.

LEVEL 2: BILATERAL PARTNERSHIPS AND
LEADER AS MEDIATOR

At Level 2 the child appears to look at the leadership of the group
from the reciprocal perspectives of both leader and followers. The first
aspect we note is a new concern that leadership be based on equal treatment as pragmatically benefiting both parties (e.g., "If everybody is
equal, then nobody bosses anybody," age 8:11). Leadership is based on a
bilateral equality and reciprocity of interests.

A second aspect is that a good leader is believed to be an "arbi-
trator," not a "dictator" as in Level 1. The leader should attempt to
organize the different claims made by members in order to produce
some coordinated effort. This allows the group to move beyond the
stalemate of conflicting interests of individual members.

IS IT GOOD TO HAVE A LEADER IN A GROUP?
Yah, you have to have a leader because you have to have someone to follow
around. If you don't have a leader you have someone saying, I am going first in the
house, I am, I am, I am, but the leader keeps organizing it so everybody gets a
chance to go in the house and everybody takes turns going in.

(8:3)

The leader is seen as a mediator, but still one who imposes his or her
perspective in order to organize the group.

A third aspect is that the child believes the leader can help group members through encouragement and friendliness, by being a group psychologist of sorts. The leader leads not only by directly imposing his or her will, but by attempting to "get along with everybody" and "be an understanding person" (age 10:3), and generally promoting good relations through friendliness. However, group leadership conceptions are still unstructured in that the leader is not yet able to create a formal organization.

WHAT KIND OF QUALITIES DO YOU LOOK FOR IN A GOOD LEADER?
If she gets along with everybody because if she doesn't, then everybody will hate her and won't do what she says or anything.

(10:3)

WHAT KIND OF PERSON SHOULD BE A GROUP LEADER?
An understanding person, because he would tell his team that it was okay, that they were going to win sometimes, if the team keeps getting upset because it is losing.

(9:3)

LEVEL 3: GROUPS AS HOMOGENEOUS COMMUNITIES
AND LEADERS AS SOLIDIFIERS

At Level 3 the subject sees the group as a social system where the function of leadership is to marshal group solidarity (e.g., "The leader helps to structure the group," age 15:3). The principal aspect of this level is that a good leader should reflect the concerns of the group itself, not impose his or her own will; he or she should promote a group's sense of community and bring the group together "as a whole."

DO YOU THINK IT IS GOOD TO HAVE A LEADER IN A GROUP?
It depends on whether the rest of the group wants a leader or not.
WHY WOULD IT BE GOOD TO HAVE A LEADER?
You probably wouldn't be going every which way. He would probably take you some place as a whole, do something as a whole together, instead of having everyone go his own way.

(13:1)

In this sense, the leader is also seen as a catalyst in the creation of a formal structure of the group as a social system.

WHY IS IT IMPORTANT TO HAVE A LEADER?
If you don't have a leader, you never get started on what you are going to do. You need somebody to give you a push, to help you a little.

(13:7)

LEVEL 4: PLURALISTIC GROUP ORGANIZATION AND DIFFERENTIATED LEADERSHIP ROLES

The first aspect we looked at was subjects' identification of leadership as a social role function, abstracted from individuals. The subject reasoning at Level 4 believes leadership to be one of many social role responsibilities which function for the collective good of the group. The individual holding the office is distinguished from the duties and expectations of the office. The leader is seen to fill a position created by the organizational demands of a complex and pluralistic organization.

WHAT KIND OF PERSON MAKES A GROUP LEADER?
She should be somebody who symbolizes the finest in the group. I think they probably selected her as the embodiment of the group spirit, the group's existence. The president would be the light of the group, so that the outside world knows what the leadership is.

(26)

In this sense the ideal leader is "an embodiment." The power of leadership rests in the nature of the role itself ("to define the goals of what the group wants"), and an ideal leader does not possess this power except as the "embodiment of the group spirit." Abuses are seen to occur when an "authority figure" personally assumes the power of his or her office ("They sort of let the power go to their head").

At this level, a second aspect also emerges. Group leadership becomes differentiated into several functions or several roles. Each leadership role serves a complementary function to the group as a complex system ("the task leader"; "the person who smooths the rough edges").

IS THERE MORE THAN ONE KIND OF LEADERSHIP IN A GROUP?
Well, there is the person who takes charge in making sure that the group's task is accomplished, and there is the person who smooths the rough edges that arise when the task is being carried out, either by supplying comic relief or emotional support.
WHY DO YOU THINK A GROUP NEEDS THESE DIFFERENT KINDS OF LEADERSHIP?
When the group is carrying out its tasks, many times it creates friction among group members who have different points of view or interests. The group action which involves compromise would leave some members disenchanted. The task leader is there to see that the task is reached, and the person providing the emotional support is there to see that group members are not so disenchanted with the group that they would leave.
ARE THESE THE ONLY KINDS OF LEADERSHIP?
I can think of the leadership role of both types being shared by a number of individuals.

COULD THERE BE OTHER KINDS OF LEADERSHIP, OTHER THAN SUPPOR-
TIVE AND TASK ORIENTED?
There could be expertise, a person could be the opinion leader because the
members see him as the most knowledgeable.

(31)

ARE THERE DIFFERENT KINDS OF LEADERSHIP IN A GROUP?
There could be—in a band you have different kinds of leaders, there might be
someone who is the most creative and who will lead the group on creative ventures. Then there is someone else who is an organizer and who will get the group
together to make appointments and do all the organizing kinds of things.

(34)

Subjects reasoning at lower levels may believe that more than one kind
of leader exists. However, they see those types as simple character traits
("nice," "one that you like") or stereotyped roles ("president, vice president"). At Level 4 these multiple functions or kinds of leadership are
abstract roles which come from the structural requirements of an
organized system ("providing emotional support"; "to see that the task
is reached").

Concepts of Parent–Child Relations:
Children's Rationales for Punishment[7]

Recently there has reappeared a subtle but growing ideological divi-
sion among some developmental psychologists as to the relative importance of parental and peer influences for the present and future social
behavior of children. Most everyone agrees that both influences are important, and that they are in some ways different in quality and kind.
However, behind this neutral acknowledgment of differences, one sus-
pects there sometimes lurks a belief that one of these influences is more
healthy, productive, facilitating, and important than the other. In
particular, I sense a trend toward an idealization of the peer relationship
and a deprecation of the relation between parent and child. Peer groups
are often romantically described as naturally democratic and egalitarian
and as the true source of the child's understanding of fair play and
sociocentric communication. Often overlooked is how narcissistic, insen-
sitive, and cruel children can be and are to one another. Most often emphasized in the parent–child relation is conflict, stress, and inequality of
power and resources. Here, sometimes overlooked is the essential growth
potential of a mature relation between parent and child, providing a
secure foundation of emotional and physical support.

[7] Acknowledgment is made to Ellie Bruss-Saunders for the work on this domain. Examples are drawn from Bruss-Saunder's dissertation (Bruss-Saunders, 1979).

The first step for understanding the similarities and differences in the ways the child thinks about the parent–child relation and about the other relations we have so far examined is to identify issues particularly salient to the parent–child relation and examine how children's developing thinking about these issues compares to their thinking about the issues of importance in friendship, peer relations, and individuals. Are there issues that are analogous? Are there issues that are inherently uncomparable? Most likely, the answer to both these questions is a qualified yes. For instance, although children do not choose parents in the same way they may choose friends, children believe they need parents to a far greater degree than they believe they need friends. But the basis of that perceived need may be quite different for different children, and the developmental progression may have some unique qualities. As another example, what are children's theories about the reasons parents, or more accurately, adults choose to have children and thus to become parents? How does the child's thinking on this matter compare to his thinking about the reasons children choose certain individuals to be their friends. Furthermore, children have neither the same kinds of conflicts nor the same spectrum of resolutions with parents that they have with friends. What do children view as the optimal methods for conflict resolution in the family in comparison with conflict resolution on the playground and schoolyard?

These are some of the questions underlying Bruss-Saunder's expansion of our system to the study of developing concepts of the parent–child relation. Five issues have been identified for the parent–child domain: (a) *formation* of the relationship, which refers to concepts about why adults might want children, why children need parents, and what makes a good parent; (b) the nature of *emotional ties* between parents and children, which includes both issues of affection and cooperation; (c) *obedience* and the nature of and reasons for parents' demands of children; (d) the nature of *punishment* and the child's view of its function; and (e) parent–child *conflicts and their resolution*. For our "case study" of how a perspective-taking analysis can be applied to the parent–child domain, I have chosen the issue of punishment for several reasons. First, punishment represents an issue that is fairly particular to an authority relation such as exists between parents and children and therefore speaks to something unique about this domain. On the other hand, punishment and the child's understanding of how and why a parent may choose to punish a child would seem to be importantly influenced by the child's understanding of the parent's perception of how children understand things. Finally, punishment as a general concept speaks to the child's ability to reflect on his or her own behavior as well, and this could have interesting correspondences to concepts in other domains, in particular, the clinically important issue of self-awareness.

As we did in the descriptive study of concepts in each of the other three domains, in the parent–child domain we used a combination of approaches in the constructive phase, integrating responses to a hypothetical dilemma with follow-up questions about the general nature of the domain and issues under examination and with questions directed toward the subjects' own attitudes and personal experiences. The version of the parent–child dilemma used by Bruss-Saunders with preadolescent-aged subjects follows:

I am going to tell you a short story about a girl (boy) your age and the decision she (he) once had to make. I will then ask you to tell me what this girl (boy) should do, why this would be a good decision to make and what you think about this girl (boy) and her (his) relationship with her (his) parents.

Jane is a girl your age. Every week she gets 25 cents from her parents. It is her pocket money. Jane's parents tell her to save it. She should spend it only on something she really needs.

This week Jane has seen a little doll in the toy store. It costs 25 cents and looks really nice. Jane would like to have it, but her parents think that she has enough toys and will not buy it for her. So Jane thinks of buying it for herself using the 25 cents she just got from her parents. But she knows that her parents do not want her to spend her money on toys. On the other hand, it is her money. Jane really does not know what to do.

The interview, as with interviews in each of the other domains, systematically inquires into the subject's beliefs about each of the parent–child issues. Three questions directly focused on punishment in the dilemma.

1. Let's say Jane's parents tell Jane that she should not buy the doll, but she disobeys them. If Jane's parents find out, what do you think they will do? Why?
2. Do you think that children should be punished if they disobey? Why?
3. Why do parents sometimes punish their children? PROBE: How does punishment work, what does it do for children?

These were followed by a general interview with these further questions:

When parents get upset with their children they sometimes punish them. Do you get punished sometimes? Why do you think your parents punish you sometimes? PROBE: How does punishment work? What is it supposed to do for you? Do you think your parents could bring you up without ever punishing you?

Following are descriptions of concepts at each level.

LEVEL 0: PRAGMATIC PARENTING AND REACTIVE-PUNITIVE RESPONSES

While children whose conceptions are coded as Level 0 appear to understand that punishment temporally follows a transgression or a disobedience, they do not appear to understand that parents can have *socializing motives* for punishing children or that the act of punishment is an independent action that follows *after* the parent's evaluation of the child's actions that precede it. In other words there is a confusion between punishment as cause (I did something wrong because I was punished) and punishment as effect (I was punished because I did something wrong). Thus, functionally, punishment does not even seem to be seen as a conscious retribution but as a reactive physical enforcement.

WHY DO PARENTS SOMETIMES PUNISH THEIR CHILDREN?
Because they don't do what they are told to do.
BUT WHY PUNISH THE CHILD?
To make them do it.

(6:1)

Second, the child's responses coded as Level 0 focus only on the *effects* of the punishment on the child rather than on the parent's motives for instigating a punitive procedure.

WHAT DOES PUNISHMENT DO FOR CHILDREN? HOW DOES IT WORK?
It makes us upset.
WHY DO PARENTS WANT THEIR CHILDREN TO BE UPSET?
Because the child was bad.

(5:4)

LEVEL 1: AUTHORITARIAN PARENTING AND PUNISHMENT AS A LESSON FROM ABOVE

Whereas at Level 0, a child focuses on the recipient of the punitive action, the child whose reasoning is coded as Level 1 focuses attention on the punitive agent and his motive for instigating a punitive action. Thinking at this level can, in this respect, look like an "identification with the aggressor," that is, the child is able to consider (appreciate) parental motives for a punitive action, but appears to "forget," or not (be able to) keep in mind, the recipient's reaction. Three new aspects of the punitive function emerge at this level.

First, punishment is seen as a *teaching device* for informing children what is good or bad and what they may and may not do. The child, taking the perspective of the parent who resorts to it, asserts the punitive function is to "teach the child a lesson."

WHY DO YOU THINK PARENTS SOMETIMES PUNISH THEIR CHILDREN?
Because they do bad things and they want to teach them a lesson.

(9)

WHY DO YOU THINK PARENTS SOMETIMES PUNISH THEIR CHILDREN? HOW DOES PUNISHMENT WORK?
The point of it is because they wanna teach them a lesson, to not do them bad

things, but she just did, but the parents don't want them to act that way, cause they'd go to the circus and they'd act up while they're watching the circus.

(6)

That children seem to look at punishment from only one person's point of view reflects the limitations of Level 1 social perspective taking. What is missing is a balanced concern with the child's reactions to being punished, a concern which it should be remembered played an important role in Level 0 concepts of punishment. It is not until Level 2 that concepts of punishment will include both the parent's and the child's point of view.

A second aspect is that punishment is now understood to be a device for protecting the child from danger. There appears to be a sense that punishment serves to warn children of potential injuries that parents, in their wisdom, can foresee but children cannot.

WHY DO PARENTS SOMETIMES PUNISH THEIR CHILDREN?
Because you take out your bike, you get hit by a car. And you mother say, "Don't take out your bike."

(7)

DO YOU THINK CHILDREN SHOULD BE PUNISHED IF THEY DISOBEY?
Yes, I do because children, when they disobey and do not listen to their mothers should be punished because they've been bad and they did something bad and their mothers worry about them and if they got kidnapped or something that would be worser, and their mothers don't want them to do that stuff.

(6)

Sometimes one even gets the impression that behind this reasoning seems to be the image of a "wild" child who needs to be tamed by means of punishment to be prevented from exposure to a most dangerous world.

Third, and directly related to the Level 1 perspective-taking "reciprocity of action," punishment appears to be seen as the appropriate parental reaction to the child's transgression insofar as it restores a certain equilibrium. If a child disobeys a parent's injunction, punishment is viewed as the natural way that the parent pays him or her back. This notion of "setting things straight" represents the difference between a Level 0 action–reaction and a Level 1 reaction to restore balance or equilibrium.

WHY DO CHILDREN GET PUNISHED?
Well, they done something wrong, and then they should get paid back for it.

(8)

WHEN PARENTS GET UPSET WITH THEIR CHILDREN, THEY SOMETIMES
PUNISH THEM. DO YOU EVER GET PUNISHED?
Yeah. I got punished last night.
WHAT HAPPENED?
I gave someone a candy.
AND YOU WERE NOT SUPPOSED TO GIVE THEM CANDY?
Yep.
WHY DO YOU THINK YOUR PARENTS PUNISH YOU SOMETIMES?
Cause you're bad.
HOW DOES PUNISHMENT WORK? WHAT'S THE POINT OF IT? WHAT DOES
IT DO FOR YOU?
By behaving. And if you do it the next day, the same thing will happen.

(6)

WHY DO PARENTS PUNISH THEIR CHILDREN WHEN THEY DISOBEY?
Because they deserve it.

(8)

LEVEL 2: THE PARENT–CHILD RELATION AS
A SOURCE OF RECIPROCAL EMOTIONAL TIES
AND PUNISHMENT AS A FORM OF COMMUNICATION

A major shift in the reasoning of children coded at Level 2 is the new
understanding that punishment can be a way for a parent who is concerned for the child's well-being to appeal to the child's own judgment.
Punishment appears to be seen as a mode of discourse, a method for telling the child to consider changes in disapproved behavior. One aspect
thereof is that one goal of punishment is seen to be the establishment of
or facilitation of the self-reflective process in the child, for example, to
make the child think about his or her actions before embarking on a
dangerous activity or to help the child establish controls over his or her
own behavior. In this sense punishment functions as a message sent
from one self-reflective and judging being to another.

WHY DO YOU THINK PARENTS PUNISH SOMETIMES?
I guess to make you feel . . . make you think about it . . . or something like that.
HOW DOES PUNISHMENT WORK? WHAT IS IT SUPPOSED TO DO FOR YOU?
It's supposed to make you become good.

(12)

WHY DO YOU THINK YOUR PARENTS PUNISH YOU SOMETIMES?
To let you know what point of view they are in and where they are coming from.

(15)

WHAT IS PUNISHMENT SUPPOSED TO DO FOR CHILDREN?
Make them learn. Think over what you did wrong, next time maybe you will make a
better decision.

(15)

DO YOU GET PUNISHED SOMETIMES?
Yup, I don't get to watch TV.
WHY DO YOU THINK YOUR PARENTS PUNISH YOU?
Cause if they wouldn't punish you, they wouldn't care.
THEY PUNISH YOU CAUSE THEY CARE ABOUT YOU? HOW DOES PUNISH-
MENT WORK? WHAT IS IT SUPPOSED TO DO FOR YOU?
Um . . . that's real tough. To make you think what you did wrong.

(10)

A second new aspect of thinking about punishment discerned at Level 2 is perception of the deterrent quality of punitive action. The child speculates that children who do not fear that their transgressions will lead to a punitive response will have little or no incentive to refrain from disobeying their parents. In this sense the goal of punishment is seen to be the instillation of fear, which in turn acts in part as an internal agent of control for the child. (See the description of self-awareness at Level 2 for a "cross referenced," or corresponding, conception.)

SHOULD CHILDREN BE PUNISHED IF THEY DISOBEY?
Yeah. Cause then when you tell them not to do something, they won't do it. And if she don't punish them, they're just gonna go back and do it again, and they have command of their parents.

(13)

DO YOUR PARENTS PUNISH YOU SOMETIMES?
Yes, so I won't do the same thing again. And I'll remember.
DO YOU THINK YOUR PARENTS COULD BRING YOU UP WITHOUT EVER PUNISHING YOU?
No.
WHY NOT?
Cause if they did it that way, I'd be doing the wrong thing all the time. Knowing that I get away with it.

(12)

As pointed out above, coded as Level 2 is punishment seen as a means by which parents communicate to their children their dissatisfaction with their behavior. This conception of punishment leads to a third aspect, a new concern for the effectiveness of punishment and a questioning of the wisdom of using physical or constraint punishment rather than a serious talk as a means of telling the child what is good and what is bad for him or her. Punishment is now seen either as an expression of parents' love or as an expression of parents' lack of understanding of their child, depending on whether or not punishment is considered an appropriate way of establishing and enforcing parental rules. Punishment is viewed as an acceptable teaching method only if it has a beneficial influence on the punished child. Sometimes children reasoning at Level 2 point out that punishment hurts, but that feeling hurt and learning what is good and what is bad can be two different matters. Further, it is now understood that parents can make mistakes and dole out unjust punishment. Therefore, these children recommend that parents should pay close attention to their children's thoughts and feelings about what they have done before deciding to punish them. The most effective communication regarding what is right and wrong is seen as taking place in the form of an exploration of what has transpired rather than of some retaliatory action.

WHAT WILL ANDY'S PARENTS DO IF THEY FIND OUT THAT HE DID NOT STAY AT HOME?
They will let him off, without punishment.
WHY?
They would just tell him not to do it again. Because if they punish him, all that happens when I go home is I get punished. But then he would think I really shouldn't have done it, because he didn't get punished. But if he gets a punishment he will think, "That is all that is going to happen, I just worry if I am going to get a punishment."

(13)

WHAT WILL ANDY'S PARENTS DO IF THEY FIND OUT THAT HE DID NOT STAY AT HOME?
He will get killed, because he disobeyed.
WHAT WILL PUNISHMENT DO FOR HIM?
Teach him next time not to disobey his parents.
DO YOU THINK IT WILL TEACH HIM TO OBEY HIS PARENTS?
It depends on the kid. Some kids would get killed for doing it, and they would just go and do it again.
WHAT DO YOU THINK PARENTS SHOULD DO WITH SUCH A KID?
Sit down and talk to him. Tell him what he did wrong and tell him that they will kill him the next time he does it.
DO YOU THINK THIS WOULD HELP THE KID MORE THAN JUST GETTING A PUNISHMENT?
Yes, because punishment just makes him get mad and so he would just go out and do it again.

(13)

WHAT DOES PUNISHMENT DO FOR CHILDREN?
It depends what the punishment is. But it doesn't really tell you not to do it again, it is just punishing you.

(14)

DO YOU THINK THAT YOU SHOULD BE PUNISHED IF YOU DISOBEY?
Yes, to a certain extent. But I always have a reason for not obeying, I don't just disobey.
DO YOU STILL THINK YOU SHOULD BE PUNISHED?
If she punishes me, it is just hurting me, but it will not really do anything, it will not really stop me from doing things.

(17)

LEVEL 3: PARENTS AND CHILDREN AS SEPARATE PERSONALITIES AND PUNISHMENT AS A NEED FOR CONTROL

By the time the child has reached the age at which most children are capable of Level 3, mutual coordination of perspectives, the actual nature of the parent–child relationship in which they are involved has changed radically. This is reflected in the thinking of the preadolescent and adolescent subjects in our sample who make a distinction between punishment for themselves versus the function of punishment for younger children. The older child, regardless of what level of concept he or she has attained, usually thinks of punishment within the parent–child context as something that applies less to them and more to their younger siblings or other little children. Nevertheless, it is only those older children who are able to articulate a new aspect, that punishment simultaneously serves the needs of the parents *and* the children, whom we code as having Level 3 understanding. These subjects seem to be able to see more clearly that parents have their own needs as well as interest in the needs of their children and to view the punitive act as one that in the ideal sense represents an attempt by the parent at balancing these sometimes conflicting needs. Thus when the child can paint a picture of both parent and child as having personalities, as having interests and concerns that influence punitive decision making, his thinking is coded at Level 3.

> Parents have their lives too. If a kid is always screwing up, it's not just the kid who needs to see the light. The parents don't always want to be bailing him out of trouble.
>
> (16)

A related aspect is that corporal punishment is seen as a less-than-optimal way to command obedience, a tool to which parents might resort in anger and despair because of inability to find better ways of controlling their children. A better mode of behavior management is seen to be "talking things out." (See "Friendship Conflict Resolution" for a similar strategy.) In making this recommendation the preadolescent recognizes that, in reality, the parent has less actual physical control over an older child and therefore cannot use the kinds of threats and coercions that may work for the younger child. Children or adolescents who appear to be reasoning at levels lower than 3 can also recognize this as a fact, but it is how well the child weaves this reality into the fabric of an understanding that both the parent's and the child's needs need to be recognized that differentiates Level 3 from the lower stages.

WHY DO PARENTS SOMETIMES PUNISH THEIR CHILDREN?
Punishment is not necessary; there are other techniques to achieve obedience. It

depends on the capabilities and needs of the child. I don't think punishment is necessary, but it is effective, but there are also other ways in which one can achieve obedience. It depends on the parents, what they are like as well as the children.

(17)

LEVEL 4: PUNISHMENT AND POWER, SOME SPECULATIONS

One can see that Level 3 conceptions of punishment require a fairly sophisticated level of understanding. It is quite possible to have these concepts tucked away in one's basic understanding of human nature yet not demonstrate them in the type of interview that we use to code interpersonal reasoning. In this sample, we found this to be a particular problem, since many of the subjects were both young (under 18) and from social class backgrounds not generally recorded as having great verbal facility. The low number of subjects in the sample who were able to articulate Level 3 responses made trying to go beyond Level 3 to a Level 4 coding that would parallel the highest levels we had differentiated in the other domains seem a shaky business. However, I believe that some of the responses that were originally coded as representing Level 3 themes or aspects can be thought of as actually representative of Level 4 concepts. Clearly more data are needed to make systematic claims. However, I would like to at least describe what I feel illustrates Level 4 thinking on this issue.

I would consider one Level 4 offshoot of Level 3 to be understanding punishment as an unconscious attempt to maintain psychological control or fusion. A number of the parent–child interview subjects seemed to have a sense that the act of punishment on the part of the parent might represent a displaced sense of anger or despair. For example, some subjects brought up the issue of child abuse as an example of "crazy" or inappropriate punishment and saw its roots in the unhappiness of the parent or the parent's inability to understand the nature and limits of childhood. Other subjects pointed out that punishment could serve the needs of some parents who were unable to give up control over their children for psychological reasons.

SHOULD CHILDREN BE PUNISHED WHEN THEY DISOBEY?
Not when they are older. The mother cannot keep the child, or the father, if that child is eighteen years old or so. Parents often think that they still run their child, but they can't because that person is almost the age where they can begin going on their own; they are old enough to decide that they want something.
WHY DO PARENTS DO THIS?
They don't even know they're doing it.

(18)

What makes me think this response can be coded at Level 4 is in particular the acknowledgment at the end of the excerpt that the motive for control that underlies the punishment is not known to the parent. This ability to acknowledge the double-edged function of parenting, (parenting for the parent's sake as well as for the child's) and to see the potential for unawareness of these multiple functions on the part of the parent has its complement in the understanding of punishment-eliciting behavior of children. I would code as Level 4 the responses of a subject who is capable of expressing an understanding that children are not merely passive victims of parental anger or targets for their parents' hopes and aspirations, but that some children, some of the time, have a need for punishment, insofar as punishment symbolizes for them that their parents care about them.

WHY DO PARENTS SOMETIMES PUNISH THEIR CHILDREN?
In order to make the child obey. Some kids will do something wrong just to get punished, to see if the parents really care. Some parents won't punish. But punishment can be an expression of love, because it shows that you care.

(18)

It is true that at Level 2 there was noted an understanding of punishment as a type of caring. Here the additional idea is that children "unconsciously" use behavior that provokes punishment as a means either of getting themselves under control or of obtaining a sign or symbol of parental affection. Level 4 in the parent–child domain, as in the other domains, signifies conceptions that recognize *mutualities* and *relations* at subconscious and unconscious levels of interaction as well as on the verbal surface of human discourse.

In the next chapter, I discuss each domain in more general terms.

6

Four Domains, Five Stages: A Summary Portrait of Interpersonal Understanding

Thus far in Part II, Chapter 4 presented a theory for coding interpersonal concepts into one of five developmental stages and provided examples from a model which divides interpersonal understanding into four broad domains and these into 22 more fine-grained issues, and Chapter 5 focused on four sample issues, tending to highlight the particular character of each issue at each *level*, rather than the "holistic" aspect of interpersonal understanding at each stage. In this chapter, I attempt to move from the particular to the general, providing an overview of how at each level, each of the issues in a given domain fits with the others to form, from a logical perspective, a structured whole, a *stage*.[1] I conclude this chapter with a brief discussion of the kinds of problems that arise when, as we have done during this phase of research, one attempts to paint a "still life" picture of what are obviously very dynamic and fluctuating processes.

---

[1] See also discussion of the terms *level* and *stage* in Chapter 4.

Summary Description of Stages in Conceptions of Individuals

STAGE 0: INDIVIDUALS AS PHYSICAL ENTITIES

There are several major characteristics of this stage. First, there appears to be a confusion of the causal relation between physical and psychological experience (one is sad *because* one is crying, not crying *because* one is sad). Second, overt behavior appears to be seen as defining the inner experience (subjective experience) rather than the other way around. Similarly, subjective states appear confused with physical states so that a person is seen as capable of only one emotion at a time in the same way as that person can only be in one place at a time. The child whose reasoning is coded at Stage 0 has a material conception of self-awareness. Whatever self-conceptions the child has, in the sense of being able to verbalize an awareness of self, are conceptions of a physical self, characterized by inherent bigness or strongness.

> I am a good boy.
> WHY?
> Because I am big.
>
> (4:10)

Similarly, questions designed to assess the child's conception of personality (e.g., What kind of person do you think Molly is?) are responded to with descriptions of overt physical appearance (girl, longhaired). Finally, personality change is equated with physical growth (as I get older, I get bigger). There is yet to appear to be any reflective understanding of internal changes or of the factors which might bring about *psychological* change within persons.

STAGE 1: INDIVIDUALS AS INTENTIONAL SUBJECTS

At Stage 1, the subject more clearly differentiates psychological and physical causality. Thoughts are seen to underlie actions, motives are more clearly seen as important for the understanding of behavior, different people are seen to be capable of having different reactions to similar types of events, and one person is seen as having the capacity for having several feelings within himself or herself. Nevertheless, it is still difficult for the subject using Stage 1 reasoning to understand that one person can have conflicting thoughts or feelings toward the *same* social situation at *one* time.

With regard to self-awareness, although the Stage 1 subject is aware that motives can underlie behavior, this child generally takes what persons say about their own motives at face value, that is, believes that what a person says is what a person means. It is not that the subject at

Stage 1 lacks a reflective conception of lying; such a subject does appear to know persons can purposefully distort facts. What is still difficult to understand is that persons can distort feelings, that is, feel one way and say they feel another. In general, the subject at Stage 1 appears to believe that feelings are not easily hidden, and that overt behavior will generate clues to inner feelings.

Personality is still context-specific, but rather than only being a function of overt appearance, personality is now seen as being manifest in abilities and skills. Likewise, personality change is seen as improvement of skills with age; however, the categories of improvement still tend to be those of overt behavior, or the learning of specific facts. At Stage 1, people are understood to be capable of change simply by saying they want to change; then, what is needed is, for instance, practice of new skills.

STAGE 2: INDIVIDUALS AS INTROSPECTIVE SELVES

The Level 2 perspective-taking understanding that one's perspective of others must take account of others' perspective of self corresponds in the *persons* domain to the understanding that although other can take account of the self's inner thoughts, the self can also conceal his or her own inner subjective reality from other's view. Put another way, the child generates a dual-layered conception of persons as having an inner and an outer self and realizes that people can present an overt appearance of self that may or may not identically correspond to the inner subjective reality. Being capable of self-reflection, the child understands that thoughts, feelings, or motives toward one object or within one individual can conflict or be ordered in a hierarchy. There may be multiple albeit separate subjective reactions to the same situation or acts. (A gift of a new puppy can make one happy because one wants a puppy and sad because it reminds one of one's old dog.) Similarly, the child now recognizes that persons may do things they don't want to do or say things they don't believe because other thoughts or motives so dictate. ("He may pretend he likes the gift but he really doesn't. He is only saying that to not hurt Tom's feelings.") Here the child is viewed as self-aware in the sense that the child can weigh the relative value of his or her feelings toward his friend and his or her feelings toward the gift. However, this conception of persons as self-aware appears limited in the sense that such self-reflection is always seen as potentially available to the self; if one does not know something about the self's attitudes it is because of "forgetting" or "not paying attention" to this inner experience. One can trick others but not oneself.

Although still context-specific, personality appears to be understood in terms of a person's feelings or mood as well as actions. Persons are described on the basis of how they feel about specific social situations; people can have different personalities in the same sense that they can have different moods or feelings at different times. Personality can change in the sense that one can change how one feels or how one thinks about things. Sometimes, however, change in personality is understood as being difficult because the specific habits that one picks up and which are seen as the personality itself are, themselves, difficult to change. These habits are not abstracted traits, but specific ways of acting. Finally, change in personality (as change in habit) is understood to be possible through self-reflectively trying harder. The idea is to simply apply one's newly developed notion of self-reflection to the self's moods or motives and thereby, through effort, to change the particular mood or motive.

STAGE 3: INDIVIDUALS AS STABLE PERSONALITIES

At the previous stage, different subjective aspects of experience are understood to exist by the child separately but coterminously. Now people are seen as able to have mixed thoughts, feelings, or motives toward the same object at the same time. (Mike can hate and love the dog at the same time.)

The significance of this achievement in understanding can be interpreted in terms of the perspective-taking levels. We noted at Stage 2 a concept of an inner or real self emerged defined as an understanding of one's own subjectivity as seen from the point of view of other or of "self-as-other." At Stage 3, "mind" appears to have a third-person concept, a concept whereby the self can observe its own reflections on subjectivity. This ability to observe or reflect upon the inner coherence of self's subjective life leads the child to the idea of a psychological trait as an organization or "pulling together" of subjective inner attitudes as well as to the recognition of ambivalent motivational states.

Ironically, enthralled by the underlying psychological realities, the child making use of Stage 3 reasoning often appears to overgeneralize simple or unidimensional (stereotypic) traits as the primary features of the psychological aspects of persons. Another limiting aspect of this stage is that subjectivity within the person still is understood to occur on one plane, the plane of conscious awareness. The powerful idea that the mind, the conscience, or the "little person inside" can organize the self's inner psychological life leaves no room for psychological phenomena unavailable to this roving eye.

Coded at Stage 3 is the subject's belief that it is possible to fool the self, but only in the sense that the mind makes a *special effort* to trick itself, that is, fooling oneself is understood to be possible only if one *wills* it; and even then, once one pays attention to the concern, one can no longer truly fool the self. Understanding of true unawareness in human nature emerges at Stage 4. And although conflicting motives, thoughts, or feelings are seen to exist within persons hand-in-hand with one another, it is not until Stage 4 that these conflicts are seen to lead to new forms of thoughts, motives, or feelings, qualitatively distinct from the component parts.

Because the concept of personality is understood to represent a predictable set of character traits, it is also viewed as relatively stable and unchangeable. Individuality is acknowledged beyond specific attitudes or habits. Furthermore, there is a recognition of the qualitative difference between changing one's personality (Stage 3) and changing one's habits (Stage 2), the latter being a relatively easy process and the former a much more difficult one which requires a basic "personality" reorganization.

STAGE 4: INDIVIDUALS AS COMPLEX SELF-SYSTEMS

Stage 4 represents a new form of understanding which integrates the elements which emerged at Stage 3. For example, at Stage 3 the subject is aware that persons can have mixed feelings toward the same social situation or action. At Stage 4, there emerges an understanding that mixed feelings themselves may be psychologically integrated to form qualitatively distinct emotions (e.g., ambivalence is not just a mixture of two conflicting feelings, but a distinct psychological experience).

With regard to self-awareness, at Stage 3, the subject understands both that there are certain aspects of the self's behavior of which the self is not in control and that the self is able to examine its own motivations and behaviors. By putting together these concepts, the subject moves at Stage 4 to construct a new psychological process, the *unconscious,* to explain the observation that persons are not always aware of their behavior, that even introspection may not yield the psychological causes which best explain behavior, and that external causes cannot explain all of the self's behavior either.

Just as specific feelings and motives are integrated into a new system at Stage 4, so is personality as a system seen to be an integration of various traits and values. At Stage 3, the subject tended to overgeneralize one trait or system to define each person as a unique personality. At Stage 4, the subject sees that persons have sometimes conflicting and complex traits which need to be integrated at a more basic level into a more complete descriptive system. ("He is sometimes passive with his boss, but a very bossy person with his own staff. I guess he is pretty authoritarian when it comes right down to it.")

This tendency and attempt to integrate various facets of personality into an "integrative core" can also be seen in the area of personality change. Stage 3 represents an understanding of the difficulty of personality change, but it refers to a conception of personality as a simple trait. At Stage 4, there is recognition that change may occur at a number of levels: superficial behaviors, stronger traits, or deepest and most basic core aspects of one's personal and interpersonal orientation.

Summary Description of Stages in Conceptions of Friendship

STAGE 0: CLOSE FRIENDSHIP AS MOMENTARY PHYSICAL INTERACTION

The physicalistic social thinking of the young child is characterized first by the failure to recognize or differentiate the psychological from the physical qualities or attributes of people and their relations and second by the inability to define friendship beyond the momentary or repeated incidents of interaction between two persons who come together to play. For example, reflections upon how to go about making a friend tend to emphasize the physical reality of proximity and propinquity at the expense of or through ignorance of psychological considerations. Similarly the qualities of a person who might make a good friend are attributes such as physical and functional similarity.

WHAT KIND OF PERSON MAKES A GOOD FRIEND?
Boys play with boys, trucks play with trucks, dogs play with dogs.
WHY DOES THAT MAKE THEM GOOD FRIENDS?
Because they do the same things.

(5:1)

Also observed at Stage 0 is admiration of a person as a friend for observable valued physical attributes such as fast running or strong play.

This physicalistic orientation also pervades conceptions of intimacy and trust. It is difficult for the child reasoning at Stage 0 to differentiate degrees of friendship; good acts are friendly, bad acts are not. Hence friendship relations themselves are not perceived along a continuum, except on a naively physicalistic and literal basis ("close friends live close by"). Trust, to the extent that the concept is familiar to young children, appears to be accommodated to this nonsubjective orientation. Trust is limited to faith in physical capability, that is, the belief that to trust a friend is to know he is capable of playing with one's toys without breaking them. Not until the next stage are a person's motives or intentions considered.

WHO IS YOUR BEST FRIEND?
Eric.

DO YOU TRUST HIM?
Yes.
WHAT DOES IT MEAN TO TRUST ERIC?
If I give him a toy I know he won't break it.
HOW DO YOU KNOW?
He isn't strong enough.

(6:2)

The momentary quality of friendship in Stage 0 conceptions is highlighted around issues of jealousy and intrusion–exclusion. Jealousy is not interpersonally oriented in the sense of a concern for the losing of a friend's affection or attention. Rather, jealousy is directed to the loss of toys or space. Strategies for resolving conflicts between two playmates tend to center around the same simplistic reliance on physical force or movement.

IF YOU AND YOUR FRIEND ARE EACH TRYING TO PLAY WITH THE SAME TOY, HOW DO YOU DECIDE WHO GETS IT?
Punch her. Or just go play with something else.

(5:3)

Finally, because friendships are physicalistic, momentary, or both, physical battles ("when he hits you") or physical qualities ("I don't like her voice") are seen as both the cause of and the justification for playmate separation at Stage 0.

STAGE 1: CLOSE FRIENDSHIP AS ONE-WAY ASSISTANCE

There are two underlying organizational developments at Stage 1: (a) the new awareness of the functions of motives, thoughts, and feelings, internal psychological phenomena which serve to direct or influence external or observable social actions of persons; and (b) the new understanding that these "psychological" perspectives of self and other need to be seen as separate and independent, that is, differentiated. However, the child is still not capable of understanding the reciprocal relationship between these viewpoints. Hence interpersonal conceptions tend to be one-way, that is, focused on only one person at a time, and on that person's subjective perspective in the social relationship.

Thus, friends are understood to be important because they perform specific overt activities which the self wants done ("You need a friend because you want to play some games and you have to get someone who will play the way you want him to"). To make a friend requires attention to inner likes or dislikes; one has to know what a person likes as an activity in order to be his or her friend. In return, a good friend to the self is someone who knows what the self likes to do and will do it with the self. In other words, one person's interests or attitudes are set up as a fixed standard, and for the friendship to form, the other person must tune in to the standard thus formulated. However, it is not until the next stage that the child is able to take a somewhat more relativistic perspective and to see that each party has a set of likes or dislikes that need to be coordinated, and that friendship may be more than the accommodation of one person's behavior to the other's will.

Intimacy and closeness in a friendship are now understood to rest on more than simple demographic credentials (lives close by). Close friendships are rank ordered on the basis of how closely each friend matches the self's interests, for example, "A closest friend is the one who knows which games you like to play the best." This one-way conception is also applied to the issue of trust. Trust is recognized as more than a Stage 0 confidence in another's capabilities; it is now understood to include a faith in a person's motives and intentions. However, a trusting relationship is still seen as one in which one party, the friend, has good intentions or motives toward the self. Still missing is the perceived sense of reciprocity. The causes of conflicts are also seen as unilateral; one person acts in such a way as to cause a problem for the other. The resolution of these conflicts is also one-way; the actor needs to undo or negate the action and restore the partner to a more comfortable state.

WHAT CAUSES FIGHTS BETWEEN FRIENDS?
If she calls you a name or something like that.
HOW CAN YOU GET TO BE FRIENDS AGAIN?
Make her take it back; make her say she was lying.

(7:9)

The basic mechanism for restoring the peace is here forcing of a retraction; whether she means it when she takes it back is not considered relevant at Stage 1.

Finally, Stage 1 reasoning includes that friendships can break up on the basis of unilateral decisions as well as on the basis of physicalistic confrontations. One person can decide independently that a friend no longer "does what I want him to do," and so decides to terminate the relationship ("You get tired of playing her games, the ones she likes so you tell her not to be your friend anymore").

STAGE 2: CLOSE FRIENDSHIP AS
FAIR-WEATHER COOPERATION

With this stage comes the ability to see the reciprocal relation between interpersonal perspectives; each person is seen as capable of taking into account the other's perspectives on the self's motives, thoughts, and feelings. The resulting underlying conception of friendship relations focuses on a context-specific, fair-weather reciprocity. This understanding of the necessity for a "meeting of minds" is seen as necessary only around specific incidents or issues rather than as the underlying system upon which the relationship is structured. The basic limitation of this stage is that the subject still sees the basic purpose of reciprocal awareness as the serving of the self's interest, rather than as the service of mutual concerns.

Friendships are viewed as important at Stage 2, not just because the child wants to have things done for him or her, but because the child believes people need companionship, need to be liked. Hence we see a more truly interpersonal orientation. There is a dim but growing recognition that persons need relations for the social interaction itself, rather than only for the sake of getting what they want (Stage 1) or allowing them to play a game (Stage 0). Making friends requires the coordination of context-specific likes and dislikes rather than the matching of one person's likes and dislikes to the fixed standard of the other. A good friend is understood to be one who reveals inner or true feelings about things rather than one who fronts or presents a fake image.

Intimacy and sharing is also understood as reciprocal at this stage; each party finds out what the other likes to do. The fair-weather aspect of close friendship once again is seen in an orientation to the benefits for the self rather than for the relationship itself. Trust is also understood as a reciprocal relation in thought as well as in deed. It implies that a friend is someone to whom one can reveal inner thoughts (e.g., secrets) which will be safely stored away, not revealed to outsiders.

In concepts of jealousy and exclusion we see the same new interpersonal understanding that we see in general at Stage 2. Jealousy is not viewed as just the self feeling sad because an event or activity was missed, or because the self did not get to do *something* the self wanted to do. It is recognized at Stage 2 that one may feel bad because a friend actively chooses *someone* else to spend time with over the self.

Because conflicts are more clearly understood as *between* parties rather than simply caused by one party and affecting the other, resolutions of conflicts must be generated which are satisfactory to each participant. It is not viewed as enough, as it was at Stage 1, to simply negate an action to undo a conflict. At Stage 2 each party must make sure that the other person really means it if he or she apologizes, that is, that underlying intent is in accordance with the overt expression of a desire to resolve the conflict. Just as the child at Stage 2 can recognize the need to mean what one says, the child also recognizes that persons sometimes don't mean what they say, particularly if they are angry at that moment.

A final but dominant feature of Stage 2 friendship concepts is the difficulty subjects at this level have in seeing friendship as a system which can transcend the immediate, context-specific conflicts or cooperative ventures of each party. When dyads are in disagreement, they are "not friends," but just as these relations are easily dissolved, so they are easily reformed when conflicts are forgiven or forgotten.

STAGE 3: CLOSE FRIENDSHIP AS INTIMATE AND MUTUAL SHARING

At this stage it is understood that the individual can abstractly stand outside the friendship relationship (at Stage 2, it is understood that the individual could stand outside the self, but not the relation itself) and view it as an ongoing and stable system. Hence the major focus or orientation is on the relationship itself, rather than on each or either individual separately. This leads to a general shift in orientation from a Stage 2 view of friendship as reciprocal coordination with other for the self's interest to a Stage 3 notion of collaboration for mutual interest and sharing (Sullivan, 1953). The primary function of friendship at Stage 3 is viewed as a general mutual support to be upheld over a period of time, as opposed to lower stage concerns for immediate activity or the serving of the self's immediate interests, for example, boredom or loneliness. Although at Stage 3 the subject is aware of the phenomenon of "hitting it off" right away, in the subject's general thinking about the process by which persons make friends, good friendships are seen as developing over a period of time in which the parties get to go through mutual experiences, get to discover each other's "personality" and traits, and become familiar with each other's complementary and common interests.

Closeness within a friendship at Stage 3 is seen in the degree to which two persons share intimate personal concerns and the effort they make to maintain the relationship. Trust is a major conceptual force in the vocabulary of subjects whose understanding is coded at this stage; it signifies that each party is willing to share these intimate thoughts and feelings with his or her partner, thoughts and feelings that are not shared with less intimate friends or acquaintances.

One senses that at Stage 3, friends are viewed as part of one another. As Sullivan noted, each party gains a personal satisfaction from the awards and accolades that are gained by the other. The intensity of the felt "in-group of two" which characterizes Stage 3 conceptions of friendship is also felt in the subject's understanding of issues such as jealousy and exclusion. Relationships of closeness are perceived in a particularly possessive perspective. Aware of the amount of effort and interest involved in the formation of a close friendship, the subject also understands that good friends are protective of their relation, that they do not readily allow others to intrude for fear of losing the relationship altogether.

Conflicts between friends are also viewed somewhat abstractly which in turn leads the subject at this stage to realize that a particular conflict adequately worked through can strengthen the relationship. Talking things out is seen as a common strategy for conflict resolution at Stage 3.

Finally, at this stage, the subject more clearly differentiates between the kinds of conflicts which are relatively minor and which the relationship itself serves to help ameliorate, and the types of conflicts which threaten the very foundation of the relationship itself. The latter types of conflicts are usually understood to be those which break the bond of trust established over a period of time by the two friends, for example, when a personal confidence is exploited or not taken seriously. ("A lot of times you will tell a friend some real private thing, something about your girlfriend or how you feel about somebody. If he goes out and asks that girl out, then you just can't trust him anymore, and you really can't be very good friends.")

STAGE 4: CLOSE FRIENDSHIPS AS AUTONOMOUS INTERDEPENDENCE

At Stage 4 the subject understands persons to have, in a psychological sense, complex and sometimes conflicting needs, each of which can be met by a different kind of relationship (close intimate relations, business relations, casual acquaintances, etc.). The ideal or close friendship relation is seen at Stage 4 as being in a constant process of formation and transformation. Friendships are seen as open relational systems available to change, flexibility, and growth in the same way that persons are susceptible to such development. At Stage 4, one important function of a close friendship (as differentiated qualitatively from a casual or superficial relation) is to help provide the self with a sense of personal identity. At this stage, the subject is aware that one tends to define oneself through the company one keeps. Similarly, the *process* of making a friend is seen as a series of phases of coming to know one another. ("At first you really are just feeling each other out. Then you build up a certain amount of trust. Then there comes a time when the relationship is really a commitment between the two of you.") The concept of the "ideal friend" is not understood to be some absolute good person but rather a person whose personality is compatible with one's own, that is, a good friend is a relative concept, relative to the relationship itself.

Trust in a friendship is viewed in the context of each person having complex and multivariate needs; it is now felt that in a good friendship each partner helps the other and allows the other to develop independent relations. Each individual's needs for both dependency and autonomy are recognized in the friendship and the mutual meeting of those individual needs is seen as basic to trust. ("Trust is the ability to let go as well as to hang on.") Truly close friends perform a unique and qualitatively distinct function. They attend to the deeper psychological needs of each other.

Jealousy is also understood with some distance and perspective at Stage 4. While not denying the reality of the sometimes painful feelings of jealousy, subjects also can admire the ability of persons to form relationships that help them grow. There is less the sense of possessiveness of Stage 3 and more the sense of the positive appreciation of admired relationships.

At Stage 4 the individual makes a further distinction between interpersonal conflicts and intrapsychic conflicts. The individual understands that intrapsychic problems, for example, "problems with authority," can effect interpersonal relations. Conflicts are also understood to be resolved through mutual attempts at insight and self-reflection ("You have to have some insight into your own behavior if you really want to get along with other people").

A major new conception of the factors which cause the termination of friendships includes the possibility that people grow out of relationships, that is, that as people develop their interests change, and this may lead to the negation of old relationships and to formulation of new ones.

Summary Description of Stages in Conceptions of Peer Groups

STAGE 0: THE PEER GROUP AS PHYSICAL CONNECTIONS

At Stage 0 group organization is viewed solely on a plane of overt actions ("play games") or surface properties of groups ("They are a big team; they win a lot"). The child seems unaware of psychological relationships which might exist among group members. To the extent the interdependence of the group is objective, governed by things and actions rather than subjective feelings or interpersonal bonds, the child's conception of peer-group relations is as a series of physical connections or linked activities which are taken as literally holding the group together ("Clubs stay together by holding hands"). The linkages among group members are viewed as situational, and group cohesion is defined in terms of physical proximity. That is, the child at Stage 0 does not appear to have a concept of conscious collaboration, but only chance association.

Resting on situational factors, peer-group organization is viewed as extremely unstable, for example, groups break up "when you get called home for dinner." When matters of individual choice do arise, the child is egocentric. He confuses his own perspective with that of other members. ("Mike should join the Cougars. I like Cougars, I don't like Jets.")

At Stage 0 the child has a vague understanding of peer-group processes such as leadership and conformity. However, these "concepts" also appear to be characterized only by surface manifestation, without explanation of the social causes of a particular process. For example, the child might *know* (perceive) the actions a leader would normally perform in a group ("Leaders tell you what to do") yet not see (understand) this action as a means to some end for the group. The child appears to confuse the physical result of conformity with its psychological cause.

WHY DO PEOPLE IN A GROUP ALL ACT ALIKE?
So they will be the same.

(4:6)

Physical proximity and linked activities are milestones in the concept of peer-group organization. In the child's mind, members of a group are a loose association of entities, bound together by purely physical connections. The group is analogous to strangers riding on a subway train, together only in body, not in spirit.

STAGE 1: THE PEER GROUP AS UNILATERAL RELATIONS

The child appears to organize interaction within the peer group as a series of unilateral relations. The group is viewed as established through each member's choice to collaborate with others on a plane of jointly performed physical activities ("Clubs are good, because there are more people to do things with, so you can play more games"). Although the child now sees that to coordinate actions among members is necessary to performing simple collaborative group activities, there does not appear to be recognition of how groups can effectively organize through consciously cooperative agreements among members. The child does not seem to understand how complementary roles might simultaneously benefit all members. Instead, group collaboration is viewed unilaterally. The child justifies it on the basis of some tangible outcome for one member or for the group taken as an undifferentiated association. ("You have to do what the captain says or the team will lose and they will say you can't play with us anymore.")

Group relations are understood to be stabilized by psychologically isolated but helpful acts ("be nice," "don't fight," "share your toys") which have a unilateral or one-way effect. They appear to be aimed at either pleasing other members or benefiting the self, but not both simultaneously. Cohesiveness among group members is defined as each individual maintaining a positive feeling about some concrete group activity. This group cohesion is understood to be maintained through social niceties and unilateral actions. As yet no awareness appears of ideas like convergence of members' thoughts or psychological reciprocity among members. Reciprocity is still based on physical acts.

The child now appears to differentiate surface manifestations of group processes such as conformity from their function to the group as means to collaborative ends ("The captain tells us what to do so we can win"). However, the justification for group conformity is a rigid, sometimes arbitrary tangible or pragmatic functionalism requiring some concrete result ("You have to do the same things, you all have to hit the puck the same way or you will lose").

Group leadership appears to be seen as unilateral obedience to the dictates of authority until reaching a critical level of hurt feelings results in the leader's dismissal ("If he gets bossy you tell him he can't be captain anymore"). Instead of learning a lesson about leadership, the child seems to be conceptually limited to imposing another equally dictatorial leader who also "does anything he wants."

In sum, significant gains are made over the preceding stage in developing an understanding of the collaborative nature of groups. There is now a concern for other members' feelings and a recognition of social niceties such as "sharing" or "obeying rules." However, without being able to conceptualize group organization on a plane of deliberate mental cooperation among members, the child continues to conceive of peer groups as a series of unilateral relations. Collaboration is still defined as individuals bringing their individual skills to some group activity without consciously coordinating them into a cooperative effort.

STAGE 2: THE PEER GROUP AS BILATERAL PARTNERSHIPS

The child's thinking about peer groups can now be characterized by three elements: (a) a concern for reciprocal or bilateral feelings of affection ("friendships," "we like each other") extended in a chain from one dyad to another; (b) the establishment of context-specific exchanges of favors ("partnerships," "teamwork") based on pragmatic equality and fairness; and (c) a convergence of thoughts among group members about concrete group activities ("they should like the same things").

In describing the actual structure of peer groups among preadolescents, Sullivan (1953) uses the phrase "interlocking two-groups." It denotes that group relations at this stage are seen as a set of interlocking dyads extended in an associative fashion to other members of the group. For children whose reasoning is coded at Stage 2, the group organization is seen as a network of these interlocking dyads. Relations are viewed as based on multiple reciprocated feelings of affection. The Stage 2 child believes each member forms a dyadic friendship with every other member of the group ("Everyone has to like each other, or it wouldn't be a group"). These essentially dyadic relations are maintained by a strict equality of interests ("You help him out and he helps you out"). However, the child is unable to move conceptually outside these specific subgroup relations and view the group as a commonly shared social whole. The group remains the sum of dyadic relations which compose it. For example, group cohesion appears to be defined as cooperative effort based on reciprocal feelings of affection between members of the group, and group conformity is understood as motivated by a group member's desire to be thought well of, or to make a good impression on the other members of the group. The child believes that groups remain together through a series of bilateral exchanges aimed at directly benefiting all parties involved. Once these direct benefits break down, the group is likely to break up.

The child at Stage 2 is able to recognize the convergence of thoughts among group members, that interdependence rests on thoughts as well as actions. However, convergent thoughts are not yet fully abstract. They remain tied to some specific pragmatic effect ("You have to like the same things, because if one guy wants to play baseball and another guy wants to play football, they would get bored").

STAGE 3: THE PEER GROUP AS HOMOGENEOUS COMMUNITY

Characteristic of Stage 3 is the idea of the group as a homogeneous community or common whole forming a bond of solidarity among its members. Three important concepts of group organization arise at Stage 3: (a) the group as a *social whole* or abstract structure, (b) held together as a *shared community* of common interests and beliefs, (c) in which there is *consensus* of conventions and generalized expectations.

The subject organizes the group into an abstract, yet relatively undifferentiated social system. This group system is defined at a level of organization distinct from the particular relations between persons within it ("You don't have to understand the whole group of people and each separate person in it," "When you join, it's like they are an egg and you're a blunt fork trying to break through the shell").

In the Stage 3 view, a sense of cohesiveness is achieved through shared or homogeneous values which give members a common perspective ("They all have something in common, they all like the same things"). Because groups are believed to be held together by the *psychological* similarity of their members, the need for common values results in a high level of value conformity and a clear definition of who is "in" and who is "out" ("If you didn't do what they were doing, they wouldn't think you were their kind of person," "You don't want to be the oddball or outcast").

Given this belief in the need for common values, subjects at Stage 3 appear to develop a strong awareness of the value of group consensus and generalized expectations for governing the group ("The team has to work together as a unit," "We decide on one thing everyone wants to do"). This unanimity avoids possible differences of opinion within the group and preserves a basis for homogeneous values. However, this demand for consensus also suppresses the possibility for pluralism and diverse interests, and so despite this shared sense of community, certain problems can be caused by the limitations of Stage 3 thought. While a group is seen as a social whole, the adolescent thinking at Stage 3 is unable to differentiate the various processes which help to explain changes in that whole. The subject, overly concerned with homogeneous values, confuses role differentiation with the lack of a common perspective. For example, there is confusion of the abstract role of leadership (and its specific responsibilities) with differences in personality. Certain new aspects of leadership are generally frowned upon because they violate the unanimity of a community. ("That is like taking one kid and putting him a step higher than you. You want everyone on the same level.") However, the positive aspects of leadership are also recognized as the ability of an individual to generate "team spirit" and direction for the group as an entity. Yet there is only little notion of formal collective obligation, because the subject seems unwilling to acknowledge the need to make the hard, often controversial decisions and sanctions which come with formal duties and responsibilities of leadership. At Stage 3 obligation is synonomous with conformity to the group's conventional beliefs and values. Groups are understood to break up or terminate because something happens to upset the sense of commonality shared by each group member.

STAGE 4: THE PEER GROUP AS A PLURALISTIC ORGANIZATION

Three important organizational–conceptual perspectives emerge at Stage 4: (a) a *sociological perspective* by which group processes are treated as systems interdependent with individual differences, (b) a notion of a *pluralistic community* in which individual diversity is not suppressed but united behind common goals, and (c) the recognition of *contractual agreements* and formal regulations for organizing this plurality of interests.

In analyzing the nature of groups the subject appears to assume a sociological perspective on various processes which are viewed as endemic to peer group organization. The collective is treated as a kind of organic unity or working machine whose parts are processes distinguished and analyzed in terms of their interdependence in balancing the overall organization, rather than in Stage 3 homogeneity. The subject thinks of the group as a supraindividual system balanced and maintained by a set of abstract processes set in motion by individual members. ("A group is a continuing process and it functions for members to coordinate their activities.")

The group is recognized as a communal system, but a pluralistic one which does not suppress individual differences for the sake of homogeneous values. There is either an explicit or implicit "democratic principle" where differing interests or "points of view" are not only tolerated but also encouraged. ("Individual personalities of people, different from each other, will contribute to the group and make it more of an entity than it was before.") In considering this toleration for a diversity of interests or personalities, the subject is aware that collectives may continue to function regardless of personal animosities. ("You have personality conflicts, but that is where the group sense comes out of it.") The unifying feature is a common set of goals which bring together independent parties for the sake of a common enterprise. Group cohesion is defined as a process brought about through community effort, whereby a sense of group purpose is seen to overcome individual differences.

In that the group is a pluralistic system and consensus may not always be possible, subjects are aware of the "political" processes of compromise whereby individual differences are integrated into a unified whole. ("Sometimes people come in with their own interests and personalities so there is no agreement. Then you have to reach a compromise.")

Conformity understood only as a duty is rejected in favor of formal obligations which are reached through voluntary contractual agreements. These agreements provide an otherwise free thinking and independent membership with a "groundwork" or "structure" for operating a smooth functioning organization. ("Rules serve as guidelines so an artificial order gives some structure to the group.")

Processes of group termination are additionally understood at Stage 4 as the group subdividing into sample units. This is understood to be a potentially healthy development, but also may be a negative process, in which case the interdependence breaks down and factionalism is understood to occur.

Summary Description of Stages in Conceptions of Parent-Child Relations

STAGE 0: THE PARENT-CHILD RELATION AS BOSS-SERVANT

Young children at Stage 0 do not clearly differentiate the adult role from the parent role. Therefore, colored by confusion of cause and effect and of psychological and physical, their notions of adult motives for having children are generally of desires to do the things parents (qua adults) do (watch television late, etc.). Children's needs for parents are expressed in terms of specific and immediate needs, for example, who will make my dinner, and by definition, a *good parent* meets these physical needs. Love, as in loving a child, is also by definition a parental function; if the parent does not love the child, he is not at that moment a "real" parent. Similarly, children are understood to obey parents by definition of their relation.

Behind this unreflective attitude lies the child's concern for the parent's greater physical ability, which enables him to literally direct or force a child to take certain actions, hence our appelation *boss-servant*. Although the punishment of children by parents is understood as a physical event-reaction that follows a wrongdoing in time, the child is not clear whether the wrongdoing causes the punishment or the punishment makes the doing wrong. The function of punishment is understood to be to make the child angry or mad, or in some vaguely understood way to block the repetition of the temporally linked action. Similarly, punishment of children by adults is understood as a cause of conflicts between parent and child, and not as an intentional or planful reaction on the parent's part to the conflict per se. At Stage 0, conflicts are not resolved, they are simply and quietly forgotten. However, this is not a strategy chosen among others, but a statement of perceived reality, reality as perceived through the young child's eyes.

STAGE 1: THE PARENT-CHILD RELATION AS CARETAKER-HELPER

Conceptions of the parent–child relationship coded as Stage 1 are characterized by the child's identification with parental views and opinions, the child's acceptance of parental knowledge (wiseness), and the child's appreciation of simple, basic parental "good intentions," as expressed in material and psychological assistance rendered to the child. Children at this stage express the opinion that parents want to have children because children are useful to parents (parents want kids to do the chores); they do not appear to consider the added chores and responsibilities brought on adults by having children. Children are understood to provide fun for parents, as if they liked to play with children in the same way children like to have other children to play with, so they won't be bored, so they will have something to do, etc. Similarly, having children is viewed as solving the problems of adults who do not want to be alone.

The child's need for parents at Stage 1 is understood to be based upon the child's need for protection from danger and for material support. Love between parent and child is "one-way." Parents who love their children demonstrate this by intentionally taking care of them; children, on the other hand, express their feelings of love through acts of obedience ("doing what they are told"), hence our term *caretaker-helper*. Conceptions of *reciprocal* love are limited to *physical* reciprocity (they do things for each other).

Obedience is rationalized as necessary because parents are viewed as "knowing best," because the child must act out of gratitude for the parent's good intentions toward the child, and to avoid punishment. Punishment, at Stage 1, is understood to be a "teaching device," a way a parent imparts, through action, his wisdom and expectations. Children also appear to feel a further positive aspect of punishment is that it is a way that parents protect their children from danger. Finally, punishment is also viewed as a mechanism by which the parent "pays the child back" for the child's transgression and reestablishes the previous equilibrium.

STAGE 2: THE PARENT-CHILD RELATION AS GUIDANCE COUNSELOR-NEED SATISFIER

While at Stage 1 a crucial motive for having children was understood to be the pleasure (fun) parents derive from having a nice child, at Stage 2 there emerges the notion that children fulfill an adult's psychological needs and that a parent derives pleasure from *observing* a child's growth and happiness. Similarly, whereas at Stage 1 children understood the importance of parents' service in fulfilling the child's physical needs and difficulties, at Stage 2, they emphasize a child's need for parental advice and guidance, not as absolutely authoritative opinion, but as a "guideline" for the child in deciding what to do, hence the term *guidance counselor-need satisfier*. There is now an understanding of how children rely on parents for psychological and emotional support. Thus, at Stage 2 a good parent is defined as one who is "sensitive" to his child's psychological needs. Furthermore, the child now defines a good parent as one who willingly, consciously chooses to give up something valued by the parent, for example, the parent's time, for the sake of the child. A good child is understood to be one who can step outside his or her own interests and appreciate the parent's generosity.

At Stage 2, love or the lack of love is differentiated from mere satisfaction or dissatisfaction on the part of one party, for example, the parent, with a particular behavior on the part of the other party, for example, the child. Reciprocal feelings rather than actions define love and closeness between parents and children. These are understood to be feelings of concern with the other's well-being, and the reciprocal appreciation of the other's intentions. Good intentions and feelings on the part of the parent will evoke the same in the child and vice versa.

Obedience is now understood as but one of many mechanisms that are used to avoid upsetting the delicate balance of parent–child reciprocity. However, since at Stage 2 the parent is understood not to be always correct in his opinions and judgment, absolute obedience is not necessary. This is a different kind of understanding from that of the child at a lower stage who may disobey in practice because he or she does not want to do what the parent says, but still believes the parent to have relatively infallible judgment. Here, there is the conscious knowledge of the parental potential for fallibility of judgment.

Punishment at Stage 2 is understood to be a method by which the parent communicates or sends a message to an errant child, a message about what the parent believes is good or right. Punishment is also understood to be occasionally ineffective in its aim to "change" a child's mind or attitude, although it may still coercively modify the child's behavior.

At Stage 2 conflicts between parents and children are understood to be caused by genuine differences of opinion between parents and children, rather than simply by a mistake or error on the part of either party. Another perceived cause of conflict is "lack of concern," particularly on the part of the adult or parent. By this the child means, at Stage 2, the parent does not pay attention to (role take) the concerns and needs of the child. The resolution of conflicts is still viewed as coming from one party letting the other do what he wants. However, it is now understood that this is not a satisfactory kind of resolution. In sum, the principal new understanding of Stage 2 is of the quality of emotional ties between parents and children.

STAGE 3: THE PARENT–CHILD RELATION AS TOLERANCE–RESPECT

At Stage 3, it is understood that parents may want to have children as an extension of themselves, or as in some way a part of themselves. This understanding rests in part on the child's ability to take a third-person perspective, to see how a psychological self can be distinct from its physical boundaries, and that the expansion of the self is manifest through influence on other people, shaping others' lives. The parental role is understood as a source of potential gratification through the mutual satisfaction that can be obtained raising children, as well as a source of potential self-doubt and defeat. Children are understood to need parents to help them with psychological concerns and self-esteem, and good parents do not simply observe their children's development, they foster traits of psychological competence and maturity.

In particular, ideal parents manifest tolerance and ideal children are sensitive to parents' psychological needs, or become so as they grow older, hence the term *tolerance-respect.* Love and closeness between parent and child is understood to have an important impact on the child's personality development. A lack of such love is believed to have the potential to cause children to grow up to be troubled adults who have difficulty loving others.

At Stage 3, natural conflicts are understood to occur between parents and children by dint of their unequal relation and different needs and expectations. Getting along is not characterized by absolute agreement but by respect for the other's position. For instance, the parental demand for obedience is understood to be related to the adult's need to be respected and acknowledged as a source of authority in the family system. Conflicts between obedience to parents and the need of growing children for autonomy and independence are also articulated at Level 3.

More subtle psychological functions of punishment are also understood at Stage 3. For example, it is understood that parents may be reluctant to give up control or may express the frustration in their own lives through "taking it out" on their children. On the other hand, it is understood that some children sometimes have a need to be controlled or punished and in fact receive reassurance from parental limit setting. Conflicts between parents and children may also be caused by these or other individual or personal problems. Resolution may be obtained through a third-party arbitration.

STAGE 4: SOME SPECULATION

Our data, as noted in the last chapter, were insufficient to warrant detailed description of Stage 4 thinking in this domain. However, we would speculate, on the basis of our analytical perspective and fragmentary data, that a major emerging theme would be a conception of the parent–child relation as an ongoing changing system, unique in human experience, in which autonomy and interdependence are established, but fluctuate throughout the life cycle.

Some Directions and Difficulties

In this part (Chapters 4–6), I have attempted to demonstrate how our system, consisting of 5 perspective-taking levels, 4 relationship domains, 22 associated interpersonal issues, and numerous emerging ideas, themes, or aspects, was derived at this phase and fits together to yield a developmental map of the growth of certain aspects of interpersonal conception or understanding. The presentation of a system of this complexity can, hopefully, contribute to better understanding of social development. However, it also raises problems as it suggests solutions, generates questions as it provides answers. I will discuss three of these questions here, even if they cannot be dealt with thoroughly and finally.

First, how fixed is the descriptive system just described and how open is it to change and revision? Second, how and to what degree does inference play a crucial part in this type of analysis? And third, how is the construct of stages applied to individual reasoning in this model?

Regarding the first question, of the descriptive fixity and accuracy of the system, it must be made clear that in Phase 1 of the research we are talking about the ontogenesis of social concepts in general, not the particular social concepts of a particular individual. Although we endeavored to make a broad-ranging search and thorough classification of developmental themes for each of our four manuals, in our subsequent inquiry, as well as that of researchers who adapt or use this system, new themes or aspects not originally included are discovered; furthermore, we occasionally find evidence that previously included themes are ambiguous or may better be classified as examples of a level different from the one originally proposed. What strategy can we adopt to deal with this research reality?

One option is to keep the manual open as a "working draft" and view it as always in a state of flux or potential revision; however, this would be effectively impracticable if we are to move at a reasonable pace to subsequent phases of the research. So even as we continue to make note of potential future manual revisions, we need a policy for the present. That which we have adopted rests upon the assumption that the examples presented in the manual are best seen as limited, static, representations of what in reality is a very dynamic process. It would be a mistake to think that an individual's responses could be "stage scored" simply by matching up responses to specific examples provided in the manual in testlike fashion. In my view the manuals, as explicit as they may appear, are still painted with impressionistic brush strokes rather than with the style and stroke of the absolutely clear-cut, photographic empiricist portrait painter. The manuals cannot be used in classical cookbook "matching" fashion for the simple reason, among others, that the words particular individuals use to communicate *can* have different meaning from the words used in the manual to communicate social-conceptual levels.

The manual examples, then, are properly viewed as leads to help the skillful interviewer and coder understand the developmental aspects of the meaning attributed to interpersonal concepts by the individual being interviewed. It is for this reason that no matter how detailed it becomes, the manual alone is not and cannot be a "complete" or "objective" test. In other words, a structural–qualitative analysis will always require relatively more skilled interpretation than will a purely quantitative one.

This leads us to the role of inference in stage coding. In our system the role of interpretation and inference about an individual's conceptions *is* critical. Such inference is based on the structural and dynamic relation between levels of perspective taking and interpersonal conceptions. Required is a method that takes a deep look into the underlying meaning of the words that a subject uses to represent his interpersonal concepts. In our method, manual or no, the interviewer must always have the explicit theory in mind. One must always be asking questions such as the following while conducting the interview: Is there in the subject's responses an indication of a fusion or lack of understanding of the individuality of perspectives (Level 0) or are individuals seen by the subject as having separate perspectives (Level 1)? Is the subject using a concept in a way that indicates only a reciprocity of actions (Level 1) or is there recognized, implicitly or explicitly, a reciprocity between individuals' thoughts and mental operations (Level 2)? If there are mental coordinations invoked by the subject, are they only the momentary matchings of beliefs and opinions (Level 2) or does the subject seem to understand the need for a temporally and psychologically stable system of coordinations between perspectives (Level 3)? To what degree does the concept, as used, imply a mutuality of understanding at only a surface, verbalized level (Level 3) or how much of the reciprocal dynamics between individuals are understood to be taking place on multiple levels of understanding corresponding to multiple levels of awareness, understanding, and communication within and between individuals (Level 4)?

The inferential process begins with the interviewer's questions, then goes to the words the subject uses to respond. Through careful probing, the interviewer must explore with the subject the subject's meaning as it is conveyed by these words. Words like *loyalty* or *closeness* in a friendship may well have developmentally different meanings to different people. This is particularly likely across different ages. For example, both a 5-year-old and 15-year-old will agree that close friendships are important. However, for the adolescent closeness may mean someone with whom one can mutually share and explore a personal experience, whereas for the 5-year-old closeness may mean someone who lives next door. Thus, the trained interviewer must know that it is not merely closeness that defines a stage conception of friendship, but what is entailed in the meaning, thinking, and interpretation the concept of closeness invokes or represents for the subject.

This brings us to how to move from a developmental model of concepts to an assessment of individuals. So far, we have discussed a formal model of interpersonal concept development, and touched briefly on some of the issues involved in tapping an individual's conceptions as they pertain to this model. But we have not yet examined, directly, the question of the functional reality of stages for a subject. According to our formal model, the locus of a stage is in the *interaction* between perspective taking (as a skeletal, underlying, core structure) and each of the various concepts in each domain. The term *level* has been used to refer to the *core structure* while the term *stage* has been used to refer to the *complete system* of concepts in a domain that are manifest around each level.[2] But do individuals actually have a coherent theory of interpersonal conceptions that can be characterized or captured by a single stage? Is an individual whose concepts are coded as Level 3 on conflict resolution in friendship likely to have his or her concepts of punishment in the parent–child relation similarly coded? And if so, will this theory be applied to practice with the same coherence?

Most cognitive psychologists are interested in how individuals reason and conceptualize, not a description of how concepts themselves are naturally sequenced. And many cognitive psychologists are skeptical about the utility of the stage construct, especially when it comes to the idea of structured wholeness. For example, John Flavell (1977), in the final pages of his typically lucid text on cognitive development, probably spoke for many developmental psychologists when he concluded (in reference to Piagetian stages):

> Same-stage cognitive acquisitions (e.g., concrete–operational ones) ought to develop in a closely-interdependent, temporally concurrent fashion, according to most interpretations, if Piaget's concept of stage-by-stage development is to have any real meaning or validity. While diagnostic problems make it difficult to tell for sure, it does not appear that they do normally develop in this tightly-knit, concurrent fashion. The existing evidence suggests to me that cognitive growth is not as stage-like a process as Piaget's theory claims it is. It should be added, however, that a number of developmental psychologists would not agree with this conclusion [p. 255].

At this point, at the end of Phase 1, our research lends support to neither the psychologists who agree with Flavell nor those who Flavell thinks disagree with him, for we have so far simply presented a formal descriptive model of interpersonal concept development, a method for eliciting the individual's reflective interpersonal conceptions, and a procedure for assigning them to one of five developmental levels. If, with proper safeguards against bias, it can be shown that in expressing concepts about each of the various issues in our system, the individual tends

[2] Elsewhere I have discussed the relativity of the terms *content* and *structure* (Selman, 1976b). There I have made the argument that that which is structure at one level of analysis may be content at another. For instance, the perspective-taking levels can be considered content for Piaget's deeper, more formal logicomathematical stages, but structure to the more on-the-surface, content-bound interpersonal conceptions. That is, when a child thinks about coordinating his or her own and other's perspectives, the child's thoughts are the content and the deeper underlying logicomathematical operations are structure. Yet when thought is directed toward social concepts content (friendships, etc.), the child's ability to coordinate perspective acts as the structure of his or her thinking.

to do so at one consistent stage, then the criterion of structured wholeness would seem to be validly met by our model of interpersonal understanding. If, on the other hand, individuals' levels of expressed conceptual competence appeared to vary considerably across issues and domains, we would begin to reformulate our research to look at questions of whether there is any regularity in those variations. For example, do concepts of friendship emerge consistently earlier than concepts of peer relations? Might concepts about such issues as trust and loyalty develop more rapidly or earlier than concepts about such issues as conflict resolution and punishment?

While it strikes me that at the first or constructive phase of research, the structural model has great utility for providing a way to describe the developmental aspects of social concepts, its applicability to how individuals actually use their concepts has remained largely unexplored. This is the direction we have opted to take. In the next part (III) we look at the second phase of the research, the exploration of our system's validity. Then in Part IV we return to questions of application.

INTERPERSONAL UNDERSTANDING— PHASE 2: CONSTRUCT VALIDATION

7

A Developmental Analysis of Interpersonal Understanding: The Measures, Their Reliability, and the Design

As reported in Part II, Chapters 4–6, the result of the first, constructive phase of our research was a formal stage-by-issue description of interpersonal concept development derived from both empirical interview data and structural–analytical use of social perspective-taking levels. The goal of the second phase, as reported in this part (III), is to evaluate whether interpersonal conceptions as described actually fit the proposed stage model. To do this, data were gathered more formally to determine whether or how well the interpersonal conceptions of growing children meet the cognitive–developmental criteria of structured wholeness, invariant sequence, and generalizability.[1] At the core of this phase of the

[1] In Chapter 4, I listed four first-order concerns. Two of these, structured wholeness and invariant sequence, are addressed directly in this section. The other two, qualitative differences and hierarchical organization, have been addressed in the constructive phase as well as in the theoretical formulation of perspective-taking levels. Chapters 9 and 10 insofar as they provide a glimpse of the natural functions of expressed reasoning (the uses of understanding) also touch upon issues of developmental hierarchies of social decision making. Criteria of qualitative differences and hierarchical organization *are* amenable to formal empirical analysis, but interview data are not well-suited for this purpose. The concern for universality, for the applicability of a descriptive model across individuals who have wide ranging sub- or cross-cultural experiences is also addressed in this section through clinical–comparative and normative analyses.

psychological research process are the instruments and procedures for data gathering and the techniques and rules for scoring or coding the data so gathered. In this chapter, I describe the sample, the assessment procedures, and the reliability of scoring and coding. In Chapter 8 I present results of five analyses which speak to various aspects of the validity of our system.

The term *research phase* by no means implies that once a phase has been passed through, phase-specific questions and concerns cannot or need not be raised again. In fact, the research process and findings being reported in this section have twice been through a Phase-2-like period. In an earlier study (executed in 1974–1975 and then published: Selman, 1976b), we committed ourselves after several years of exploratory work to using a set of procedures (instruments and scoring methods) with many important similarities to and yet some significant differences from the ones that are described in this chapter. That period of data collection was designed to be the inaugural project in what was to become a longitudinal study of the growth of children's interpersonal conceptions. But as is commonly the case with longitudinal research, be it on a grand or humble scale, the results of looking at our initial data led us back in spiral fashion to a period of Phase 1 reconceptualization and methodological revision (Jones, Bayley, MacFarlane, & Honzick, 1971).

For instance, although in this earlier work we sketched out the framework we now use in the four interpersonal domains, formal descriptive work had actually been undertaken for only two of these domains (individuals and friendship). Furthermore, our data-gathering procedures were devised to look at interpersonal conceptions as subjects applied them to resolving four specific interpersonal dilemmas. Our interest was in looking at stability of the use of interpersonal concepts across variations in the *content* of the interpersonal dilemma to be resolved. There are some advantages to this method. For example, our results suggested that variation in the content or theme of the dilemmas presented to the subject had little effect on the overall level of conception the subject used to resolve them.

However, this technique is also a potential source of bias, when concepts in separate domains are collected with the *same* interview and at the *same* time, it is possible that concepts in one domain (e.g., individuals) might influence level of concept in another (e.g., friendship, cf. Damon, 1977). This kind of artifactual confound-bias could occur in a number of ways at a number of points in the process: in the subject's mind whereby thinking about questions in one domain might influence thinking about questions in the other, in the questions and probes asked by the interviewer as he or she hears responses to questions in one or the other of the domains, or in the scorer's coding of responses, responses throughout the protocol influencing the assignment of a developmental score to specific items. Thus, although in this earlier research we took some safeguards to prevent scoring bias (e.g., by dividing up protocols and scoring each domain blind, without knowledge of scores in the other domain) we were less able to control for the other two of the aforementioned sources of bias.

Therefore, in collecting the subsequent data reported here, it was decided that *separate* interviews for each domain would, on balance, be more valid and useful. In addition, separate dilemma–interview sessions for each domain are critical to the success of the more in-depth, intensive interviewing required for the more detailed stage-by-issue analyses. In addition to these methodological concerns, there are both theoretical and practical factors that also dictated the current methods.

Theoretically, it is quite important to our current research to know the extent to which the subjects' interpersonal conceptions are unitary, or same-stage, when examined from a structural developmental point of view; therefore, a method that did not start with confounding across domains was needed. From a practical standpoint, it is also important to gain some sense of how stable, developmentally speaking, an individual's interpersonal understanding is across a range of "thought-about" experiences. If research indicates that synchrony (i.e., understanding or conceptualizing each issue at roughly the same developmental level) is the norm, what does this say about the individual with a dissynchronous or fluctuating stage pattern across issues? Or if research indicates that certain issues (or domains) consistently appear to develop more rapidly than others, what does this imply about the nature of the experience children have with the phenomena these issues represent or about the child for whom this is not true?

Finally, I believe that an intensive method for interviewing subjects, children in particular, about each of four very important kinds of relationships—one intrapsychic, three interpersonal—may eventually have some real clinical payoff; in addition to being a research tool for looking at the characteristics of and relationships among psychological processes, it may prove to be adaptable as a clinical tool which can be used to shed some light on the thinking of particular individuals.

The first specific aim of this chapter is to describe the methods and procedures we ultimately devised for assessing the ways subjects conceptualize the issues in the interpersonal understanding system. In addition, I discuss how these methods were designed also to be appropriate to the reanalysis of data collected during the initial longitudinal interviews. Concerns for the reliability of data collection and coding are also dealt with here as are the reasons why it may make more sense to consider our procedure a standardized research or clinical interview rather than an attempt to meet the stringent, less flexible criteria of a psychometric test.

The primary aim of the next chapter, Chapter 8, is to report the findings generated from analysis of data collected with these procedures. Five types of data analysis have been applied to data from several overlapping samples of subjects. The five analyses speak to issues of internal validity, for example, structured wholeness, developmental sequence, etc., in developmental theory.

I want to make one last comment about the organization of this chapter. In most reports of research, the description of an instrument's characteristics, most specifically its reliability, are placed after the sample and methods of data collection have been described, usually at the beginning of a "results" section. However, I provide some reliability findings directly following a discussion of coding and scoring procedures. There is one basic reason for this. The development of the method has been an ongoing process, not used only for the data collected and the samples described in this section of the book. Parallel and collaborative work of colleagues and project associates has added valuable information to our knowledge of what are the stable characteristics of these measurement procedures. In particular we shall draw from some of the results of a carefully implemented intervention study undertaken by Ellen Cooney (1978). As she points out, it is quite difficult to unravel the often intertwined threads of theoretical and measurement issues. This is particularly true when one wishes to sort out theoretical questions about the degree to which developmental aspects of interpersonal concepts are coherent or unitary in nature from questions about measurement procedures that may bias findings toward or away from such conclusions.

The Assessment of Interpersonal Conceptions: Psychological Test, Clinical Interview, or Both

In 1976 a set of scoring rules and procedures was devised that could be used to reanalyze and score previously collected data at the same time as it made full use of the three revised issue manuals. (The parent–child manual was not completed until 1978.) We faced the task of generating a standardized scoring procedure with some misgivings. For one thing, many contemporary researchers had appeared fairly content to orient their work to the first or descriptive phase of research only, or sometimes erroneously to merge Phases 1 and 2, even using the same data in the service of both description–construction and validation. For another, by Phase 2, it became abundantly clear that scoring could never be reduced to a simple matching of a subject's verbal response to some empirical criterion. Valid and reliable administration and scoring would always require individuals to be well trained in interviewing, quite familiar with the manuals and the scoring, and well grounded in the theoretical basis of the structural analysis.

For instance, when an individual untrained or unfamiliar with our system first looks at a single interview, he or she usually has great difficulty "seeing" developmental stages in a subject's statements about each issue or across issues. In part, this is a question of our need to communicate to the uninitiated our own way of orienting or organizing social concept data. However, it is also a "distance" question of learning how to compare data in a developmental frame of reference. It is not until an individual has the opportunity to *compare* the variety of responses to the same questions given by subjects at different ages that he can get a sense of distance, that the data begin to take on developmental properties, that the observer begins to be able to differentiate developmental and non-developmental differences in the responses of subjects to questions such as what makes someone a good friend or what keeps a group united. In this sense a well-trained interviewer must, by definition, be a well-trained scorer, must know what questions and inquiries to make to arrive at scoreable responses.

In the Appendix, I have excerpted from our scoring manuals some of the instructions we provide for beginning interviewers. In reading this Appendix, one begins to see that the scoring process is in some respects akin to clinical assessment and also has some qualities in common with psychometric testing. As in a clinical orientation to assessment, interviewing experience is an important factor. It is necessary for the interviewer to have a great deal of familiarity with a wide range of potential responses (or reasons) that any individual might provide and to be able to match these responses to what the interviewer knows are criteria for assigning responses (or reasons) to specified levels. On the other hand, as in psychometric measurement, the interpersonal concept manuals do function as sets of possible signs of what developmental stage a particular reason or justification most likely represents. However, it is still up to the interviewer–scorer to know when to probe deeply enough to feel comfortable interpreting obtained responses in terms of developmental stages.

We needed an assessment procedure that could code data collected with differing questions and methods (e.g., in 1974 and 1976). However, there is a second reason why our manuals emphasize standard *scoring procedures* rather than standardized *administration procedures*. It is my belief that each researcher poses questions that have a certain uniqueness, an individuality that requires that an investigator feel able to adapt data collection and coding procedures to meet the needs of his or her particular study. Cognizant of the time and effort required to obtain reliability of coding schemes, researchers are often fearful of tampering with previously validated procedures, concerned that such tampering might artifactually invalidate the instrument. But as Cronbach *et al.* (1972) and Gottman and Parkhurst (1979) have pointed out, reliability requires the investigator to think about the use of an instrument or procedure in the context of a particular study; it is not an automatic calculation using some universally agreed upon statistic independent of the specificity of a project's goals and needs. Thus, in our brand of developmental psychology, unlike the psychometric model, the focus of reliability and validity is on rigorousness of the method of *coding* and *interpreting* a subject's reasoning, not on rigorously asking every subject exactly the same questions in exactly the same order.

Another reason for emphasizing the methods of interpretation is the lengthiness and expense of our procedure. For example, we now have a system that consists of 22 issues across four domains. To complete an entire interview across all issues usually takes upwards of 2 to 3 hours. Transcription of this material can take up to 10 hours, and scoring, another 2 or 3. Few researchers have that kind of time to spend on one measure. Therefore, although a standard interview is used in the studies *we* describe, the *potential* user of the *system* described in this book must feel free to experiment, adapt, and decide how the procedures described here might best fit his or her purposes. For this reason, if no other, the relative emphasis here is on scoring rather than test administration. In fact, it is my belief that one criterion by which to judge the success of a research endeavor is the degree to which other researchers are able to *adapt* methods and procedures to their own interests and purposes, rather than simply *apply* them.

Procedures for Assigning and Computing Stage Scores for Interpersonal Conceptions

THE ISSUE-CONCEPT

We call the basic unit of analysis in our scoring system the issue–concept. As described in Chapter 4, each issue (e.g., conflict resolution in friendship) is seen as a critical process, important quality, or major area in (the conceptualization of) each domain in the interpersonal system. But as also pointed out earlier, issues, although they are the key part of a category system, are usually too abstract for most subjects to deal with directly and must be translated into operationally more meaningful and manageable units. One cannot expect, for example, to gain a fair assessment of a child's level of understanding of a concept such as *cohesiveness* by just asking the child to define it. In addition, for scoring purposes, simply identifying an issue does not provide a way to set up markers designating when the expression of reasoning about that issue begins or when it ends. Furthermore, within any given interview, it is possible that thoughts about or concepts of a given issue may appear more than once. This is particularly true when interviewing procedures do not systematically cover each issue in a defined order. (The way the assessment we are describing is designed, issues *are* dealt with systematically, but this not necessary.)

The issue–concept, as it is used in our interview procedures, is *any codable response about an issue* in an interview, whether a response to an initial issue-oriented probe question, to subsequent follow-up probes that serve to clarify the subject's level of usage, or to general conversation in the interview. Issue–concepts can in fact be identified in any discussion in which an issue can be identified and a level of understanding assigned. I have devoted some energy here to expressing the opinion that the less a scoring procedure is bound to a specific manner of data collection or instrument, the greater its flexibility. The use of the issue–concept allows for this kind of flexibility. For example, recall that in our initial study (1976) two domains were assessed, but one of them, the friendship domain, was divided into only three broad categories (formation, maintenance, and termination) rather than the six more recently identified, more specific issues. Use of issue–concept analysis allows us to return to these data and with confidence recode them for the present six issues whenever discussion of them occurs.

THE ISSUING PROCEDURE

We devised a standard procedure for scoring interview material from three domains called the issuing procedure. The interpersonal conceptions manuals provide specific details of scoring and computational rules. These can be summarized as follows. Based upon a computation of issue–concepts, each issue is scored as either a pure stage (e.g., Stage 2) or a major(minor) stage [e.g., Stage 2(1)]. For each domain, a quantitative score can be computed by averaging all issue scores to obtain the total stage score for the domain. For example, in the individuals domain, issue scores of Subjectivity 2(3), Self-Awareness 3, Personality 3(2), and Personality Change 2(3) would be averaged into a quantitative score of 2.58. (When averaging major[minor] scores, major scores receive a two-thirds weight and minor scores a one-third weight.) In addition, an overall quantitative *Interpersonal Understanding Maturity Score* (IMS) can be computed by averaging all issue scores from all interpersonal domains. For example, if a subject was interviewed on three domains, all 17 issue scores would be averaged to yield an IMS score. If a subject was interviewed on only two domains, the subject's IMS score would be the average of his issue scores in those domains. For qualitative analysis

TABLE 7.1
Conversion of Numerical IMS[a] Score to Global Stage Score

IMS range	Global stage
0.00–0.24	Stage 0
0.25–0.49	Stage 0(1)
0.50–0.74	Stage 1(0)
0.75–1.24	Stage 1
1.25–1.49	Stage 1(2)
etc.	etc.

[a] Interpersonal Understanding Maturity Score.

this numerical IMS score can be translated back into a stage score, a global interpersonal understanding stage, as shown in Table 7.1.

Reliability of Scoring Procedures

I have just briefly described procedures (described in greater detail in the manuals) that can provide a single score, either a global stage score or a numerical IMS score, from one or more domain–interviews. But is there empirical support or justification for such a merger of domains? As noted, difficult measurement issues make this theoretical question more complex. For example, as pointed out earlier, whether or not an individual actually does reason synchronously (at the same developmental stage) across issues, certain data collection and coding procedures may tend to distort the picture one way or the other.

In general, it is thought that bias in measurement would tend to present a picture of conceptual development as more synchronous than it really is. For instance, the first general scoring instruction is to read through the entire protocol for a domain before going back to identify issue–concepts. Practically speaking this is a necessary step in reliable scoring, that is, in achieving adequate interrater agreement. But what effect does such a first step have in biasing results toward overly synchronous (same-stage) scoring across issues? To safeguard against this "overgeneralization effect" across domains we can interview the same subject at different times for each domain, and then score each individual protocol without knowledge of the subject's scores on other protocols. But what about scoring issues *within* a domain; what safeguards can be taken at this level of coding? To ascertain the extent to which there appears to be some validity to combining issues to achieve a global *stage score* for a domain, it is not only necessary to know whether there is an adequate degree of same-stage synchrony across issues, but also the extent to which synchrony is truly a function of the phenomenon under investigation rather than of certain biases in measurement procedures.

An attempt to control for possible measurement bias was undertaken. From the larger sample, to be described shortly, were drawn the transcripts of 40 subjects, ranging in age from 6 to 20. Each transcript included three interviews, on the individuals, friendships, and peer-group domains. The wide age-range was used to insure our getting scores representative of all stages. For each subject, issue–concepts across all three interviews were marked but not coded. Then each issue–concept was excerpted from its protocol and randomly assigned to a set of issue–concepts excerpted from the protocols of the other 39 subjects. Each issue–concept was then stage scored without knowledge of which subject offered it or of what that individual said in response to questions about the other 16 issues.

Once scoring was complete, the hundreds of issue–concepts were put back together like 40 jigsaw puzzles and scored in the normal manner. The correlation between IMS scores obtained through this precautionary method and those obtained through the normal procedures (whereby each domain is scored essentially as a whole unit) was .86, a strong and encouraging correlation, because it suggests that degree of found stage synchrony of issue–concepts, issues, and domains is not a function of the scoring process itself.

In addition to the "safeguard study" just described, we have focused reliability analyses on three other areas: correlational and absolute agreement between (or within) scorers with varying levels of experience and expertise (inter- and intrarater reliability), the temporal stability of the interview (test–retest reliability), and other possible kinds of interviewer or scorer bias. Information on the reliability of the procedure originates in several studies, both within our project (Chapter 8; Brion-Meisels, 1977; Cooney, 1978; Jaquette, 1979; Lavin, 1979) and outside it in work by independent researchers using our procedures (Enright, 1977; Lieberman, 1979). In reporting these results, I shall be referring to scoring using the general procedures in the manual.

In particular, attention is called to the fact that the computational basis of the reliability analyses is the IMS score, the numerical *average* across issues, as distinct from a procedure that might focus on the *highest* level of conception. (In the latter case, one would look across the issues within it for the highest score given in a domain. This score would be higher than an average.)[2]

---

[2] In discussing averaging procedures (the IMS score), it should be noted that the transformation of qualitative (stage) scores into quantitative numerical scores gives them an appearance of being equal interval data, making Pearson correlational analyses appropriate. However, we felt this was possibly inappropriate. As a result, in our project's analyses, Spearman correlation coefficients were also calculated for all analyses where Pearson correlations were used. Since the results were substantially the same throughout, separate reports will not be presented.

INTER- AND INTRARATER RELIABILITY

More and more, researchers have come to recognize that to a degree, reliability, particularly among observers or scorers, is in part a function of degree of training. Using protocols from interviews in three domains of 15 subjects ranging in age from 6 to adulthood, the correlation of IMS scores assigned by two "expert scorers," that is, two project workers involved in the manual construction, was .96. Exact agreement of experts' IMS scores, defined as a difference of not more than .25 IMS points, that is, one-quarter stage, was 93%.

The average of correlations between an expert scorer and three individuals trained only through reading of the manuals was .92 ($N = 15$), while the average correlation between an expert and three workshop-trained individuals was .94 ($N = 15$).[3] Exact agreement (within .25 points) in all cases was over 82%.

Interrater reliabilities have also been calculated separately for each domain. The average Pearson correlations between an expert and three trained scorers were .97 ($N = 15$) for individuals, .87 ($N = 15$) for friendship, .97 ($N = 15$) for peer groups, and .82 ($N = 10$) for parent–child relations. (With respect to this last finding, see Bruss-Saunders, 1979, for specific details.)

Using an interview schedule that was focused on the friendship and individuals domains, Cooney reported an intrarater reliability between an original score and a blind rescoring 6 months later of 25 randomly selected protocols of .91 with a range from .64 to .93 across issues (Cooney, 1978). Exact agreement (as defined above) in the intrarater reliability was reported at 92% with a range across issues of 81 to 96%, with no scores greater than one .25 interval apart. It should be noted that Cooney's data come from a sample of 32 second and third grade middle and working class children, so the range of scores is much narrower than for the other samples in our project.

TEMPORAL STABILITY OR TEST-RETEST RELIABILITY

Estimating the test–retest reliability of a method that is designed to assess a continually changing developmental process is a delicate affair, one that requires retesting over two occasions separate enough in time so that the first administration would not be expected to influence the second, but near enough in time that results would not be confounded by natural age- or experience-related developments. Our own estimation of the temporal stability of the interpersonal conceptions interview procedure comes from control groups in four studies whose primary foci

---

[3] A workshop consisted of a 2½-day session starting with theoretical issues and including practice interviewing and discussion of scored protocols.

have been the effects of various types of interventions on the assessed change in level of interpersonal conception from pre- to post- to follow-up testing.

In Cooney's (1978) study, Pearson correlations of control group ($N = 32$ middle- and working-class public school children) scores on pretest and posttest (2-month interval) and on pretest and delayed posttest (5-month interval) were calculated. The Pearson correlation of blind scores (using the same scorer) at the shorter interval was .51 ($N = 32$) and at the longer was .63. Exact agreement (as defined) was 70% between pre- and posttest, and 73% between pre- and delayed posttest. Two factors other than measurement error in the interview procedure might serve to lower correlations. For one, in assessing children at two adjacent grade levels (second and third), the limited range of the initial scores tends to lower correlation. For another, some variation in upward change might naturally be expected, particularly over the 5-month interval, which even if it did not influence correlation would influence percentage of exact agreement.

In a study undertaken outside our project, Enright (1977) reported test–retest reliability correlations of .92 in fifth and sixth graders across a 22-week period. Brion-Meisels (1977) reported correlations of .61 in the same age-range across a 6-month period. These studies support the short-term stability–reliability of the measure, although the results show variation and are limited to elementary grade children whose scores are primarily at Stages 1, 2, or 3. Data that speak to the test–retest stability of the interview for older subjects and higher stages are still required.

In this regard, results from one other independent study, within limits, can add some information to our estimation of our procedure. Using the responses of 63 eighth-grade public school children, Lieberman (1979) found a correlation of .69 ($p < .00001$) between assessments administered 10 weeks apart. The limitations on the applicability of these results stem from Lieberman's use not of an interview method, but of a written form of the measure, subjects reading dilemmas and responding alone on paper, without the challenge to articulate provided by interviewers' questions.

RESISTANCE TO INTERVIEWER BIAS

There are a number of other factors stemming from the interviewing and scoring characteristics of the measurement procedure which are not generally considered issues of reliability but which nevertheless may be sources of unreliability of results. Blind scoring can usually be arranged to eliminate scorer bias. However, it is not always possible to control for interviewer bias in the same way. Knowledge of the time of administration in a longitudinal study or of whether a subject is in a control or experimental group in an intervention study would have little effect on how a "data collector" would interpret data in some measures, for example, of changes in physical strength or stature or in spelling skill or in resistance to infection. However, in collecting data with our interview procedure, such knowledge on the part of an interviewer could be a source of bias if, for example, the interviewer were rooting, consciously or unconsciously, for developmental advancement. Although such sources of potential unreliability are well known, the question can be raised as to the "degree of susceptibility" of a particular measure to such sources of bias. How *resistant* a procedure is to methodological bias is a fascinating area of study for those concerned with a method's stability.

For instance, in the Cooney study, for practical reasons it was impossible for interviewers not to be aware of the group (experimental or control) into which a subject was placed. Therefore, some means was necessary to estimate how resistant the interview procedure was to this bias effect. Cooney took 20 interviews (10 experimental and 10 control) and examined them for traces of interviewer bias. Her check was to compare the number of questions asked in experimental and control groups. Cooney reasoned that if more questions were asked of the experimental group, this would be an indication of an interviewer's attempt to draw out these subjects' higher level reasoning. Here, Cooney found no *quantitative* differences in one-way analyses of variance for pretest [F (1,18) = 3.85, ns] or posttest [$F(1,18)$ = .929, ns] samples. To ascertain whether any *qualitative* differences in interviewing could be detected, a second sample of 20 posttest protocols (10 experimental, 10 control) were given to two trained interviewers who, without knowledge of the group (experimental or control) from which the protocols were drawn, were asked to rank them as to how much the interviewer seemed to "lead" the subject to higher level scores. The rankings by these scorers bore no significant relation to the groups from which the protocols were selected, as measured by a Mann–Whitney U test (U = 30, ns). Of course, in any study care must be taken to guard against interviewer or scorer bias. Still, these particular analyses indicate that a trained interviewer can function in an objective manner, despite the latitude the procedure allows in deciding how fully a subject's initial responses need to be probed.

A final state-of-the-art note with respect to the reliability of the interview procedure. One traditional kind of reliability—alternate form —has received little of our attention. This is in part because results from our earlier study (Selman, 1976b) did not show much variation in individuals' scores across differences in the content of dilemmas. This is also in part because of our desire to emphasize that the foundation of the procedure is the interview and scoring, not the resolution of a specific dilemma.

Validation Analyses: Samples and Measures

Evaluating the reliability of an instrument or scoring procedure does not *end* with establishing that two or more observers can agree on what they observe or how they code that observation or that subjects will "test" about the same over a short interval. However, the confidence that decent reliability provides *is* an essential step in the validation process. I now move forward to description of studies undertaken with project members, one by Ellen Cooney (1978) and one with Debra Lavin and Daniel Jaquette (reported here for the first time in full) (Selman, Jaquette, & Lavin, 1977). These studies were designed to validate the construct of stages of reflective interpersonal understanding, a superordinate construct that organizes into developmental levels or stages an individual's expressed interpersonal conceptions across and within each of the four domains as they are elicited through an interview procedure.[4]

The studies will be reported in Chapter 8 as five analyses which have applied to some or all of four overlapping samples of subjects interviewed since 1974. Here I describe the samples and the data, other than the social reasoning interviews, that were gathered.

CHARACTERISTICS OF THE FOUR SAMPLES

The *normative sample*[5] (Sample A) consisted of 225 interpersonal understanding interviews, 48 of which were 2-year follow-ups of the same individuals (see Sample B). The ages of these subjects ranged from 4½ to 32. Forty-six were female and 179 male. Sixty-one came from working-class backgrounds and 164 from middle- or upper-middle-class backgrounds, as defined by parental- or self-occupation and educational level. Thirty-three individuals of the normative sample were black and 192 white.

The *longitudinal sample* (Sample B) is a subset of Sample A composed of 48 boys interviewed in 1974 and again in 1976 as a 2-year follow-up.[6] In 1974 their ages ranged from 6:0 to 12:1 and in 1976 from 7:11 to 14:3. Thirty-one subjects of the longitudinal sample are middle- or upper-middle-class and 17 come from working-class backgrounds. Thirty-eight are white and 10 are black. The average IQ of the group is 105 with a range from 85 to 133.

---

[4] It should be noted that at the time most of the analyses to be reported here and in Chapter 8 were undertaken, only three of the four domains had been adequately described. Work on the parent–child domain was still at a formative stage, and so the results to be reported only partially pertain to it.

[5] As of September, 1978.

[6] As of the time of this writing 40 subjects for the longitudinal study have been reinterviewed a third time. Where meaningful and appropriate, the partial findings from this third follow-up will be included.

The *clinical-comparative sample* (Sample C) was made up of 21 additional boys in the Sample B age-range who in 1974 attended day schools for children with emotional and interpersonally-related learning problems. They were from either working-class or middle-/ upper-middle-class backgrounds, and had intelligence scores within the normal range as assessed by the WISC. In most cases these children came from urban environments. These 21 "disturbed" boys were matched with 21 of the normal longitudinal sample (B) on the basis of age, sex, race, socioeconomic status, and IQ. Eleven of the 21 matched pairs came from middle-class families and 10 from families of working-class background. Four of the pairs were black and 17 white. Since 1974 *and* 1976 data exist for both the disturbed and matched normal member in each pair, the clinical-comparative sample is also an additional longitudinal sample.

In particular, the clinical sample was composed of children whose major referral symptoms included poor interpersonal relationships (has no friends, plays with younger children only, etc.). Children with active or current psychotic symptoms (severe thought disorders, excessive difficulty distinguishing fantasy and reality) or obvious neurological problems were excluded from the sample. Although diagnostic labels are eschewed in the description of the children in Sample C, behavioral descriptions differentiating them from their public school peers can be attempted. First, the children referred to the clinic schools appear to be in greater need of and respond positively to a more structured learning environment than is necessary for their public school peers. Second, these children appear to have greater difficulty in delaying immediate gratification and display lower levels of frustration tolerance. Third, these children appear to be less able to take full responsibility for their own acts, particularly when functioning in group situations. Fourth, they appear to have less adequately developed social abilities: to give appropriate peer feedback, to control overly excessive attention-seeking behaviors, or to display age-appropriate group discussion skills. Finally, their academic skills are more poorly developed, both in overall achievement level and in the study skills necessary to settle down to complete their assignments autonomously.

The *supplementary normative sample* (Sample D)[7] was drawn from the control groups of a study (Cooney, 1978) of an elementary grade social developmental intervention constructed by the Social Reasoning Project. The subjects were 32 public school children of both sexes drawn from four classes divided between second and third grade and between schools serving upper-middle-class and working-class populations.

---

[7] The subjects in Sample D were interviewed on only two domains (friendship and individuals but not peer groups), whereas the subjects in the other three samples were interviewed on all three.

OTHER DATA COLLECTED

In addition to the interpersonal understanding interview, several other assessment procedures were administered to some subjects from each of Samples A, B, and C. One hundred and twenty-one subjects (parts of Samples A and B) were administered a procedure designed to assess level of Piagetian logicophysical reasoning (Forbes & Selman, 1974). Seventy-four children, including the 21 children in Sample C, were also rated by their teachers on two scales, one designed to specify school-related difficulties, the other school-related strengths. Finally, psychometric intelligence data were available through school records for 48 of the subjects in Samples B and C. The reasoning and teacher rating measures will be briefly described here.

Logicophysical Reasoning Tasks

A propositional logic task was adopted (Forbes & Selman, 1974) from Piaget and Inhelder (1954) to assess at both test periods logicophysical reasoning within the context of Piagetian cognitive stage theory. Each child was given a rod suspension box with rods differing in length, material, and thickness. The child worked with the rods two at a time, hanging weights on the ends, to discover the factors involved in differing amounts of flexibility. If performance on this task clearly indicated a child had achieved concrete operational functioning, no further logical assessment procedures were administered.

However, if a child's performance was equivocal in this regard, two easier tasks adapted from Piaget and Inhelder (1964) were given: the *concrete-operational class logic task* and the *concrete-operational logic of relations task*. In the former, the child is presented with 32 triangles in two sizes, two materials, and two colors and asked to sort them in various ways. In the latter, the child is asked first to draw, then to place, a series of colored rods in size order. The child is asked to match a set of circles, graded from light pink to dark red, with a set of size-graded sticks, the shortest going with the lightest.

The measures were scored according to Piaget's system of three stages (preoperational, concrete–operational, and formal–operational) and three substages of operative reasoning, generating a range of six levels (1A through 3B). Interviews were scored both at the time of administration and later from the transcript of the interview. An interrater reliability of .90 was obtained by correlating two raters' scores for 15 subjects. Perfect agreement between scores assigned at the time of the interview and those assigned from scoring transcribed interviews was 81%. For final scoring, disagreements were resolved through further discussion and the highest level agreed upon to be clearly expressed by a child was the assigned score.

Teacher Ratings

Two instruments designed by the University of Rochester Primary Mental Health Project (Gesten, 1974; Lorion, Cowen, & Caldwell, 1974) were used by teachers to rate students' classroom behavior. Specifically, these instruments were designed by their authors to provide teachers with a systematic means of communicating (a) the specific areas of *concern* a teacher has about a child's classroom behavior and (b) the specific areas of *strength* or competence observed in that child.

The *Classroom Adjustment Rating Scale* (CARS) allows the teacher to evaluate a child's difficulty in three areas: (a) learning difficulties; (b) problems of withdrawal, dependency, and/or undersocialization; and (c) disruptive or overly aggressive behavior. The CARS consists of 41 behaviorally oriented items (e.g., "reacts poorly to disappointment"), each rated along a 5-point scale ("1 = not a problem" to "5 = very serious problem"). It is scored for each of three scales, corresponding to the three aforementioned areas of difficulty, as well as for a T or total score summarizing each child's degree of adjustment difficulty. Norms for elementary grades are available (Clarfield, 1974; Lorion *et al.*, 1974).

The Health Resources Inventory (HRI) provides a measure of the child's school-related competence by use of items in five areas: (a) good student (e.g., does well in reading, does original work); (b) gutsy (e.g., defends own views under group pressure); (c) peer sociability (e.g., shares things with others); (d) rules (e.g., is polite and courteous); and (e) frustration tolerance (e.g., copes well with failure). As with the CARS, each item in the HRI is rated from 1 (not at all) to 5 (very well). The emphasis of the HRI is on positive adaptive aspects of a child's functioning in contrast with the usual emphasis of teacher rating–observation scales on symptoms of maladaptation. With the HRI, higher scores indicate better functioning, whereas with the CARS, higher scores are indicative of greater social adjustment problems (Gesten, 1974).

Having described the samples and measures used, I go on to the reporting of our validity analyses in Chapter 8.

8

The Development of
Interpersonal Understanding:
Five Analyses of Validity

In this chapter, I report our validity analyses, using data from the four samples described in Chapter 7. The characteristics of the samples are summarized in Table 8.1, to which the reader is encouraged to refer in reading this chapter. At the end of this chapter, I summarize our findings to date before I move to Part IV (Chapters 9 and 10), which deals with applications of our model.

Analysis 1: Structured Wholeness and Variability—
Cross-Sectional Correlations, Cross-Tabulations,
and Factor Analyses

Most structuralists enjoy the task of puzzling over the way reasoning about different areas of social knowledge is coordinated in the child's mind. This applies both within systems (as in looking at the development of relations among issues in the interpersonal understanding system) and across systems (as in looking at the relation of logicophysical stages to interpersonal stages). This type of analysis is not undertaken through correlation alone, but also in terms of the inner logic of each stage in each system. Understanding of the "structural" relation of levels or stages of

TABLE 8.1
Summary of Characteristics of Four Samples Used in Validity Analyses

Sample and title	N	Age (years)	Sex	Race	SES	Normal or disturbed
A. Normative sample	225	4½ to 32	79% Male 21% Female	85% White 15% Nonwhite	73% Middle–upper-middle-class 27% Working-class	Normal
B. Longitudinal sample	48	6 to 11: Time 1 8 to 13: Time 2 11 to 16: Time 3	Male	79% White 21% Nonwhite	65% Middle–upper-middle class 35% Working-class	Normal
C. Clinical-comparative sample	21	6 to 11: Time 1 8 to 13: Time 2	Male	80% White 20% Nonwhite	52% Middle–upper-middle class 48% Working-class	Disturbed
D. Supplementary normative sample	32	Second and third grade	50% Male 50% Female	Predominantly white	50% Upper-middle-class 50% Working-class	Normal

development across issues, domains, or systems is of theoretical importance because it makes models more coherent and integrative.[1]

There remains, of course, some uncertainty as to which methods and
analyses will allow conclusions as to degree of synchrony attained and as
to what degree constitutes enough "togetherness" to demonstrate structured wholeness or find it a useful idea. But in general, and in the
analyses to follow, the rule that greater synchrony means greater structured wholeness is a generally accepted working guide.

RESULTS

When attempting to explore the logical consistency of a developmental system, it is usually useful to keep variations in the type of task used
to a minimum in order to maximize the possibility that any intrain-
dividual consistency will show itself without confound. One way to hold
task difficulty or context constant for a clearer look at relations among
concepts is, in our case, to work in the mode of reflective reasoning. The
data reported in this first analysis speak to the developmental coherence
of interpersonal concepts usage but caution is suggested in generalizing
beyond the reflective interview context used.

Three kinds of analyses were performed: full and partial correlations,
factor analyses, and cross-domain comparisons of level of interpersonal
reasoning within subjects. Optimally the analyses of issue and domain
coherence and variability should be based on scoring procedures
whereby a subject's response to one question cannot influence scorers'
assessments of responses to other questions. In this respect, the data
analyses presented here may be somewhat limited because independent
scoring was done only across domains, not within. However, the independent, blind scoring operations reported in Chapter 7 were performed
across issue–concepts and suggest scorer bias is minimal.

Full and partial correlations can help to inform about the degree
of coherence across domains. Sample A IMS scores correlated .76 with
chronological age ($N = 225$), .77 with psychometric IQ ($N = 48$), and .62
($N = 121$) with Piagetian logicophysical reasoning stage.

Table 8.2 presents Sample A and B first-order correlations and partial correlations among the three domains when variations in chronological age, Piagetian logicophysical reasoning ability, and psychometric
intelligence are controlled. (Time 2 data are presented as a replication of

---

[1] Actually, contrary to popular belief, lock-step development across domains is not
seen as a crucial condition for the validation of the theoretical stage model. In fact,
developmentalists are beginning to realize that variation in patterns of development
across areas may themselves be of some psychological interest. Damon (1977), for instance, reports that in his study of authority and justice concepts, children do not
automatically think at corresponding levels across all concepts.

TABLE 8.2
Correlations among the Domains of Individuals, Friendship, and Peer Group at Time 1
and Time 2, Partialling out IQ, Age, and Logical Stage

	Individuals/Friends	Individuals/Group	Friends/Group
Time 1 (1974, Samples A and B, age 6-12)			
First-order	.87 (74)[a]	.81 (72)	.73 (72)
Controlling IQ	.87 (70)	.81 (68)	.73 (68)
Controlling age	.75 (71)	.60 (69)	.37 (69)
Controlling logic	.78 (70)	.67 (68)	.52 (68)
Time 2 (1976, Sample B, age 8-14)			
First-order	.80 (47)	.78 (46)	.86 (46)
Controlling IQ	.80 (44)	.77 (43)	.86 (43)
Controlling age	.65 (44)	.60 (43)	.71 (43)
Controlling logic	.69 (43)	.65 (43)	.78 (43)

[a] Sample size in parentheses.

the correlational results.) At both Time 1 and Time 2 the correlations among the domains remain high even when each external variable is controlled. Controlling for IQ has the least effect on the interdomain correlations; this is what one might predict insofar as the IQ score is designed to hold relatively constant across chronological age while social–cognitive stage varies (develops) with age. Holding logical ability constant decreases the correlations among the domains, and so, to a greater extent, does chronological age. However, the interdomain correlations remain relatively high, indicating considerable independent, internal coherence across domains.

In the blind-scored reliability study reported in Chapter 7, the issue-by-issue correlational matrix generated by comparing each issue score with each of the other 16 issue scores across 40 Sample A individuals generated a range of Pearson correlations between .52 and .96 with a mean correlation of .81.

To evaluate the coherence of reasoning levels across domains at different ages, first-order correlations were computed at four age-ranges (7:11–9:2, 9:3–11:3, 11:5–13, and 13:1–14:3) for the 48 Sample B subjects at Time 2 (1976). These data (Table 8.3) indicate that the overall pattern of high correlations among domains appears to hold at most of the age-levels. The major exception is the individual–group correlation at the early age-period. One possible explanation is the relative lack of experience with groups on the part of young children. Results of partial correlations controlling for Piagetian and psychometric intelligence at each age-level were similar to those found using the entire age-range.

Factor analysis provides a summary statistic for characterizing variation in level of interpersonal understanding across the 17 interper-

TABLE 8.3
First-Order Correlations among Three Domains (Individuals, Friendship, Peer Group)
at Four Age-Periods (Data from Sample B at Time 2, 1976)

Age-range	Individuals/Friends	Individuals/Group	Friends/Group
7:11–9:2	.44 (11)[a]	–.19 (11)	.66 (11)
9:3–11:3	.73 (13)	.90 (13)	.79 (13)
11:5–13:0	.89 (11)	.85 (10)	.75 (10)
13:1–14:3	.84 (12)	.79 (12)	.96 (12)
Overall	.80 (47)	.78 (46)	.86 (46)

[a] Sample size in parentheses.

sonal issues assessed. Using Sample B, a first factor of issue correlations accounted for 61% of the variance at Time 1. At Time 2 the first factor accounted for 66% of the variation. At Times 1 and 2 the second factor was far smaller, accounting for only 14% and 6% respectively. A factor analysis of the blind-scored issue-by-issue matrix indicated a first factor accounted for 59% of the variation in scores, with no other factor accounting for more than 10% of the additional variance.

Although correlational and factor analyses support the unity, synchrony, and coherence of a cross-issue interpersonal *system,* they do not demonstrate structural (i.e., same-stage) synchrony across issues or domains *within subjects.* Developmental stages across interpersonal domains or issues could correlate strongly *across* subjects while stages of reasoning *within* subjects in a particular domain or issue could still systematically develop at an earlier or later age than in other domains. To investigate this possibility, mean stage-by-age graphs were plotted for three domains. Figure 8.1 is a cross-sectional representation of stage of understanding in individuals, friendship, and group domains in Sample A subjects aged 6 through 15. It shows that for young children, individuals concepts generally emerge first, followed by friendship and finally by group-relations concepts. By age 14 or 15 conceptual development across all three domains appears to be more closely integrated. Of course, it is possible that this trend for the younger children to think at slightly lower levels about group concepts may be an artifact of the group dilemma itself, that is, the group dilemma may be less familiar or more difficult. However, this is unlikely because the interviews are not focused only on discussion of a particular dilemma, but also on a general clinical overview which covers the subjects' personal experiences as well. A more likely explanation, as mentioned earlier, is that young children do not generally have systematic peer-group experiences.

Another way of approaching the question of structured wholeness in social–cognitive stages is to record the degree to which variation in stage responses is likely to be found within all given individuals across all

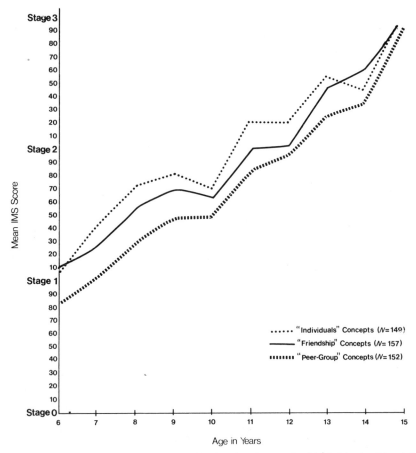

Figure 8.1. Mean stage-by-age trends in the development of individuals, friendship, and peer-group conceptions.

issues. If an individual's responses tend to be distributed broadly, one could question the central tendency predicted by structural social–cognitive analyses. If, however, issue responses for each subject tend to cluster around his or her modal stage, this would support a claim of structured wholeness, at least within a reflective interview setting. To this end, the stage range of issue scores of each subject in Sample B at Time 2 was examined in relation to the subject's major or global stage. Put in terms of a cumulative frequency, on the average, 38% of subjects' issue scores were *at* their global scores, 85% were within (plus or minus) *one-third* of a stage [one transitional step, e.g., 2(3) to 3(2) or 2], 99% were within *two-thirds* of a stage [two transitional steps, e.g., 3(2) to 2], and

100% were within *one and one-third* stages [four transitional steps, e.g., 3 to 2(1)].

The final examination of structural consistency in interpersonal understanding was an analysis of its relationship to the formal structure of Piagetian logicophysical cognition. One hundred twenty-one Sample A and B children were interviewed within a 2-week time period on both logicophysical reasoning and interpersonal understanding. The overall correlation between logicophysical and interpersonal awareness was .62 ($N = 121$, $p < .01$) and with age controlled, .51. These correlations should not be surprising given the common theoretical base between systems.

However, another way to understand the relation between these social and nonsocial domains is through cross-tabulated contingency analyses which allow for the examination of each subject's scores in each domain in relationship to one another. Table 8.4 shows the relation between each subject's global Piagetian logicophysical stage (preoperational, concrete operational, and formal operational) and the subject's global interpersonal understanding stage.

It is interesting to note that no subject whose global score indicated even minimal Stage 2 interpersonal reasoning was scored below concrete operations (II A-B) and that no subject given any indication of Stage 3 interpersonal reasoning was scored as reasoning below formal operations (III A or B). These data suggest that perhaps Stage 2 interpersonal understanding can be thought of as concrete operational–social thought and Stage 3 interpersonal understanding as formal operational–social thought. Perhaps Stage 2 interpersonal understanding requires certain concrete operational reciprocal logical ability and Stage 3 interpersonal understanding requires certain abstract, reflective, and formal operational logical ability.

TABLE 8.4
The Relation of Interpersonal Understanding to Physicological Ability in 121 Sample A and B Cases

| | | Global Interpersonal Understanding Stage | | | | | | | |
		1	1(2)	2(1)	2	2(3)	3(2)	3	Totals
Global	IB	2	—	—	—	—	—	—	2
Logical	IIA-B	11	15	14	13	—	—	—	53
Stage	IIIA-B	1	3	7	33	11	9	2	66
Totals		14	18	21	46	11	9	2	121

DISCUSSION

Taken as a piece, these results suggest that although there remains some interest or value in the examination of each domain or issue independently, there is clearly justification for calculating the numerical global interpersonal understanding or Interpersonal Understanding Maturity Score (IMS) from an average of the scores across issues.

From the differentiation or "separatist" perspective, it is clear that individuals, particularly young children, become familiar with and are able to express their understanding of certain social concepts earlier than others. Figure 8.1 and our statistical analysis suggest that for the younger subject in our sample familiarity radiates outward, starting with the ability to express developmental knowledge about the self, then moving out toward dyadic relations such as friendship, and finally to the socially organized experiences represented by group life. It appears that with time and normal development in our culture, understanding of these domains becomes more integrated.[2]

From the unifying or "integrative" perspective, there are both empirical and logical rationales for the utility of a summary score (the IMS). Empirically speaking, under reflective conditions statistical analysis points to a high degree of synchrony in the minds of subjects across issues. Of course it must be emphasized that this synchrony is found under relatively benign conditions; a trained and sensitive interviewer is attempting to elicit from the subject his most facile thinking under the relative calm of an interview about a hypothetical situation. Logically speaking, the rationale stems from the realization that there appears to be a great deal of cross-fertilization among issues, and this appears to increase at the higher levels. For example, to see that friendships may terminate because of personality changes in one or both of the parties requires an integration of concepts of individuals and friendships.

There thus appears a time and place for both the differentiated and the integrated perspective. In the analyses to follow I focus on the integrative aspects of interpersonal understanding and make use of the IMS as a summary statistic. In Part IV, describing research under naturalistic conditions, the emphasis shifts somewhat toward individual domains or issues, oscillation and variation, suggesting, somewhat paradoxically, that developmental stability or structure and situational oscillation are *both* useful constructs in a cognitive–developmental social psychology.

[2] As part of the Time 2 follow-up interview of Sample B, 18 subjects aged 8 to 13 were given the parent–child interview. There was no statistically significant difference between the level of reasoning of these children as a group on the parent–child interview and their reasoning on the other three domains [t (17) = 1.9, two-tailed].

Analysis 2: The Uses of Demographic Data

It is not unreasonable for consumers of cognitive–developmental research to want some indication of "natural" or "normal" age-ranges for the emergence of stages of reasoning. Similarly,·questions about developmental differences in understanding between boys and girls, men and women, whites and nonwhites, or those of different social classes seem equally important. However, when doing stage descriptive work, many developmentalists have eschewed such questions, their concern being more for the *universal* or structurally similar, sequenced qualities of social thought in children and adults than for the specifics or differences among individuals. Nevertheless, these norms are necessary information if the developmental approach is to move from a primarily descriptive-philosophical (Phase 1) orientation to an orientation in which study of functional use of conceptions and structural aspects of understanding go hand-in-hand.

Ironically, where consistent demographic data have been provided, they have provided more than mundane norms; they have stimulated important discussion and thought about the theoretical bases for and accuracy of stage descriptions. To take one example, using Kohlberg's system, research reports have generally indicated that adult American women on the average score at Stage 3, whereas comparable samples of American men score at Stage 4. Kohlberg has interpreted these results as an indication of the importance of "role-taking" (perspective-taking) opportunities. He suggests that men's greater opportunity for interaction in the sociopolitical world of work stimulates advancement to a Stage 4 sociopolitical moral view; such opportunities do not abound for his housebound female cohort. However, rather than accepting this social–psychological explanation of the inferiority of the moral thought of the "isolated American housewife," researchers have challenged this interpretation on two counts. First, some have challenged the validity of the Kohlberg measurement and scoring procedures (Holstein, 1976). Second, and perhaps more accurately, others have challenged the basic descriptive model itself, realizing that method and model cannot be divorced entirely from one another. Gilligan (1977) claims that women may think *differently* about moral issues but not necessarily less adequately and that these *developmentally equal* (same-stage) but contextually different ways of thinking are incorrectly categorized as unequal (lower stage) in Kohlberg's measure and characteristic structural net. Rather than providing mortal wounds to the basic theory, these empirical investigations, if used constructively, can serve to generate the antibodies that are essential for the health and vigor of a cognitive-developmental approach.

RESULTS

Age

In Figure 8.2, IMS scores for all 225 assessments in Sample A are used to plot a mean stage-by-age progression in interpersonal development.

Table 8.5 represents the range of ages for any one global stage in Sample A; informal interviews with six very young children (ages 2 to 8) are also included.

As a more complete picture of age-by-stage norms is obtained, a question of interest in any developmental assessment is how constant is the *rate* of social-conceptual growth with age. As with any system which defines, at least for the moment, a highest level or ceiling which is achieved in early adulthood, the *rate* of development will eventually decrease as adulthood approaches. Nevertheless, there may be a steady *stage rate* of growth within certain boundaries.

To obtain a preliminary cross-sectional approximation of the degree of linear development in interpersonal understanding, the IMS score of each Sample A subject was divided by his or her age in months and multiplied by 100 to yield an *Interpersonal Understanding Quotient* (IUQ). For example, three 8-year-olds whose IMS scores were 1.00, 1.50,

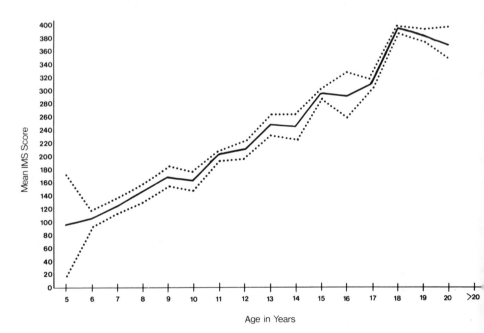

Figure 8.2. Mean IMS-by-age development (outer lines represent two standard deviations from mean).

TABLE 8.5
Range of Ages of Sample A Subjects for Each Global Stage of
Interpersonal Understanding

Stage	Range in age	N
Stage 0	2:4–5:11	6
Stage 1	4:6–12:4	60
Stage 2	6:9–15:10	98
Stage 3	11:3–Adulthood (+20)	31
Stage 4	17:8–Adulthood (+32)	36
		N = 231

and 2.00 would have IUQ scores of 1.04, 1.56, and 2.08, respectively. Table 8.6 presents the mean IUQ score of children at each year of age across the range 5 to 14. Despite variations in sample size, the IUQ appears relatively constant in this age-range, with a mean of 1.52 and a range of between 1.38 (age 10) and 1.61 (age 5). A one-way analysis of variance (1 × 10) yielded no significant differences across the 10 age-levels. This would appear to indicate fairly steady linear development across this period, on the average.

Social Class

A second demographic interest is the relation of social class to level of interpersonal understanding. Using the two-factor index devised by Hollingshead (1965), subjects were assigned to either working-class (Levels 4,3) or professional-class (Levels 2,1). Figure 8.3 presents an age-by-stage progression of interpersonal understanding in working and middle-class Sample A children, ages 7 to 14. The graph indicates that working-class children generally express lower levels of interpersonal

TABLE 8.6
Mean IUQ Scores in Sample A for Each
Age 5–14

Age	Mean IUQ score	N
5	1.61	2
6	1.43	15
7	1.50	20
8	1.50	27
9	1.57	18
10	1.38	16
11	1.54	30
12	1.47	24
13	1.60	12
14	1.46	10

understanding until about age 11 at which time their understanding develops to match that of middle-class peers. A 2 × 2 analysis of variance was performed by dichotomizing social class (middle versus working) and age (7–10 versus 11–14). Posteriori Scheffe tests were used to compute differences between particular cell means. The results indicate an interaction effect, $F(1) = 5.07$, $p = .024$, where significant differences in interpersonal understanding between middle- and working-class children occur in the age range 7 to 10, but not between the ages of 11 and 14. These findings were replicated to a degree in Sample D. Pretest IMS scores for upper-middle-class children averaged 1.82 ($SD = 30$), for working-class children 1.66 ($SD = 33$). The difference between these mean scores was significant ($p < .05$).

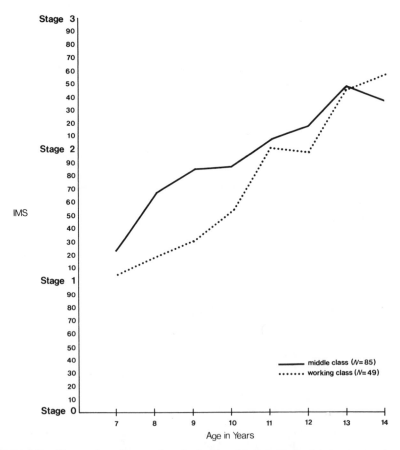

Figure 8.3. Mean stage-by-age trends in the development of interpersonal understanding in working- and middle-class children, ages 7 to 14 years.

Similar results, such that middle- or upper-middle-class subjects were found to reason at an average level that was higher than that of their working-class counterparts until early adolescence but then to reason at a similar level, were found in Sample B at Times 1 and 2. In Sample D, which did not include older children, similar results were found for younger children.

These data, as in the demographic analyses in general, are presented with the understanding that the results are suggestive, and that more systematic sampling procedures are necessary to test the hypotheses that the analyses of these initial samples suggest. However, since similar results appear in three sets of data, confidence in their replicability is increased.

A couple of speculative interpretations of these findings can be made, each of which would await further testing. First, the early advancement of middle- and upper-middle-class children over working-class children could be seen as a function of a precocity which is in turn a function of the higher average general intelligence associated with their class, a precocity that is eventually matched by working-class children. That is, the verbal precocity of the middle-class child in comparison to his or her working-class counterpart may serve the expression of concepts when those children are young, but with age be a less significant factor. Second, perhaps some relative deficits in early social experience experienced by working-class children are compensated for by increases in intensity and quality of peer interaction across social class boundaries during preadolescence which may serve as an equalizing force in the development of interpersonal understanding for both working- and middle-class children.

Sex

To assess the possibility of sex differences in interpersonal understanding, 46 Sample A female subjects were matched with 46 Sample A males on the basis of age, race, and social class. Using a two-tailed t-test for matched pairs, the difference between the male and female samples is insignificant [t (45) = 1.49, p = .20]. To evaluate the possibility of a sex-by-age interaction effect on interpersonal understanding scores, the 46 pairs were divided into four age-groups. The mean IMS scores for these age-by-sex groups are presented in Table 8.7. An interesting trend in the age-by-sex table is the early spurt in developmental scores among the youngest girls (ages 5 to 7). A t-test for the 10 matched pairs in that group was calculated; it indicated this difference was just short of significance [t (9) = 1.76, p < .10, one-tailed]. This age-related trend is consistent with other findings concerning early social development of girls which is only later matched by boys.

TABLE 8.7
Mean IMS Scores for Forty-Six Matched Pairs of Sample A Males and Females in Four Age-Ranges

Age-range in years:months	Sex		Total N
	Female	Male	
5:1–8:0	1.31 (10)[a]	1.10 (10)	20
8:3–12:8	2.08 (12)	1.97 (12)	24
15:3–18:3	3.22 (11)	3.29 (11)	22
18:6–32	3.90 (13)	3.78 (13)	26
Total N	46	46	92

[a] N's in parentheses.

No differences in IMS were found between sexes across Sample D (1.79 for boys, 1.70 for girls) at either second or third grade. These children were between 7 and 10 at the time of the assessment, corresponding most closely to the 8 to 12 range in Table 8.7; these findings replicate those obtained in Sample A.

This analysis of sex differences is also only preliminary, performed more to affirm the appropriateness of the measure for both sexes than to uncover meaningful trends in sex-related social development. Further sex-related interpersonal understanding research, as with social class analyses, must be based on more carefully selected samples from across a wide range of ages and social experiences.

Race

Differences in interpersonal understanding by race with variation in social class controlled were not found to be significant. Mean IMS scores were computed for black and white middle–upper-middle- and working-class children, and a 2 × 2 analysis of variance (race × social class) was computed. Although a significant main effect due to social class was observed [F (223, 1) = 34.1, p < .001], effects due to race [F (224, 1) = .003, p = .99] or the interaction between race and social class [F (1, 223) = .802, p = .992] were not significant.

Discussion

Several comments are in order with regard to the demographic analyses. First, as Table 8.5 demonstrates, the wide age-range at which any particular global stage may be observed makes the assumption of complete homogeneity across individual or interpersonal understanding at any particular age appear unwarranted. Second, this table indicates that the breadth of age-range found for any given global stage increases with movement up the developmental scale. This increasing breadth of age-range at higher stages suggests considerable importance is associated with social experience in stimulating individual differences in verbally expressed interpersonal understanding. Also it should be stressed that thus far, development in this area seems to be steady and linear on the average.

Perhaps the most interesting and unexpected finding is not only that there is a slower growth rate of expressed social-conceptual level in the younger working-class children as compared to middle-upper-middle-class cohorts, but also that it is rapidly remediated by the adolescent years. To the speculative interpretations made earlier, I would add that there seems to be little evidence from these data of a "critical period" for development of social understanding in "normal" children. Furthermore, the importance of natural peer-group experiences of various samples of children at different ages needs to be more closely examined to better understand the mechanisms which correspond to or facilitate higher level interpersonal understanding. It is likely that the generally observed move from family to peers as socialization agents in the preadolescent years is an important factor in providing further understanding.

In general, demographic results, when replicated repeatedly on large and varied samples should prove most useful by providing *approximate* norms or benchmarks for those who work with children whose social adjustment is inadequate. As I have repeatedly stressed, these reasoning skills and assessment methods are unlikely ever to be susceptible to precise and rigid demographic–normative description.

Analysis 3: Longitudinal Data Analysis

Longitudinal data are generally viewed as the sine qua non among findings of developmental approaches; such data are often viewed as essential if the claim of invariant sequence is to be validated. Because social understanding is a continuously but slowly developing process across major portions of each individual's lifetime, it is not surprising that longitudinal evidence is quite difficult to obtain. Existing reports of 1- and 2-year follow-up studies (Damon, 1977; Turiel, 1975; Selman, Jaquette & Lavin, 1977; Rest, 1979) support claims of sequentiality by showing that reasoning scores assigned to individuals at Time 2 are generally at a higher stage than the scores assigned at Time 1. More recently, Kuhn (1976) has made some persuasive arguments for collecting shorter term longitudinal data, measured in intervals of weeks or months, as a complement to information obtained through longer-term longitudinal studies where sampling is obtained yearly or less frequently. We have collected information on interpersonal conceptions at both "long" and "short" intervals, which I report here.

LONG-TERM DEVELOPMENTAL PATTERNS

Two follow-up assessments over 5 years do not constitute an exhaustive test of invariant sequence; still, results could be supportive or suggestive. At the least, few, if any, subjects would be expected to regress during such a time interval.

Scoring of longitudinal cases in Sample B was done blind so as not to bias assessment in favor of developmental progress. The results support an initial conclusion of longitudinal growth and invariant sequence. Table 8.8a–c illustrates the changes in global stage of interpersonal understanding from Time 1 (1974) to Time 2 (1976) and to Time 3 (1979) and from Time 2 to Time 3. As seen in Table 8.8a, over the first two years, of the 48 subjects in Sample B, 8 remained at the same global level, 20 advanced one-third of a stage, 17 advanced two-thirds of a stage and 3 moved up a full stage.

When these longitudinal data (Time 1 to Time 2) were examined separately for each of the three interpersonal domains, "stage regression" was found in 4 of 144 cases, which appears to be within the range of measurement error, given the levels of test–retest and interrater reliability reported earlier.

Table 8.8b shows the further progress of 40 of the 48 Sample B subjects from Time 2 to Time 3. One subject was coded one-third stage lower at Time 3 than at Time 2.[3] Four subjects remained at the same stage, 10 moved up one-third of a stage, 15 moved up two-thirds of a stage, 9 moved up one full stage, and 1 moved up one and two-thirds stages. The average rate and variation in rate appear to be roughly equivalent at both intervals.

Table 8.8c shows the change from Time 1 to Time 3, a 5-year interval, during which time no subject stayed at the same stage and only 7 of 40 failed to move at least one full stage. This table suggests that on average it takes children in this sample roughly 4 to 5 years to move

---

[3] As much as an anecdotal comment on adolescent life as a defense of the coherence of our system, I note that this 16-year-old subject confided to the interviewer that he was "very stoned" at the time of the interview. If his claim was not apocryphal, I believe the measurement error so engendered could be akin in magnitude to that occasioned by timing a runner when he had a broken leg. This example "in the extreme" applies also to less blatant cases. For this reason, when research moves from interview methods for descriptive purposes to interviews for assessment purposes, extreme caution is recommended.

TABLE 8.8
Changes in Global Stage of Interpersonal Understanding over Three Time Intervals in Sample B

a. Changes from Time 1 (1974) to Time 2 (1976)

		Time 2					
		1	1(2)	2(1)	2	2(3)	3(2)	3
	1	1	3	4	2	x	x	x
	1(2)		2	4	3	x	x	x
Time 1	2(1)		-	x	8	1	x	x
	2				5	4	8	1
	2(3)					x	1	1
	3(2)						x	x
								48

b. Changes from Time 2 (1976) to Time 3 (1979)

		Time 3							
		1	1(2)	2(1)	2	2(3)	3(2)	3	3(4)
	1	x	1	x	x	x	x	x	x
	1(2)		x	x	2	2	x	1	x
Time 2	2(1)			x	1	3	2	x	x
	2				3	4	6	5	x
	2(3)					x	x	3	x
	3(2)						x	4	1
	3						1	1	x
									40

c. Changes from Time 1 (1974) to Time 3 (1979)

		Time 3							
		1	1(2)	2(1)	2	2(3)	3(2)	3	3(4)
	1	x	1	x	3	4	x	1	x
	1(2)		x	x	x	5	3	1	x
Time 1	2(1)			x	3	x	3	3	x
	2				x	x	3	9	1
	2(3)					x	x	x	x
	3(2)						x	x	x
	3							x	x
									40

from Stage 2 to Stage 3 (10 of 13 subjects who were initially Stage 2 moved to at least Stage 3), but that the move from Stage 1 to Stage 2 may be accomplished more quickly [8 of 9 subjects initially at Stage 1 moved to at least Stage 2 and 5 moved beyond Stage 2 to 2(3) or even Stage 3]. Of course, most of the subjects initially at Stage 1 were younger than those at Stage 2, a fact not shown in these tables.

Our longitudinal data also provide information on the nature of the progression in logicophysical reasoning over the period from Time 1 to Time 2. Only one case of "regression" was observed out of 46 cases.

A crucial question which the collection of longitudinal data raises is to what extent does empirical evidence from longitudinal data validate or invalidate the claim of invariant sequence. Is one "aberrant case" sufficient to reject a model, or, assuming some measurement error, should reliance be placed more on statistical probabilities to make statements of confidence? Clearly such decisions must take into consideration a number of factors, such as number of longitudinal samplings (in this case, three), the time between sampling (here, 2–3 years), the method of sampling (interviews), and the demographic nature of the population sampled (urban and suburban New England children). The results presented here must be considered one step, one piece of evidence in a necessarily long- and broad-reaching effort to understand the sequential aspects of social–conceptual development.

SHORT-TERM DEVELOPMENTAL PATTERNS

Following an initial interview (Time 1), the 32 children in Sample D were reinterviewed 2 months later (Time 2) and again 5 months after the initial interview (Time 3). Table 8.9 presents the amount and direction of change from Time 1 to Times 2 and 3 for 31 subjects.[4] Over 2 months, 19 of the children interviewed stayed at the same level, 6 moved down, and 6 up. Those moving up gained up to one-half stage (+.25–+.49 IMS points). Over 5 months, about the same number (21) remained at the same level (although these may be partly different subjects than in the first comparison), none moved down, and 10 moved up one-quarter to one-half stage.

Taken as a piece, these data suggest that in this short time period, the upward shift represents the slight movement of about one-fifth to one-third of the children assessed, depending on the interval between assessments. However, it should be noted that six subjects had one-quarter stage lower scores at Time 2 than at Time 1. This needs to be considered, even as it is pointed out that we are describing a relatively small amount of downward movement.

[4] Data were unavailable on 1 of the 32 subjects.

TABLE 8.9
**Amount and Direction of Stage Change in Interpersonal Understanding in
Sample D Subjects**

Time interval	Stage change (by quarter stages)						
	$\geq -3/4$	$-1/2$	$-1/4$	0	$+1/4$	$+1/2$	$\geq +3/4$
Time 1–Time 2 (2 months)	—	—	6	19	2	4	—
Time 1–Time 3 (5 months)	—	—	—	21	6	4	—

Does the evidence for such downward movement contradict the theoretical expectation of invariant developmental sequence? Putting factors such as scoring or measurement error aside for the moment, these findings suggest that even under interview conditions, there may be more "short-term" fluctuation in the development and expression of interpersonal understanding (or of social cognition, generally) than is represented by long-term longitudinal data gathered over longer assessment intervals.

Analysis 4: Clinical–Comparative Analysis

Comparisons of developmental patterns of social reasoning across various kinds of groups, populations, or cultures are important with respect to both theoretical and practical issues. The theoretical claim of universality of stages is a bold one indeed, although in principle, formal arguments for universal characteristics of development of social reasoning can be made.

These theoretical arguments can be bolstered by empirical comparisons. Comparisons for cross-cultural differences, even from a developmental perspective, might reveal gaps so great as to weaken searches for universals. (For example, how would developmental conceptions of friendship be surveyed in a society based totally on communal relations, one that does not actively value or encourage dyadic relationships at all?) Or they might reveal close correspondences.

A second form of developmental comparison juxtaposes specific groups that may be expected to function at developmentally higher or lower levels than the general population. Thus, in addition to defining levels of interpersonal understanding, an extensive part of our research has been clinical–comparative work. Children in Sample C, referred to special schools for emotional or interpersonal difficulties, as described in

Chapter 7, were matched case-by-case with better functioning public school peers on the basis of sex, race, age (± 4 months), social class (middle–upper-middle-class or working-class), and psychometric intelligence (± 15 points) as ascertained through public school records. If an interpretation of interpersonal dysfunction in children is construed as, in part, a developmental lag in interpersonal understanding, socially troubled children should progress in interpersonal level, but lag behind their peers; however, the hierarchical and invariant characteristics of stages should still obtain.

RESULTS

Table 8.10 presents the global stage of interpersonal understanding of the 21 Sample C children at Time 1 (1974) and Time 2 (1976). In all cases, interpersonal global stage either remained the same (8/21) or increased by one (5/21), two (6/21), or three (2/21) transitional (one-third stage) steps. Twenty subjects were also assessed at both times on their logicophysical reasoning ability. As with the interpersonal understanding assessment, data indicated progress through logicophysical cognitive stages, the mean degree of change over 2 years being about one substage.

That the longitudinal evidence suggests the clinic sample develops through the same interpersonal sequence as the normative sample provides some support for our developmental model, but is not particularly informative about the function of interpersonal conceptions for disturbed children. To approach this problem, several other analyses were undertaken.

First, Sample C age–stage relations were compared with those in the

TABLE 8.10
Changes in Global Stage of Interpersonal Understanding from Time 1 (1974) to Time 2 (1976) in Sample C

		Time 2							
		1(0)	1	1(2)	2(1)	2	2(3)	3(2)	3
	1(0)	x	1	x	x	x	x	x	x
	1		4	x	2	2	x	x	x
Time 1	1(2)			3	1	1	x	x	x
	2(1)				x	3	1	x	x
	2					1	x	1	x
	2(3)						x	x	1
									21

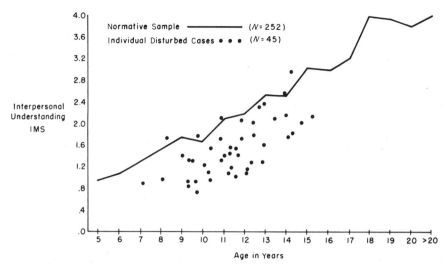

Figure 8.4. Scattergram of Sample C (clinic) cases (Time 1 and Time 2), plotted against the mean stage-by-age development trend from the normative sample.

"normal" samples. It was found that of the 45[5] Sample C interviews only five (11%) were above the age norms of the "normal" samples. Thirty-six (80%) fell two standard deviations below the age norms. Figure 8.4 indicates that in the normative sample, by approximately age 10½ years, Stage 2 interpersonal understanding is well consolidated for the average subject in the general sample. For the Sample C children, however, Stage 2 is not being used consistently until near age 13. The lag in usage for the clinic sample is about two years at that particular age and stage.

Second, matched t-test comparisons were made of the 21 public school–clinic pairs on their level of interpersonal understanding at Time 1 and Time 2. At both times the difference was significant on the basis of a one-tailed probability. At Time 1 the mean IMS among the 21 "disturbed" cases was 1.36 [Stage 1(2)] and was 1.83 [Stage 2(1)] among the 21 public school matches [t (20) = 6.23, p < .0005]. At Time 2 average IMS for the disturbed group was 1.69 [Stage 2(1)] and was 2.25 [Stage 2(3)] for the public school matches [t (20) = 5.73, p < .0005]. This pattern of a Sample C lag in interpersonal understanding recurred in each of the three interpersonal domains assessed (Individual, Friendship, Group) at

[5] Sample C originally contained 24 subjects. At Time 2 three subjects were no longer available. Thus the sample for longitudinal purposes was reduced to 21. However, the three additional Time 1 interviews provide useful data for looking at stage–age relations and are therefore included.

both Time 1 and Time 2 (see Table 8.11). All comparisons are significant using a one-tailed matched-pair t-test.

In addition, at Time 2, 11 of the 21 Sample C subjects were given the parent–child interview. A direct comparison with the matched sample is not possible here because few subjects from that sample received the parent–child interview. Nevertheless, it is possible to compare for each clinic subject the level of reasoning expressed in this domain with the reasoning expressed in the other three domains. Whereas for 18 Sample A subjects (reported earlier) no statistical difference was found between this domain and the other three, within the clinic sample, children on the average were significantly less mature, developmentally speaking, in their understanding of the parent–child relation than in their general interpersonal understanding [t (10) = 2.23, $p < .05$, two-tailed].

Third, in Table 8.12 t-tests of the statistical differences (one-tailed) between clinic and matched samples for each of the 17 assessed interpersonal issues at both Time 1 and Time 2 are presented. Of the 10 issues at Time 1 where sufficient data were accumulated to score across the entire sample, Sample C as a group performed at significantly lower levels on 8 issues. At Time 2, all issues could be scored. Out of 17 interpersonal issues, the "disturbed" group was significantly lower on 15 and close to significantly lower on a sixteenth ($p = .06$). The one issue on which the groups did not significantly differ at either testing time was "self-awareness."

TABLE 8.11
A Comparison of Twenty-One Clinic (Sample C) Subjects and Their Public School Matches— Mean Stage of Concepts in Individuals, Friendship, and Peer Group Domains

Domain	Time 1			Time 2		
	Means	SD	t-test	Means	SD	t-test
I. Individuals						
Clinic:	1.50	.48	$t(20) = 4.73$,	1.96	.60	$t(19) = 3.3$
Matched:	1.96	.40		2.35	.42	
			$p < .0005$			$p < .0015$
II. Friendship						
Clinic:	1.32	.47	$t(20) = 5.81$,	1.65	.59	$t(18) = 6.0$
Matched:	1.84	.31		2.27	.46	
			$p < .0005$			$p < .0005$
III. Peer Group						
Clinic:	1.19	.55	$t(16) = 4.72$,	1.48	.58	$t(20) = 5.8$
Matched:	1.69	.34		2.13	.43	
			$p < .0005$			$p < .0005$

TABLE 8.12

t-tests of Interpersonal Issue Scores for Twenty-One Sample C Matched Pairs at Time 1 and Time 2

Interpersonal issue	Time 1 t-tests			Time 2 t-tests		
	t value	df	p value	t value	df	p value
Subjectivity	4.61	18	<.0005	3.53	16	.0015
Self-awareness	.82	12	(not significant)	1.02	18	(not significant)
Personality	4.89	18	<.0005	1.95	18	.0335
Personality change	1.94	8	.044	3.23	15	.003
Formation (friendship)	4.20	15	<.0005	4.46	18	<.0005
Closeness–intimacy	4.10	18	<.0005	5.72	18	<.0005
Trust–reciprocity	1.71	16	.053	6.20	16	<.0005
Jealousy–exclusion	(insufficient data)			1.65	11	.0635
Conflict resolution	4.31	19	<.0005	2.70	13	.009
Termination (friendship)	(insufficient data)			2.24	14	.021
Group formation	(insufficient data)			5.06	20	<.0005
Group cohesion	(insufficient data)			3.80	18	.0005
Group conformity	1.11	7	(not significant)	3.19	11	.0045
Group rules	(insufficient data)			2.19	10	.0265
Group decisions	(insufficient data)			4.63	12	.0005
Group leadership	2.11	11	.029	2.01	15	.0315
Group termination	(insufficient data)			3.25	12	.0035

DISCUSSION

Although the aforementioned data indicate a general social–conceptual lag in the clinic sample, at the same time it should be pointed out that not all "disturbed" children function below their public school counterparts in interpersonal stage as measured through a reflective interview method. Of 21 possible comparisons, 4 clinic subjects functioned at a level comparable to their peers while the other 17 fell one transitional stage step (one-third stage) or more behind public school matches.

It is also important to compare the longitudinal growth in interpersonal understanding between the two groups. Are the "disturbed" children developing at a rate which will help bridge the gap in interpersonal understanding? Does the lag appear to be increasing as the clinic children become older? Difference scores computed between each child's IMS at Time 1 and Time 2 indicate that the gap is not growing at a significant rate. The disturbed group gained an average of .32 IMS points over 2 years while the normal group gained .42 [t (20) = 1.35, p = .191, one-tailed]. It must be remembered that children in Sample C had already been identified as "at risk" and were receiving several forms of remedial treatment (e.g., special schooling, individual psychotherapy, etc.), in ways which were not systematically controlled or examined in this study. Whether or not the gap would have been greater for a group of similarly troubled but untreated children is as yet unknown.

We have evidence of a generally lower level of expressed interpersonal understanding in the clinic sample. However, some practitioners and theorists (e.g., Redl, 1956) have described the child with interpersonal difficulties not so much as lagging in social acuity as being more inconsistent in utilization of interpersonal insights. The child may occasionally demonstrate high-level abilities, but more often than a normal child will regress to use of less adequate interpersonal conceptions. This distinction calls to mind differences between performance and capability. Because the IMS here is the *average* stage of interpersonal conception across 17 issues, it might be said to measure *performance* under *interview conditions*. A measure of *capability* can be obtained by looking at the child's *highest* individual score, without averaging it with other lower scores. For the 21 pairs, the highest stage score found for a single issue at Time 2 was recorded. In comparing these *highest capability* scores in each pair, it was found that in only six cases did the public school child demonstrate a higher interpersonal *capability*, as compared to the previously mentioned 17 pairs in which the public school match's *overall* interpersonal global score was higher than that of the clinic child. In other words, in only 6 out of 17 matched pairs in which there was a clinical lag in *performance* was the difference associated with differences in maximum *capability* as assessed. The other 11 cases of clinical lag (in

IMS) appeared to be a function of the disturbed child *performing* across the issues at a level lower than his capacity; nevertheless, this difference in capability is still significant using a one-tailed matched pair t-test $[t (20) = 2.82, p < .02]$.

The qualities of interpersonal understanding among disturbed children may, therefore, be marked by an inconsistency in functioning, whereby higher capabilities are accompanied by lower stage oscillations. If this is true, one would expect a greater frequency of large-scale departures (among disturbed children's issue scores) from their overall global scores. To assess this possibility, the percentages of issue scores one full stage or more from a subject's global stage were recorded for the 21 disturbed children and their matches. For example, a subject with a global score of Stage 3(2), and issue scores of 3(2), 3(2), 2(3), and 2(1), would be recorded as having one out of four or 25% of issue scores one stage or more away from his or her global stage. Such departures from global stage were relatively rare, but significantly more prevalent among the disturbed children than their matches. Seven percent of the disturbed group's issue scores departed one stage or more from global scores while only 1% of the normal children's issue scores did so $[t (20) = 2.40, p < .023$, one-tailed].

An interesting finding in issue-score comparisons of clinic and matched children is the lack of a significant difference between groups on the issue of self-awareness. With comparisons on 17 issues, one might expect to find one nonsignificant difference in issue-score at the .05 level of chance alone; however, the fact that conceptions of self-awareness did not differ significantly in the two samples at either test period suggests it is a stable occurrence. This result may be a function of the individual psychotherapy received by most of the clinic sample and focused on helping these children to be aware of thoughts, feelings, and insights (see Chapter 10). If so, these findings point to ways in which structured experience can stimulate social–cognitive development. This finding also points to the distinction that needs to be made between the maturity of *reflective thought* about social or psychological experience (e.g., "concepts of self-awareness," etc.) and the *functional expression* of that experience or phenomenon (e.g., "self-concept" in the sense of self-esteem or how one feels about oneself). While these clinic children showed good understanding of the human capacity for self-awareness, they still tended to have difficulty acting in a way that could be described as self-aware. In addition sensitivity to the process of self-awareness did not indicate anything about these children's self-concept or self-esteem. The general question which is raised here is what is the relation between a child's developmental level of reflective understanding about an issue or category and how that child functions or operates within that category, a question to be addressed in Part IV, Chapters 9 and 10.

Analysis 5: Relating Interpersonal Understanding and Behavior Ratings

In an earlier study using data collected on Sample B at Time 1, it was reported that *positive* peer sociometric ratings did not correlate significantly with interpersonal understanding stage, but that increasing *negative* judgment by peers of a child correlated negatively and significantly with an increasing level of interpersonal conception (Selman, 1976b). This evidence was interpreted to mean that those children who could express only relatively low levels of interpersonal understanding were, in general, thought poorly of by peers, but that children with adequate or "normal" levels of expressed interpersonal conceptions might be either liked or disliked by peers. In this sense adequate or "normal" level of interpersonal understanding was viewed as a necessary but by no means sufficient condition for positive peer evaluation. Good interpersonal conceptual ability does not differentiate children in their peers' judgment although poor interpersonal conceptual ability apparently does. To parallel these positive and negative *peer* sociometric ratings of Time 1, *teachers* were asked to assess positive and negative behaviors at Time 2.

RESULTS

At Time 2, using 44 Sample B subjects and 17 Sample C subjects, the relation between teacher ratings of children's strengths and weaknesses and their level of interpersonal understanding was examined, using two student rating scales for teachers, the Health Resources Inventory (HRI, rating strengths) and the Classroom Adjustment Rating Scales (CARS, rating weaknesses).

These teacher ratings are not developmental, that is, the 1 to 5 ratings as to how well adjusted a student is are used across all grades, and therefore, in effect, students are being evaluated relative to other students in their age–class cohort. Furthermore, the sample consisted of subjects from a range of grades. Therefore, correlations between the IUQ (IMS score divided by chronological age) and teacher ratings are reported rather than the correlations of IMS scores and teacher ratings. Tables 8.13 and 8.14 report the correlation between IUQ and the CARS and HRI, for both Sample B and Sample C subjects.

The results are striking; they indicate that the IUQ scores had little systematic relation with the teachers' assessments of *negative* social adjustment problems (CARS), but consistently, positively, and two-thirds of the time significantly correlated with teachers' perceptions of children's *strengths* (HRI).

TABLE 8.13
Correlations between CARS Ratings (by Categories and Total) and IUQ Scores (Global and Each Domain) for Public School (B) and Clinic School (C) Samples

CARS Scales	IUQ	Individuals	Friends	Group
Sample B (N = 44)				
Acting out	-.08	-.08	.06	-.10
Shy/anxious/moody	.02	-.11	.31	-.02
Learning problem	.01	-.04	.22	-.10
Total	-.01	-.08	.26	-.06
		None significant at .05		
Sample C (N = 17)				
Acting out	-.11	-.07	-.10	-.17
Shy/anxious/moody	-.12	.13	.20	.02
Learning problem	.10	.15	.20	-.04
Total	.09	.12	.16	-.03
		None significant at .05		

TABLE 8.14
Correlations between HRI Factors and IUQ (Global and Each Domain) for Public School (B) and Clinic School (C) Samples

HRI Factor	IUQ	Individuals	Friends	Group
Sample B (N = 44)				
Good student	.48 (.03)[a]	.57 (.008)	.25 (.16)	.38 (.07)
Gutsy	.50 (.02)	.72 (.001)	.07 (.38)	.43 (.04)
Peer sociability	.57 (.007)	.74 (.001)	.51 (.24)	.52 (.02)
Rules	.51 (.01)	.46 (.03)	.46 (.02)	.40 (.05)
Frustration tolerance	.43 (.04)	.49 (.02)	.21 (.20)	.39 (.02)
Sample C (N = 17)				
Good student	.50 (.02)	.29 (.12)	.54 (.01)	.48 (.006)
Gutsy	.38 (.06)	.24 (.18)	.34 (.09)	.50 (.01)
Peer sociability	.30 (.11)	.26 (.15)	.33 (.10)	.29 (.12)
Rules	.46 (.02)	.28 (.13)	.57 (.01)	.42 (.02)
Frustration tolerance	.53 (.01)	.42 (.04)	.55 (.01)	.53 (.01)

[a] Significance levels in parentheses.

To better understand the factors that contributed to the significant HRI–IUQ correlations, in each sample the mean HRI and IUQ figures were calculated. Subjects in each sample were then categorized: high IUQ–high HRI, high IUQ–low HRI, etc. Subjects then fell into cells as shown in Table 8.15. Chi-squares reveal significant relations between IUQ and HRI, confirming the findings in Table 8.14. Beyond this, however, we hoped to characterize the students falling into each category (high-high, high-low, etc.). If a general necessary but not sufficient relationship exists between higher levels of interpersonal understanding and greater maturity or adequacy in some forms or aspects of social functioning, then one would expect few if any subjects to be found in the low IUQ–high HRI cell. However, some children did fall there, and we were especially interested in looking closely at them.

A clinical analysis of each subject was undertaken, including an examination of each teacher's ratings on each item on the CARS and HRI. As might be expected, the 15 Sample B and 6 Sample C subjects who scored high IUQ–high HRI were the most socially effective and competent and best functioning children in their respective groups. In Sample C, they proved to be children who, from a clinical perspective, had the least pervasive social–emotional problems, and were viewed by clinic staff as ready for reentry into the public schools. The 15 Sample B and 6 Sample C subjects who scored low IUQ–low HRI tended to be at the bot-

TABLE 8.15
2 × 2 Contingency Analysis of High and Low IUQ and HRI Scores (Mean Splits) in Samples B and C

Public School Sample (B) (N = 44)

HRI ($\bar{X}$ = 175)

IUQ ($\bar{X}$ = 1.52)		High	Low
	High	15	6
	Low	8	15

χ^2 = 4.53, p < .025

Clinic School Sample (C) (N = 17)

HRI ($\bar{X}$ = 146)

IUQ ($\bar{X}$ = 1.16)		High	Low
	High	6	4
	Low	1	6

χ^2 = 2.24, p < .05

tom of the heap in their functioning relative to their peers, with "normal"–"disturbed" differences being of degree. The 6 Sample B and 4 Sample C students who scored high IUQ–low HRI tended to be older children (in junior high school) and somewhat anti-authority in attitude (low on items such as "follows class rules," high on "clowns around"). In the "disturbed" sample, this group was particularly unstable and rebellious. The 8 Sample B and 1 Sample C students in the low IUQ–high HRI category tended to be younger children with modest learning skills and who were quiet and conformist in class behavior (e.g., high scores on "overconforms to rules," "is polite and courteous"). These children, our particular interest, will be discussed.

DISCUSSION

These data exemplify the complexities of trying to understand the relationship between level of interpersonal understanding and behavioral assessments. The "hypothesis" that adequate interpersonal reasoning is necessary but not sufficient for mature or adequate social behavior is hard to examine without a detailed specification of what constitutes such behavior. As the data indicate, even though positively rated classroom behavior relates to higher level of interpersonal understanding, some students with low level understanding were judged by teachers to "behave quite well," if not maturely. I would like to suggest that one reason for the presence of subjects in this low IUQ–high HRI cell is that the HRI does not for these children reflect truly mature behavior, but "well-behaved," low-profile behavior which would not seem to require especially good social reasoning. Be that as it may, it is still difficult to assess such issues, even with more accurate definitions and measures. The relation of reasoning and behavior, taken up in Chapters 9 and 10, is an extremely important area for further investigation.

The closer analysis also indicates that the clinic sample comprises several categories of children. While, as a group, the clinic children express lower levels of interpersonal understanding than matched peers, it also appears that *within* that clinic sample the student seen as "better adjusted" from a clinical perspective also conceptualizes social relations better. Clearly, what is needed for a more meaningful analysis of the relation of social–cognitive level and behavior is a way to characterize the structure of interpersonal behavior within a developmental framework, to try to identify ways of understanding and assessing age-related pro- and antisocial manifestations of social maturity.

The finding that positive teacher rating related positively to interpersonal level but that degree of negative adjustment did not relate either negatively or positively is difficult to interpret. One partial explanation may be the same as was put forth for the findings with relation to peer sociometric choice. Although children with poor understanding also have behavioral difficulties, children with an adequate or normative level of interpersonal understanding still may exhibit school adjustment difficulties related to factors other than their social–cognitive competence, thus reducing direct correlations of the CARS to IUQ. However, as we saw in a clinical examination of the individual HRI–IUQ scores, simple explanations are not sufficient.

An Interim Summary

The information from projects such as ours studying social development speaks to various concerns along a continuum bounded on one end by theoretical models (generating questions such as whether development is continuous or discrete) and on the other end by behavioral description (generating questions such as what the average 5-year-old thinks makes someone a good friend). That these poles are seen as connected in a continuum rather than as independent concerns is one of the guiding principles behind our research.

However, it is sometimes refreshing to shelve theoretical considerations for a while and consider, without too much qualification, what data suggest about the social realities and capabilities of growing children. In concluding this chapter and Part III, I first review what are, to me, the more interesting "child-study" findings from our research. Then, in part as a way to introduce Part IV, I consider what theoretical questions have been raised by our research findings and some alternative methods for their study.

SOME THOUGHTS ON CHILD DEVELOPMENT

From the point of view of childhood development, five areas of our findings merit repetition and further discussion: (a) the ages at which the average child is capable of the kind of interpersonal understanding characterized by each stage; (b) the differential growth rate in interpersonal understanding across the three domains assessed, and what these differences might mean about the social *experiences* of the average American child; (c) the differential growth rate in interpersonal understanding between two broadly defined socioeconomic groups, middle–upper-middle- and working-class; (d) the susceptibility of interpersonal understanding to planned stimulation, as suggested by findings from our clinical–comparative analysis; and (e) the shift from one stage to the next, particularly from Stage 2 to 3, whether in synchrony with one's peers or not.

Age Norms for Stages

Our data indicate that by the age of 6 the average American child is capable of expressing Stage 1 interpersonal concepts, by 11 Stage 2, and by 15 Stage 3. Under interview conditions, there appears to be some developmental coherence in each individual and as Figure 8.2 suggests, (group average) interpersonal understanding development is fairly linear (with a regression coefficient of .79 and this linear trend accounting for 71% of the variance in stage over time). Furthermore, there does not appear to be any particular age at which a new stage rapidly emerges for children as a group.

Of course, it is important to remember that these norms, in keeping with the data collection procedures of these studies, describe the child's growing ability to *reflect* upon interpersonal experience, and not necessarily the earliest age at which children "have" certain interpersonal concepts. Having a concept and being able to reflect upon and express that concept are related but distinct modes of functioning. Therefore it should not be surprising to find that children, or adults for that matter, sometimes demonstrate in their natural social discourse and conversation, more mature conceptions than those they seem able to express in the context of a clinical interview.

These norms are best thought of as rough benchmarks for when the average child has *consolidated* a particular stage of interpersonal understanding, and is in fact probably on the way to making the conceptual discoveries inherent in the next level. It seems useful to suggest, using broad brush strokes, that the late preschool and early elementary grades are characterized by a one-way or action-reciprocity orientation, that the middle childhood and early preadolescent years are generally characterized by an orientation focused on interactions made possible by coordination of bilateral thoughts and social relations, and that preadolescence and early adolescence are marked by the construction of a theory of interpersonal relations based on the understanding of collaboration and mutual expectations.[6]

As very rough norms, these age-ranges can give educators and clinicians very rough notions of "deviant" development in this area, whether it is retarded or advanced. But as of yet this must be approached with caution, because as is suggested in Table 8.5, across individuals, there

---

[6] Our data on earlier and later stages (0 and 4) are more sparse. However, if we draw on the works of other researchers who have used the structural approach in domains closely associated with those we have chosen (cf. Broughton, 1978; Damon, 1977; Kohlberg, 1969), it seems safe to suggest that Stage 0 physicalistic notions grossly but fairly characterize the younger preschoolers' attitudes toward friends and relations and that for those who will indeed develop to Stage 4 thinking, adolescence is the time at which that transitional process will begin.

are wide variations in the age-period at which each stage emerges, and not surprisingly, these variations appear to increase with age and experience.

Unlike our evidence that level of perspective taking does not appear to show great variation in adulthood (data reported in Chapter 2 indicated most adults we sampled achieved Level 4), what limited adult evidence we do have suggests much greater individual variation in the highest stage of interpersonal understanding achieved by adults in our contemporary society. The work of Loevinger (1976), which has important parallels to our own, particularly in adulthood, also suggests this.[7]

Cross-Domain Asynchrony in Younger Children

It is both practically and theoretically interesting to note that although there are fewer *overall* differences in level of reasoning among children in the early years, there is also at this period evidence of greater developmental isolation *among* concepts *within* the minds of any one child. As Figure 8.1 suggests, young children apparently show the greatest variation in developmental level across the three domains studied. As suggested earlier, this variation appears to be largely a function of the poorer understanding, relatively speaking, that young children have of peer-group experiences and concepts.

From a theoretical perspective this finding is compatible with both Wernerian and Piagetian notions of greater synchrony and integration of parts into wholes with development. From a practical or child psychology perspective, this finding raises a different question. To what extent is the observed early lag in the development of peer-group understanding a function of the experiences of the children in our sample, a sample that is fairly representative of children in America, and to what extent is it a function of some inherently greater complexity of the nature and therefore the conceptions of group dynamics? It is not necessary that these two "explanations" be seen as mutually exclusive. If the experience of group organization is inherently more complex, universally, than that of dyadic relations, this might be reflected in the rate at which concepts in this area develop. One cannot help but wonder, however, how well these findings would hold up in a social milieu more consciously oriented to providing planned group experiences for children at an early age (cf. Bronfenbrenner, 1970).

---

[7] If these norms are accurate, the implications for endeavors such as psychotherapy, counseling, or consciousness raising, which are often based on the assumption that a client can understand some very sophisticated interpersonal concepts, may need to be reexamined more carefully (see also Chapter 10).

Social Class, Social Experience, and Interpersonal Understanding

In our data there is evidence that broadly defined social-experience variables are related to variations in the development of interpersonal understanding. For instance we twice found that *younger* children from working-class backgrounds were expressing lower stage concepts than their middle–upper-middle-class cohorts but that by the age of about 11, these social class differences began to disappear. (Judging from the slopes in Figure 8.3, it appears that the working-class children begin to "catch up" with their middle-class peers rather than that the middle-class children "catch down.")

An examination of the themes and aspects used by subjects from each social-class sample in discussing interpersonal issues did not reveal any obvious differences in the *content* of the responses between these two groups. Working-class children did *not* suggest themes and aspects that differed from those middle-class children used. Even so, one might wonder whether the system itself was biased to code those themes, attitudes, or perceptions which tended to be used more often by working-class children as being lower level. If so, the observed developmental differences would actually be artifactual.

There are several reasons why I think this is not the case in this instance. First, our reliance on a structural perspective-taking model guards in part against this kind of possible content or value based bias. In an earlier study (Selman, 1976b) perspective-taking level, as defined here, was found *not* to relate to social class differences. To the extent that our interpersonal concept stage code rests upon this formal or "neutral" social–cognitive model, it receives some protection from the accusation of social-class value bias. Second, if these social class findings represent only a content–structure confusion, how does one explain the catch-up effect we have twice observed? It is hard to account, other than developmentally, for the fact that the themes, aspects, and concepts used by the 7- (or 9-) year-old working-class child tend to be the same concepts used by the 5- (or 7-) year-old middle–upper-middle-class child. In other words, we do not find *different* themes, aspects, or concepts for the two different social classes, but the consistent use of the *same* concepts by the different social classes at different ages.

Assuming then a lack of class-value bias, how is the catch-up phenomenon to be understood? If this is not a representation of the homogenization of the American culture to middle-class values through media, school, and other forces of socialization, what is an alternative explanation? It has been suggested by the early research of workers such as Hoffman and Saltztein (1967) that middle–upper-middle-class parents use early childrearing techniques that are oriented heavily toward reflection. Such an atmosphere would not only be good training for doing well on a reflective interview, but generally an advantage or head start for young children in stimulating the kind of thinking (and verbal skills) necessary to ordering social experience in general. In addition, it is possible that the peer interaction of young children from middle–upper-middle-class backgrounds, while although no more frequent than that of children in working-class neighborhoods, may be more structured and planned on the part of adults, for example, nursery school, etc. This would probably give the younger middle-class child an experiential advantage in thinking about and responding to the kinds of questions we ask in our interview (e.g., in talking about "group time").

By preadolescence, however, children from both social classes may be literally out of the house and into the streets. Perhaps it is the street life of the working-class preadolescent that provides the experiential impetus for the catch up we have twice observed. While one can argue that working-class children are "out in the street" interacting with peers at a much earlier age than their middle-class cohorts, it may be that it is not until preadolescence, when "in the street" takes on a kind of stoop-sitting reflection, that the working-class children become involved in the kind of street talk that would facilitate competence on an interview procedure such as ours.

Stimulation of Interpersonal Understanding

If, in our clinical–comparative study, we could have obtained a sample of the interpersonal reasoning of a group of children similar in all critical respects to the clinic (C) and matched (from B) samples but who were *not* in some kind of special treatment, we might have been able to get a better estimate of the diagnostic power of our analysis. However, one unexpected and highly suggestive finding was that the Sample C children did as well as the matched group in their thinking about the issue of self-awareness. On the one hand this result suggests that development of social or psychological concepts is amenable to stimulation. The process of psychotherapy with the children in our clinic sample may have oriented them to focusing on self-awareness and self-reflection, thus raising their consciousness on this issue. On the other hand, the developmental immaturity of these children on the other issues in the interpersonal system makes one speculate that the focus of psychotherapy is too narrow to be considered both an *intensive* and a *broad-reaching* treatment program.

These results also point to the importance of keeping clear the difference between the child's conception of some social or psychological experience and that child's actual functioning in that area. To understand the nature of self-awareness does not guarantee that an individual will be *functionally* self-aware. On the other hand, not to have a developmentally adequate conception of self-awareness would, I believe, eventually make for a distorted perception of self.

Speculations on a Stage Transition

It is well known to developmental psychologists that a cross-sectional analysis across ages can mask critical individual growth patterns and their correlates. A particular developmental hypothesis that would not necessarily be evident in cross-sectional data analyses was posed by Sullivan 25 years ago in his interpersonal theory of psychiatry (1953). Drawing upon his clinical observations, he called attention to the importance of the transition in preadolescence from the juvenile (roughly equivalent to Stage 2) to the preadolescent (similar in nature to Stage 3) periods. Sullivan labeled this healthy shift in preadolescence a continental divide in the sphere of interpersonal relations and he predicted that for those who do not negotiate this transition successfully, other people would continue to be viewed only as sources of self-gratification or frustration. Behaviorally, Sullivan described the successful shift from the juvenile to the preadolescent period as a shift from *cooperation* to *collaboration.*

> Now this preadolescent collaboration is distinctly different from the acquisition, in the juvenile era, of habits of competition, cooperation, and compromise. In preadolescence not only do people occupy themselves in moving toward a common more-or-less impersonal objective, such as the success of "our team". . . but they also move toward supplying each other with satisfaction and taking on each other's successes in the maintenance of prestige, status, and all things which represent freedom from anxiety [1953, p.246].

The shift from cooperation to collaboration in interpersonal relations appears to have properties structurally parallel to the shift from reciprocity to mutuality in interpersonal reasoning. Within Sullivan's framework this preadolescent shift occurs as a function of the development of intimate chumship relations. Data from our Time 3 interviews in our longitudinal sample may help us to more closely examine this transition. For example, are there identifiable patterns whereby children whose interpersonal concepts are at first advanced and later stay advanced, or children whose concepts are at first advanced and later fall behind, or children whose concepts are at first behind and later become advanced, etc.? Can a group of children be identified who have a great deal of difficulty negotiating this transition?

DEVELOPMENTAL THEORY, METHODS, AND APPLICATION

The transition between this chapter and the forthcoming ones marks a shift from the second phase, designed to evaluate whether the stage analyses of developing interpersonal conceptions satisfy the essential formal and theoretical criteria of structured wholeness, invariant developmental sequence, and universality, to a third phase wherein the model of interpersonal understanding is applied to an analysis of the functional, spontaneous, and natural social comments and social interactions of individual children. The data in this part (III) indicate our method of assessment is reasonably reliable and our model does appear thus far to meet criteria of structured wholeness, invariant sequence, and some limited "universality" (cross-class and cross-social adjustment rather than cross-cultural universality). Parts II and III on Phases 1 and 2 have stressed data and theorizing whose major purpose is the *description* of the formal characteristics of a developmental sequence of social conceptions. The next step is research directed toward understanding the functional *applications* of the developmental model.

By distinguishing between formal and functional analyses, the intention is to emphasize the need to understand the individual's application of developmental levels of interpersonal understanding in actual or natural social settings and interactions. Formal or structural developmental descriptions are by no means seen as incorrect, but as insufficient to the task of understanding how each *individual* uses his or her concepts and reasoning abilities in everyday behavior (Flavell & Wohlwill, 1969; Selman & Jaquette, 1978). The research described in Part IV highlights three critical, recurring, and interrelated methodological and conceptual concerns which require both further conceptualization and fresh empirical approaches.

Hypothetical versus Natural Reasoning

A major concern is the relation of the level of interpersonal understanding expressed in a reflective interview about a hypothetical situation and the level of understanding expressed in natural conditions, that is, during the course of the child's daily social interactions. Can one expect the two levels to be the same, or would one predict that reflective reasoning would generally be at a higher level "use" following "capacity"?

These questions are critical to a better understanding of the distinctions between capability and performance. Further evidence is needed to be able to say that a child "is at" a particular stage or "has a specific concept" in real-life functioning.

Fluctuations in Interpersonal Understanding

Although many developmental psychologists recognize that formal analyses can be applied to social concepts, many of the most thoughtful are hesitant to accept the claim that stage models capture the complexity of social development in a psychologically realistic way (Flavell,

1977). Research reviews appear to indicate too much variability when either context or content are manipulated (Shantz, 1975). Therefore, another concern of those using stage models as working hypotheses is whether or to what extent fluctuations occur in an individual's level of reasoning under various variations in conditions. Do some people fluctuate in reasoning level more than others? Do certain situations tend to create greater fluctuations than others? What are the interactive processes involved? Can research generate information which will help to characterize either typical or abnormal degrees of fluctuation, consequently informing as to the functional utility of the model?

Observation of Level of "Interpersonal Action"

Naturalistic observational approaches are needed to allow researchers to investigate whether over time certain interpersonal strategies, behaviors, and interactions can also be logically structurally analyzed and developmentally ordered in such a way as to characterize and compare actions developmentally and whether behavior (qua nonverbally expressed natural reasoning) so described can be meaningfully related to reasoning as described.

In Part IV I describe ways that each of these major concerns, derived from the analytic review of developmental theory and research, are explored within a naturalistic–developmental–clinical paradigm that emphasizes the design of planned social experiences and assessment procedures in a way that will provide direct feedback into theoretical questions. It should be stressed that I perceive the studies to be described in the next two chapters as clinical in three ways. First, they are clinical in the psychiatric sense that most of the subjects whose "applied" level of interpersonal understanding is being explored are socially and psychologically troubled children, children with a track record of interpersonal difficulties with peers and adults alike. Second, the studies are clinical in that they are case studies, the first a case study of one small group of preadolescent children observed weekly over a year-long period in class meetings and discussions and the others case studies of single children. Finally, they are clinical in that they are exploratory; the tools used to assess interpersonal understanding-in-use are still in their methodological infancy. Not only do these clinical reports explore ways to stretch stage analysis to the limits of practicality and tolerance, they also stretch the model and methods to new contexts such that one begins to see more clearly the most vulnerable parts of the fabric of which the model is constructed.

Part IV

INTERPERSONAL UNDERSTANDING— PHASE 3: APPLICATION

A Case Study of
Social-Cognitive Development
in a Naturalistic Setting

Daniel S. Jaquette

Harvard Graduate School of Education
Cambridge, Massachusetts
Charles River Counseling Center
Wellesley, Massachusetts

Background

In discussing ontogenesis, Flavell and Wohlwill (1969) distinguish between what they call *formal* and *functional* analyses of development. Formal analyses are descriptive characterizations of "the successive outputs" composing an ontogenetic sequence. Functional analyses deal with how individuals progress through or utilize a given formal scale. A formal analysis provides the researcher with an ordinal, developmental scale. However, it does not predict how individuals will perform. A functional analysis is dynamic, referring to processes of individual change and performance. This distinction has been stressed throughout this book. However, the majority of research in social cognition has been formal with little energy devoted thus far to functional analyses of how individuals utilize the formal sequences. This lack of follow-up functional analysis seriously hampers the ultimate utility of the formal analysis. The study I report in this chapter was designed to address the problem of functional analysis of social reasoning in naturalistic settings.

In the reflective interview used in formal analyses, a subject meets with an interviewer in a situation carefully structured to reduce anxiety associated with testing and minimize outside distraction and stimulation. The rationale is that this structure helps to control factors that might influence the child's cognitive performance. The researcher either introduces a hypothetical situation as a stimulus or begins by asking structured questions. The reflective interview method is probably the best choice we have so far when the goal is a formal analysis of stage development, because it allows the researcher considerable flexibility in helping the child to articulate social concepts. However, the reflective interview also imposes specific limitations on the conclusions it permits beyond formal stage description.

A particular characteristic of the reflective interview is that it appears to tap social cognition under optimal conditions, providing more a measure of competence than performance (Brown, 1975). Two aspects of the interview approach differ from what might be considered real-life reasoning. First, the *content* of questions usually pertains to distant or hypothetical situations. Second, the *context* of the interview is in most cases a private, one-to-one setting. Because of its "unnatural" content and context, as well-suited as the reflective interview method is for formal, stage-descriptive analysis, it is often only marginally relevant to the conditions under which most people normally *utilize* or develop their cognitive abilities.

For this reason, the study of interpersonal understanding, as it evolves into a study of naturalistic interpersonal functioning, needs a method better suited to functional analysis. Just as it can no longer suffice to say that a child "is at" a particular level or "has" a particular ability, a method in which performance factors are not considered is no longer adequate. A more flexible assessment strategy which allows for naturalistic observation is required to assess functional development.

The three objectives of this study were (a) to develop a method for observing natural social reasoning; (b) to relate reflective reasoning to natural reasoning; and (c) to examine transition in natural reasoning "close up" with a time series analysis of weekly observations over an 8-month period. In the rest of this section I discuss naturalistic methods and some ideas about studying developmental transition.

METHODS FOR ASSESSING DEVELOPMENT IN THE NATURAL ENVIRONMENT

Developmental research should reflect conditions within the natural environment, especially considering the importance of an ecological perspective for understanding human development (Blurton-Jones, 1972; Kuhn, 1974; Willems, 1973). However, McCall (1977) concludes that the methodology required for a naturalistic approach has been neglected in favor of more contrived manipulative approaches.

We essentially lack a science of natural development processes because few studies are concerned with development as it transpires in naturalistic environments. This problem is believed to derive from the veneration of manipulative experimental methods, which have come to dictate rather than serve research questions [1977, p. 333].

Two areas of developmental research traditionally have employed naturalistic methods of observation: cross-cultural studies of cognition (Cole, Gay, Glick, & Sharp, 1971; Cole & Scribner, 1974) and research with preschool children (Mueller & Brenner, 1977; Wellman & Lempers, 1977). In both cases, subjects have little understanding of the "testing" situation. Therefore, alternatives had to be developed to tap performance in a systematic way.

More relevant for us, however, is the status of structural–developmental research using naturalistic methods with older children, adolescents, and adults. Three naturalistic approaches so far employed are of interest here. First, Kuhn and Brannock (1977) designed the "plant problem" to assess Piaget's stages of intellectual development naturalistically. They claim that previous assessment devices required the subject to manipulate a single variable while holding all others constant. Four live plants are presented to the subject, two quite healthy and two obviously in poor health. The subject is required to determine which variables (plant food, water, or "leaf lotion") affect plant health. The goal of this study is to duplicate the multivariate characteristics of the natural physical environment. The authors report emergence of formal operations is delayed in the more naturalistic problem because of the greater complexity of the natural environment.

Although this study moves towards more naturalistic methods, I feel it fails to match the content and context of the natural environment in three important ways. First, the problem is imposed on the subject and does not represent the individual's spontaneous use of intellectual operations. Despite countless studies of cognitive development, little research to date has simply gone to the field to observe how the child employs his intellectual talents on the playground, how the auto mechanic isolates the problem in a faltering car, or how the student uses formal operations in a physics problem. A second limitation concerns the "multivariate" nature of the problem. Despite the presence of several variables, one factor, plant food, accounts for the total outcome, just as it did in Inhelder and Piaget's (1958) original pendulum, rods, and chemical problems. This single-solution characteristic is too simplistic to match naturalistic conditions. A third limitation is the assessment context itself. An isolated setting, a facilitating interviewer, and a generally motivated subject are hardly the naturalistic conditions under which cognitive activity normally proceeds.

A second study is Kohlberg's assessment of moral atmosphere (Kohlberg, Sharf, & Hickey, 1972). The approach used is to interview a subject concerning various aspects of some relevant real-life situation, for example, the moral atmosphere of a prisoner's correctional institution or a student's school. While the interview pertains to the subjects' real environment, including questions about specific justice and community concerns, for purposes of assessing natural functioning, however, moral atmosphere interviews have one serious limitation. They are interviews. The subject's perceptions of the justice structure are obtained in a one-to-one reflective discussion with a trusted participant–observer. Follow-up questions facilitate the subject's thinking processes. If the goal is to understand how individuals *employ* social–cognitive abilities, then the reflective-interview assessment procedure is perhaps not the best choice. A naturalistic context for eliciting and observing social reasoning should look at the individual *in the act* of solving problems.

Reflective interviews about real-life events provide a rather simple extension of previous methods for studying "real-life" social reasoning. But is it real-life? This problem is well demonstrated in research on "real-life" sharing reasoning reported by Damon (1977) and Damon and Gerson (1975). Children aged 4 to 10 were placed in groups of three with one additional younger child and instructed to make bracelets in order to earn a prize of candy. After 20 minutes, the younger child was removed from the group. The three remaining children were asked both individually and then again as a group how 10 candy bars should be distributed among the bracelet-makers. Each child's "real-life" distributive justice reasoning during both individual and group sessions was tape-recorded. However, Damon (1977) reports "though it was not possible to obtain reliable scores for children's reasoning in the group sessions, a 'real-life' reasoning score was obtained for each child from the *individual interviews* [p. 105]." Thus, ultimately it is a reflective, one-to-one interview about a contrived event which forms the basis of Damon's observations of "real-life" reasoning. His attempt to study the effects of naturalistic factors such as self-interest on children's real-life moral judgment rests on the assumption that situational effects produced in a peer group context carry over to a reflective one-to-one interview. This assumption may well be unwarranted, because some of the specific constraints on reasoning within a real-life group setting, such as peer conformity effects, cannot be reproduced in the reflective interview debriefing. Thus in the last analysis, neither content nor context are truly naturalistic.

In summary, to more closely approximate a naturalistic content and context, three conditions must be met. First, the assessment problem should be one spontaneously encountered by the subject and not imposed by the experimenter. Second, the entire spontaneous activity of the subject should be observed without interference as a complex of naturalistic conceptions rather than dismantled in favor of more unidimensional variables. Third, and most important, naturalistic interpersonal functioning should be assessed as it occurs in the subject's actual, real-life environment.

SHORT-TERM STUDY OF DEVELOPMENTAL TRANSITION

The central thesis of this section is that developmental research often neglects the study of microgenetic development over short periods of transition in favor of long-term intermittent longitudinal research and assessment of pre- and posttest changes. Wohlwill (1970a, 1970b, 1973) argues that the main goal of developmental psychology ought to be the analysis of growth patterns over time. This change is not simply the difference between two scores, but rather a continual relationship of age, time, and the developmental process under investigation.

What approaches have been employed to describe patterns of development? A first method has been to approximate developmental progression by cross-sectional assessment of individuals at various ages. However, the analysis of group differences suffers from a number of methodological problems, such as cohort effects, which reduce its usefulness in describing developmental change. A second approach has been to design long-term longitudinal research which samples development intermittently at 1-, 2-, or 3-year intervals, which informs about the sequentiality of the formal progressive scale. In addition, combining cross-sectional and longitudinal approaches helps to weed out cohort effects from truly developmental responses. However, the description of long-term development provides little detail of the actual functional processes of change and stage transition, nor is it intended to.

Inhelder and her colleagues (Inhelder & Sinclair, 1969; Inhelder, Sinclair, & Bovet, 1974) utilize a third method, intensive short-term observations, to capture the process of developmental transition. Children undergo short-term learning procedures pertaining to the development of conservation and transitivity. The goal is to gain "insight into the transition mechanisms" of development (Inhelder *et al.*, 1974) through careful microanalysis. Inhelder and Sinclair (1969) conclude about this analysis of developmental transition: "As in all our learning experiments, the reactions of the children during the learning sessions show us, as through a magnifying glass, the step-by-step developmental processes [p. 18]."

A fourth approach to the process of developmental transition is the short-term stimulation study (Blatt & Kohlberg, 1975; Brion-Meisels, 1977; Chandler, 1973; Cooney, 1977). Specific instructional materials or techniques are thought to be representative of a general agent of development. Control and experimental groups are randomly selected and pretest–posttest change scores are analyzed to test the effectiveness of such materials. The major shortcoming of a pretest–posttest design is that it only confirms or disconfirms whether change has occurred. It provides no information about the nature of developmental progression or the pattern of change during the intervention. For example, none of the developmental evaluation studies can answer the question of whether change occurs gradually over the course of an entire program or at one crucial point.

For this reason a growing number of developmentalists have sought to describe the process of developmental transition. Kuhn and Angelev (1976) report an intriguing methodology for observing developmental progress. Fourth- and fifth-graders took part in a 15-week intervention aimed at developing formal operational thought. The authors observed *weekly changes* in the strategies used by individual children during the intervention itself. They noted, "successful experimental induction of change does not explain the process by means of which the change occurred. Toward this end, a close observation of changes in subject's cognitive strategies over the intervention period is essential [p. 705]." While the Kuhn and Angelev data are anecdotal, their approach clearly implies that to obtain a detailed microgenetic picture of developmental transition in the application of interpersonal understanding repeated observation of the same individuals dealing with interpersonal problems must be made.

To describe transitional patterns of growth, the present study uses a time-series analysis. A time series involves many successive observations of one or more variables on the same individual or group over time. These observations are potentially related to one another owing to some underlying, and presumably developmental, process (Campbell & Stanley, 1963). The time-series approach was initially designed for the fields of economic forecasting and description (Box & Jenkins, 1970). Since developmental psychology, like economics, uses largely a descriptive and forecasting approach, this method provides a way to characterize development. The most obviously useful methodological yield of the time-series design is detailed individual growth curves, which are immediately superior to cross-sectional comparisons of children at different ages (Porges, 1976). The time series provides a continuous, descriptive record of fluctuation in the dependent variable over the course of an entire study. For a case history analysis, individual time series can be graphed (Chassan, 1965; Chassan & Bellak, 1965; Gottman, 1973). In determining both the universality of developmental functions and the specific interpersonal functioning of clinically referred children, a time-series analysis may be especially helpful.

One restriction of the time-series design is the need for multiple reliable observations on the same individual. Most instruments currently used to assess cognitive development require a formal testing session. Such multiple administration necessarily introduces instrument reactivity to the time series confounding developmental patterns (Holtzman, 1963). Naturalistic observation of interpersonal understanding in real-life settings would hopefully solve the problem of instrument reactivity, making it an especially appropriate technique for time-series analyses.

Analyses of time-series data are difficult. Repeated observations on the same individuals violate the assumption of independence underlying many conventional statistical techniques (Baltes, Reese, & Nesselroade, 1977; Gottman, McFall, & Barnett, 1969; Porges, 1976). And although certain statistical techniques such as spectral analysis (Porges, 1976) *have* been used in studies of operant learning and psychotherapy, these more sophisticated analyses require at least 100 continuous observations. Curve fitting and linear and curvilinear regression are the remaining multivariate statistical analyses with which to augment visual display of individual and group scattergrams (Campbell, 1969; Gottman & McFall, 1972; Gottman, McFall, & Barnett, 1969; Porges, 1976).

To reiterate, in the study here reported, an attempt is made to approach functional analysis of social–cognitive development, in an area where formal analysis has already taken place, stressing two major methodological issues: utilization of a truly naturalistic content and context and an in-depth analysis of transition over a short period.

Method

SUBJECTS AND SETTING

This study, because only eight subjects were involved, is in some respects most properly regarded as a case study. The subjects were students in a class in a clinic school. Their interpersonal problem solving was observed weekly for one school year. The problem-solving sessions were attended by the researcher who guided the meetings and the classroom teacher who helped in management problems and shared responsibility for directing discussion. Seven children, aged 11 and 12, were involved for the entire program with one additional student participating from March through May. These eight students made up one of nine classes in the school, a private day school for children with emotionally and interpersonally based learning difficulties. When referred, all suffered from symptoms which made their participation in a regular public school classroom virtually impossible: aggressive outbursts, incapacitating anxieties, disruptive behavior, character disorders, and poor reality testing. The group represented a mixture of sex, race, social class, and academic ability. Three of the eight returned to public school at the end of the year, and the other five remained in special placement.

To offset psychological as well as learning problems, the school's classes are small, seven or eight students. Half of the school day is spent on academic subjects, with the rest reserved for individual therapy, special group programs (fine motor skills, cooking, etc.), tutoring, and various activity groups (art, music, sports). In addition to one teacher for each classroom, the staff includes counselors, who are responsible for the activity and physical education programs and for crisis interviews and behavior management.

The emotional atmosphere at the school is very intense, expressive, and volatile. Even a researcher–observer becomes involved like the rest of the staff in the challenges of clinical intervention.

PROCEDURES

Class Meetings

1. Overview and Rationale

Weekly class meetings were instituted at the researcher's request to provide a setting for naturalistic observation of social reasoning in the individuals, friendship, and peer-group domains. These meetings were the single most important source of data in this study, representing the attempt to provide a real, or naturalistic, *content* and *context* for social problem solving and reasoning. Each meeting was tape recorded and transcribed in its entirety. From these transcripts, Naturalistic Interpersonal Understanding (NIU) was coded. (See section on measures, pages 228–232.)

Lasting from 15 minutes to 1 hour, class meetings used the existing interpersonal conflicts, individual personalities, and group goals as the basis for discussion. Discussions stressed resolutions whereby the class would be able to act on group decisions, for example, by writing a petition to address some common grievance. Class meetings had a relatively strong structure, with class leaders, discussion guidelines, extra weekly leadership seminars, crisis minimeetings, a student-initiated agenda, debates and votes on proposals, and petition procedures.

Each Friday for the entire school year class meetings were held to review the week and discuss suggestions by students and (occasionally) the teacher. Meetings were presided over by student leaders selected for 2-week periods on first an elected and then a rotating basis. Each meeting began with jointly rating the week for cooperation. The student leader first elicited examples of cooperation then asked each member for his rating and reasons. Discussion next moved to suggestions accumulated during the week in a suggestion box. The class leader read each suggestion and asked for comments and possible resolutions from other members.

The clinical rationale for the class meeting approach was based on the compatibility of naturalistic research with therapeutic and educational interventions. Class meetings establish an atmosphere where children may be able to develop more mature interpersonal styles and thought patterns through their real-life application of developing capacities. The class meeting approach also has some therapeutic advantages over the children's individual therapy. In individual therapy, the child meets with a psychologist to explore underlying causes of anxiety and stress for 1 or 2 hours each week. However, as Redl and Wineman (1952) contend, the isolation of this relationship and the poor reality insight mechanisms of the child can limit the success of individual psychotherapy for disturbed children and young adolescents. Because of the children's poor carryover abilities from therapy, one goal of class meetings was to provide immediate and consistent feedback from a peer group whose insights might offer the most pressure for positive change, when given the opportunity.

The research rationale for class meetings was twofold. First, class meetings avoid many of the problems of research reactivity accompanying experimental designs because the children perceived it as a legitimate activity or helping service of the school. Second, the kinds of interpersonal problems discussed in class meetings have considerable external validity because they are spontaneous problems of a natural peer group. In short, the class meetings appear to provide a naturalistic content and context for functional research.

2. Working Principles

Despite their benefits, class meetings severely challenge the interpersonal skills of disturbed children. Meetings often lapse into accusations, name-calling, and personal frustrations. The following are the principles developed for use in conducting class meetings with disturbed preadolescents.

Emphasis on Positive Peer Interactions and Group Discussions, on maintaining an atmosphere in which students listen to each other and give supportive feedback and each idea receives public support and clarification by staff.

Emphasis on the Adequacy of Interpersonal Problem Solving, on the applicability of suggestions to all persons involved, on the children's own ability to judge the adequacy of a particular idea.

Stress on Real-life Concerns, real-life concerns of the participating students, for example, punishment, tardiness, drugs, sharing, teasing, etc., so that interest and relevance of the discussion is increased.

Action Resolutions to Group Discussions, such that real consequences ensue from the group's debates and decisions; acting on cooperative goals can stimulate direction and cohesion, and that real-life justification is provided for the group discussion.

Decision-making Based on Democratic Principles, increasing the children's sense of efficacy and control over the meeting, adult control maintained only in cases when emotional turmoil and chaos threaten to seriously distress the children; or in some instances a total consensus is required so that an overruled minority does not feel rejected or unappreciated.

A Formal Student Organization, to avoid looseness and potentially traumatic negative behavior, without undermining student initiative: organizational components include a rotating class leader, suggestion box, weekly leadership-training seminars, rating the week for cooperation, and petition procedures for student initiatives, which rituals have a calming influence on otherwise anxious or disorganized students.

Cooperative Group Effort to Resolve Common Interpersonal Problems, trying to create a positive sense of interdependence where members care about each others' ideas, opinions, and feelings because it improves the common welfare.

3. Organizing Class Meetings

A description of some of the procedures used in class meetings provides insight into both the research and intervention aspects. The underlying goals are to: (a) increase the use of social reasoning abilities; (b) develop the real-life significance of the meetings; (c) increase the students' control over the meeting; and (d) promote action resolutions to verbal interactions among peers.

Rating the Week. To help students reflect on their week, the class leaders first ask each student to "rate the week for cooperation." These individual ratings guarantee public expression of opinions and often provide scoreable responses from each individual. This also serves as a first step for those who might not otherwise participate. As a ritual, rating the week provides initial direction on which to rely during the first shaky minutes of discussion.

Discussing Student Suggestions. Each week an agenda of student suggestions is gathered from a suggestion box, and written on an agenda sheet which is given to each participant. After the rating of the week, the class leader reads each suggestion, asks for comments and possible decision-making procedures, calls on students, and runs the meeting.

Rules for Class Discussion. Initial class meetings are used to propose, debate, and vote class rules into operation. The following rules were adopted by the class during class meetings.

1. One person should talk at a time.
2. Respect others—no hollering or swearing at people.
3. Be cool.
4. Talk to the whole group, not just one other person.
5. Pay attention; know what is going on.
6. No threats or intimidation in class.

As the group became more familiar with the procedures there was less need for specific reminders.

Class Leaders. An essential procedure is the use of student "class leaders" who organize and preside over two successive class meetings. Despite some jealousy, stage-fright, and over-control, taking the class leader role is beneficial to students. They must try to learn how to conduct themselves in front of a group and use authority without abuse. The challenge of coordinating opinions provides an excellent perspective-taking experience. Using class leaders communicates to the students their responsibility for the meetings and permits more student-to-student exchanges, thereby increasing the spontaneous expression of concepts of interpersonal understanding.

4. Role of Researcher–Group Leader

The role of this researcher was not simply participant–observer, but rather integral group member and guide to the class meeting format. Such an activist role has both its advantages and disadvantages from the point of view of naturalistic research on interpersonal functioning. The major advantage is the greater flexibility in organizing the problem-solving sessions. In addition, students take the sessions more seriously when they perceive the researcher as a legitimate school authority rather than an "outsider." In guiding class meetings, the researcher, who had a number of other duties in the school, was perceived to be part of the group and was involved in all important problem-solving sessions.

However, the benefits of greater procedural control and role acceptance come at a price. One of the most obvious costs is the loss of objectivity; however, in an exploratory study such objectivity is hardly the prime goal. A second price is time and energy. Ego-investment is high and is predictably shattered by these children whom Redl called "experts of failure." A third difficulty is the occasional contradiction between the researcher role, whereby one might *observe* how a student cannot cope with being class leader, and the "teacher" role, whereby one would *intervene* for the sake of the anxious individual and the disorganized group.

5. Interpersonal Problem Solving in Class Meetings

A content analysis of class meetings indicates that about one-quarter of the time was spent on behavior management, about one-quarter on procedure, and about one-half on actual interpersonal discussions. An example of interpersonal problem solving is presented to provide a more detailed picture of the class meetings.

Early in the year, the pervasive interpersonal problem was Daryl's[1] verbal intimidation of other students (e.g., "somebody needed to break your nose for you!"). For the first month "threats" were not mentioned, although one could easily see their negative effects. A new rule "against threats in this class" met with almost unanimous approval until Daryl began to write down the names of those whom he felt would be voting against him. While there was little real significance to this juvenile "enemies list," it was enough to dissuade three students from voting against threats. A hastily introduced "undecided" column allowed the three to avoid confronting Daryl while gaining the desired rule. Soon after, the group discussed the problem of threats, but without Daryl present.

DEBBIE: You know how sometimes all the kids in here, or certain people like Jane, you never say anything. Are they threatening you?

JANE: No [very sarcastically] . . . Daryl, when [he was running for class leader] he says vote for me! And he keeps saying it.

DEBBIE: So he is asking you?

JANE: He's telling me!

DWIGHT: You should say "Bullshit, Daryl." He shouldn't do that to you!

DEBBIE: No one say that she said anything. Cuz if he hears about it, he'll . . . .

DWIGHT: Daryl? Daryl ain't going to do that much. Daryl is the one.

RESEARCHER: Remember when we had that vote against threats? Daryl knows that if the adults hear about it he could get in serious trouble. Is he threatening as much now as he used to?

GARY: No, instead of threatening, he's using more conning people into it, like "Draw me a Continental, and I'll give you a pack of bubble gum."

DWIGHT: Daryl never threatens me or Jerry, because he knows that we will say, "You can't do nothing to us." He thinks he is the big boss. He wants to get his own way. He's a baby.

[1] All names are fictitious.

DEBBIE: You know what you can do. You can just pick him up and grab him. He never fought with me.
TEACHER: What about this peer pressure that you have been talking about?
DWIGHT: Yah, if the whole class started saying you better stop, we are going to beat you up, that is something to be careful of, the whole class.
GARY: If we got one person, like if Chuck starts going, "Hey, be quiet" and Daryl starts pushing him around, you got to have the whole class on your side.
DEBBIE: I will stay near Jane, and if he starts bugging her, then we will say you better stop bothering her, and he won't so that he won't get punished.
JANE: Suppose he asks me to draw a picture, but he said, "Draw it!" and then he threatens me, "If you don't I am going to get you after school."
DEBBIE: All you have to do is give us a call, like one of your friends.

After this show of interpersonal insight and support for more passive classmates, students openly confronted Daryl on the class's decision about threats.

DEBBIE: We know you have been threatening people and we want you to stop it. And we decided to make a rule. If we catch you threatening people we decided that we want you to be punished right away.

Confronted with his classmates' common feelings, threats were soon dropped. Daryl's popularity soared, and he was elected class leader.

Other Procedures

The class meetings provided a chance to assess children's interpersonal understanding in a *naturalistic context–real-life content.* To assess this understanding under the other three possible context–content combinations discussed, the following procedures were used.

Naturalistic Context–Hypothetical Content. Nine "social studies" group discussions were held concerning distant or hypothetical interpersonal topics, in contrast to the immediate real-life topics of the class meetings. These discussions resembled class meetings but were directed by the teacher and researcher rather than by the students. Each discussion was recorded and transcribed.

Reflective Context–Real-Life Content. At the end of the school year each child was interviewed and asked a series of open-ended questions aimed at evaluating his understanding of the class meetings. This Class Awareness Interview was designed to be similar to the Damon (1977) procedure, in that it assessed social reasoning about *real-life* events in a *reflective* one-to-one setting. In these interviews, children were posed a variety of questions about class meetings which paralleled similar questions in the standard reflective interpersonal understanding interview.

For example, "What made class meetings go well?" parallels a hypothetical question about the issue group cohesion, "What makes a group go well?" These interviews were recorded and transcribed.

Reflective Context-Hypothetical Content. A standard reflective interpersonal understanding interview on the friendship and peer-group domains, starting with interpersonal dilemmas, was administered to each child at the beginning and the end of the school year, based on procedures in the Interpersonal Understanding Manual.

MEASURES AND SCORING

Following is a summary of the scoring procedures used and the measures of interpersonal understanding derived in the various contexts and contents.

1. Reflective understanding–real-life content: Classroom Awareness Interview, spring
   Standard scoring procedure
   Measure: CA–RIU (Classroom Awareness Reflective Interpersonal Understanding)
2. Reflective understanding–hypothetical content: standard interviews, fall and spring
   Standard scoring procedure
   Measures: pre-RIU and post-RIU (Reflective Interpersonal Understanding)
3. Naturalistic understanding–real-life content: 32 class meetings
   Modified scoring procedure
   Measure: NIU (Naturalistic Interpersonal Understanding)
4. Naturalistic understanding–hypothetical content: nine "social studies" group discussions
   Modified scoring procedure
   Measure: H–NIU (Hypothetical Naturalistic Interpersonal Understanding)

The next two sections present details of scoring procedures and further describe the measures derived.

Reflective Measures

Transcribed data from both reflective contexts, the standard interviews and the classroom awareness interview, were scored according to the standard procedure (Chapter 7). Each student received pre-RIU and post-RIU scores from the Fall and Spring standard interviews and a CA–RIU score from the Spring classroom awareness interview. All scores were expressed as numerical IMS scores, that is, all reflective measures were *average* stage scores (for example, 1.38) which could be converted to global stage scores [for example, Stage 1(2)].

Naturalistic Measures

As was the case with the reflective measures, transcribed data from both naturalistic contexts (the class meetings and the "social studies" group discussions) were scored according to the same procedure, a modification of the standard procedure which is described below. And as with the reflective measures, the NIU scores, one for each student for each class meeting, and the H–NIU scores, one for each student for each discussion group, were expressed as numerical averages, for example, 2.14 (Stage 2) or 2.63 [Stage 3(2)].

The modified scoring procedure developed for scoring interpersonal understanding in a naturalistic context is described in complete detail elsewhere (Jaquette, 1978). A summary of the major details is included here. The chronological order and date of each meeting were blocked out so that scoring judgments would not be biased by time-series expectations. The names of specific children could not be blocked out because of the need to know the identity of follow-up responses and response exchanges. In each transcript, each individual's scorable speech acts were assigned to one of 15^2 interpersonal issues. Stage judgments were made by comparing responses to specific issue-by-stage aspects or through a more general characterization of the stage. Although expressions of interpersonal understanding within a group discussion may undergo surface alteration, the characteristics of the stages, the underlying nature of each stage, are still discernible. An example of scoring for the NIU on the issue group cohesion, Stages 0 through 3, using spontaneous concepts expressed during the class's evaluation of group cooperation, follows.

Stage 0: Group interdependence based on satisfaction of one's egoistic interests.
Example: "Cooperation was good, cuz I got out of class twice and I am happy."
Stage 1: Group interdependence based on unilateral satisfaction of other's concrete interests.
Example: "Cooperation was good, cuz I helped Jerry with his work."
Stage 2: Group interdependence based on bilateral coordination of two or more members' concrete needs.
Example: "Cooperation was excellent. There was a lot of cooperation and helping each other with work."
Stage 3: Interdependence based on emotional support and common feelings.

---

[2] The 17 issues of the individuals, friendship, and peer-group domains were reduced to 15 by combining 4 issues, friendship and group formation and termination, to form 2 issues: formation and termination.

Example: "Cooperation was excellent, because usually you just help on work and stuff, but mostly this week the cooperation was with helping people when they were messing up [emotional outburst], help them sit down and be quiet."

For each class meeting, each participating individual received an NIU score, which was a mean stage for all that individual's responses. In addition, a group NIU score was calculated for each meeting by averaging the stages of all *responses* across individual members.

Four particular difficulties are faced in scoring interpersonal understanding in a naturalistic context: (a) the need to be familiar with the class in order to understand the group culture and certain idiosyncratic linguistic expressions; (b) the decision of how much group discussion represents how many interpersonal issue–concept scores; (c) the decision of which interpersonal issue a speech act is to be assigned to; and (d) the identification of the characteristic interpersonal stage.

Particularly among children and preadolescents, many comments in group discussions are highly idiosyncratic, with meaning only to those who participate in the discussion. For example, one member continually used the term "messing up," which on several occasions he defined as "when people are really angry about some personal problem." The following general rule was developed for such cases. If a child gives an interpersonal concept and defines that concept according to a specific stage, further uses of the concept are scored at that stage even if the specific definition is not given a second time. This covers only the discussion during which the definition is given, and not subsequent discussions on other days.

Deciding how many issue concepts are represented in a given sequence is especially important because NIU scores are based on averaging the stages of issue concepts. The general rule developed for determining issue concepts is based on the reflective interview notion of probe questions. When certain responses or questions by either a child or a staff member set off the discussion into short coherent sequences of 2 to 10 speech acts, one issue concept is assigned. In general, new probes or responses set off new scoreable issue concepts.

In standard reflective interviews, responses are assigned to issues by virtue of the question posed. Here, no such questions exist, so deciding which interpersonal issue is represented is less straightforward. Each interpersonal issue has a short definition which can often be used in assigning the response. In addition, the following rules were employed:

1. The interpersonal issue is assigned on the basis of the subject's response rather than any question posed by other members.

2. If the subject's response offers no clear criteria, the scorer gauges the issue from the general context of the discussion.
3. If neither the subject's response or context provides suitable criteria, the scorer refers to the scoring criteria to find the issue which best fits the stage characteristics of the response.

Some issues were utilized far more than others. Frequently utilized issues were: self-awareness, group cohesion, decision-making, and organization, leadership, and conflict resolution.

In determining the stage represented by subjects' responses, two approaches were employed. Having assigned one of the interpersonal issues, the scorer turns to the manual of interpersonal understanding for the list of *aspects*. Aspects are brief characterizations of a particular issue at a given stage. For example, at Stage 0, Conflict Resolution, three aspects are listed:

1. Conflict resolution through nonintervention and avoidance
2. Physical intervention and intimidation
3. Concern with personal interests to exclusion of others

If the response is represented by one of those aspects, that stage is assigned. Where no specific aspect represents the response, the scorer relies on the general descriptions of each stage. For example, when a response shows a concern with "taking turns," the scorer finds this to be a general characteristic of Stage 1 physical reciprocity.

Two forms of stage scoring are used. If a response is clearly representative of a particular stage, a pure stage score is given (e.g., Stage 2). In cases of transition or scoring uncertainty, major(minor) scores are given [e.g., Stage 2(3)]. The major(minor) score is assigned frequently in part because of ambiguity due to the lack of follow-up probes which might clarify stage usage. Two examples of coded segments of a class meeting are provided along with analyses of the assignment of issues and stage scores.

RESEARCHER: Okay, but what happens if the election turns out to be a tie again?
DWIGHT: Then we punch them . . . Then we let them have a fight.
GARY: Yah, whoever wins is the president.
DWIGHT: And I'll help. I'll take Debbie's place.
RESEARCHER: Have a fight. Now, does anyone have a better suggestion?
GARY: So, he'll represent Debbie and Daryl will represent himself.
DWIGHT: And I'll beat up Gary.

Comment. Dwight provides an idea of how the group should resolve a tie vote by physical intervention ("let them have a fight"). Although Dwight, or any other child, may be capable of higher level conceptions, naturalistic interpersonal understanding is scored on the basis of surface conceptions. Gary enters into the concept with a strange mixture of physicalistic and organizational concepts ("whoever wins is president"). However, since Dwight initiates the concept, only he is assigned a score.

Issue. Two possible issues apply here, *Conflict Resolution* and *Decision-making and Organization.* On the side of *Conflict Resolution,* the concept implies both dyadic relations and an affective conflict. However, the general context of the discussion is concerned with more procedural matters of selecting a class leader. Hence the issue of *Decision-making and Organization* is assigned.

Stage. Dwight's concept of how class leaders should be selected is a Stage 0 aspect of "physical intervention." It involves no consideration of internal states (e.g., "feelings") or the coordination of interests (e.g., "agreements"). The concern for physical intimidation is always scored as Stage 0. Physical intervention ("fights") is seen as the simplest form of decision-making because it involves neither one-way nor two-way psychological coordination.

TEACHER: Remember that the principal said that it had to come from all of you. He wasn't talking about the counselors or teachers. He said it was to come from you.
CHUCK: Okay.
TEACHER: He was talking about a group of 28 or so people.
CHUCK: Thirty people. We're going to have to do it.
GARY: Yah, we have to get 30, at least 30 reasons from everybody.

Comment. Staff reinforces the notion that the students must come to a group decision in order to win back their lost break. Gary invokes the concept of convergent reasons ("at least 30 reasons") for a schoolwide petition among 30 students.

Issue. Staff's stimulus that the group should focus on a cooperative resolution suggests the issue–concept of *Group Cohesion.* While the issue–concept could also be scored under *Decision-making and Organization,* the concept deals primarily with the need for unity within the entire group.

Stage. The concept of "reasons" as an area of group cooperation implies a psychological plane of relations. Any convergence of thoughts or feelings (e.g., "we like the same things") is scored as minimally Stage 2. Unless higher stage conceptions are also added, the minimal score is the coded level.

Results

RELIABILITY

Seven of the class meetings were scored by both the researcher and a second rater, trained through use of the manual and about 10 hours of supervision. Interrater reliability for individual and group NIU scores was computed by Pearson correlations (.99, .89, .90, .73, .91, .97, and .93 for the seven students and .93 for group).

THE RELATION OF REFLECTIVE AND NATURALISTIC INTERPERSONAL UNDERSTANDING

In order to compare the levels of interpersonal understanding obtained in the reflective and naturalistic contexts, an average of pre-RIU and post-RIU was computed for each subject. These mean RIU scores were compared with similar overall mean NIU scores obtained by averaging each individual's 32 NIU scores. Because comparisons were between two measures obtained on the same individuals, matched t-tests were employed. Mean RIU for the entire group was 1.92 and mean NIU was 1.46. This half-stage difference was significant [t (7) = 3.248, $p < .01$]. As was expected, the naturalistic context–real-life content "constrained" performance in some manner by comparison with the reflective context–hypothetical content.

Whether the same reflective–naturalistic relation would be observed if the reflective interviews concerned real-life events was examined by comparing CA–RIU scores, which were derived from the reflective interview on the real-life issue of class meetings, and mean NIU scores. Understanding expressed in the reflective context was again approximately one-half stage higher than that in the naturalistic context, a significant difference [mean CA–RIU 1.99 and mean NIU 1.46, t (7) = 3.528, $p < .005$]. A Pearson correlation between mean RIU scores and CA–RIU scores was .97, indicating the homogeneity of understanding expressed in the reflective context, regardless of content.

These findings might suggest that it is the group versus the individual context which accounts for the discrepancy between mean NIU and mean RIU. To examine this possible explanation, mean H–RIU scores, from the nine hypothetical group discussions, were compared to the same individuals' RIU scores. Regardless of context, reasoning about hypothetical or distant issues did not significantly vary [t (7) = 0.428, ns]. However, the difference between H–NIU and NIU scores was significant [t (7) = 4.603, $p < .005$]. These results imply that the discrepancy between mean NIU and mean RIU is the product of both the real-life *content* and the naturalistic group *context* of the class meetings. See Table 9.1 for a summary of these findings.

TABLE 9.1
Summary of Comparisons of Reflective and Naturalistic Understanding

	Context		
	Naturalistic		Reflective
Real-life	NIU ◄———— sig. ————► CA–RIU		
Content ————	sig. diff.	sig. diff.	N.S.
Hypo-thetical	H–NIU ◄———— N.S. ————► RIU		

TIME-SERIES ANALYSES

For use in the time-series analyses, a group NIU was calculated for each of the 32 class meetings by averaging all responses during that meeting. The average of all responses was chosen over the average of individuals' NIU scores because different members varied in the amount they contributed to the discussions. Some expressed as few as 2 codable concepts while others expressed as many as 30 per meeting.

Both educational and clinical personnel report evidence of interpersonal regression among emotionally disturbed children toward the end of a school year as internal impulse controls wane and separation anxiety rises. Despite this, the developmental nature of interpersonal understanding would lead one to expect overall growth during the year and a time-series pattern of growth up until the last months. To assess the time-series pattern of functional or naturalistic interpersonal understanding in the group, a scatterplot of group NIU scores was computed (see Figure 9.1). A pattern of growth in level of understanding over the first two-thirds of the year was followed by a regression in the final third, with overall level at the year's end remaining higher than at the year's start. Curve-fitting techniques were used, plotting one regression line for sessions 1 through 22, and another for sessions 22 through 31. (The final meeting was not used because the two most disruptive and low functioning members were emotionally unable to participate.) The growth (first) curve accounted for 65% of the variance with a correlation coefficient of .81 between group NIU and session number. The regression–termination (second) curve accounted for 85% of the variance with a correlation between session number and group NIU of .92. (A single linear trend accounted for only 17% of the variance with a correlation of .42.)

Individual subjects' time-series patterns were also examined. Scattergrams for each subject were plotted presenting their NIU scores over time. Curves were fitted, and the slopes and correlations computed for

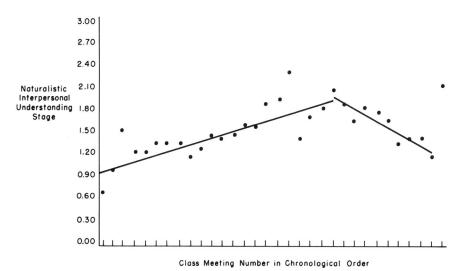

Figure 9.1. Time-series scattergram and curve-fitting for group NIU scores.

the growth (i.e., meetings 1 to 22) and termination–regression (i.e., meetings 22 to 31) phases for all eight children (see Table 9.2). Individual slope calculations showed that five members paralleled the growth and regression phases found in the group as a whole, although patterns for two of these individuals included considerable stage oscillation. The other three demonstrated progressive, albeit unstable, patterns of stage development over the entire program. No individual reflected an overall regressive trend, and all individuals showed progressive patterns during the first two-thirds of the class meetings.

Figures 9.2, 9.3, and 9.4 present three of the more interesting time-series patterns. Jane (Figure 9.2) is generally reported as a girl of

TABLE 9.2
Individual Slopes and Correlations for NIU Scores during Growth and Regression Phases

Subject	Growth slope	Growth correlation	Regression slope	Regression correlation
Jane	+.014	.302	+.012	.214
Gary	+.025	.288	−.074	.465
Debbie	+.021	.533	−.085	.863
Jerry	+.030	.459	+.059	.415
Dwight	+.037	.565	−.015	.185
Daryl	+.034	.506	−.073	.424
Billy	+.004	.041	+.052	.822
Chuck	+.330	.714	−.056	.490
Group	+.046	.810	−.086	.920

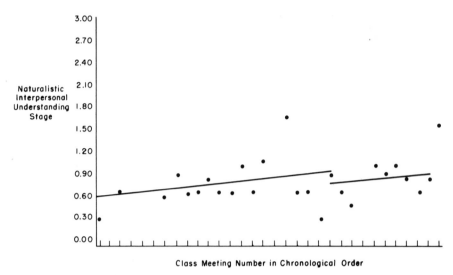

Figure 9.2.   Time-series scattergram and curve-fitting for Jane's NIU scores.

borderline retardation for whom educational and therapeutic interventions have had little effect. Her time series expresses this generally low-level consistency with little indication of fluctuation or growth. Gary (Figure 9.3) has exceptional intelligence and social sensitivity, but his difficulty in controlling anger has led him to be characterized by his teacher as a child of uneven social and academic production. His time-series scattergram reflects both his high-level competence and his

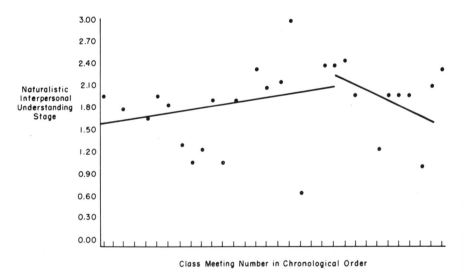

Figure 9.3.   Time-series scattergram and curve-fitting for Gary's NIU scores.

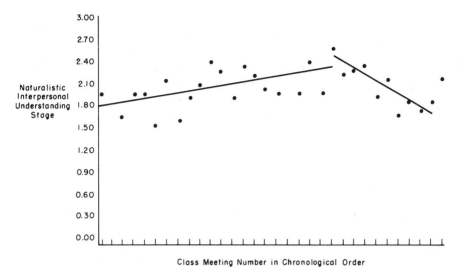

Figure 9.4.   Time-series scattergram and curve-fitting for Debbie's NIU scores.

tendency to oscillate in the level of social insight expressed during class meetings. Debbie (Figure 9.4) is characteristically a child of acute social sensitivity with seemingly good ego controls and consistent performance. However, 2 days after the completion of the school year and the class meeting program, Debbie attempted suicide, leaving a note in which she criticized her own "split personality." The time-series scattergram demonstrates consistently high performance *and* a *severe* termination–regression effect, the most pronounced and consistent regressive pattern in the class. One cannot help but speculate that the termination–regression was a barometer of her declining self-esteem. The combination of a developmental analysis of naturalistic interpersonal understanding and a time-series description of transition patterns can provide a clinical tool for helping to understand the social adjustment problems of disturbed children.

Discussion and Conclusions

REFLECTIVE AND NATURALISTIC INTERPERSONAL UNDERSTANDING

Although we studied the reasoning of only eight subjects, the evidence supports the hypothesis that real-life content and natural discussion context lower level of expressed interpersonal understanding by comparison with that expressed in standard hypothetical reflective interviews, in natural discussions about hypothetical topics, or in reflective interviews about real-life topics. The findings in this study support the long-standing observation that real-life situations generally constrain an individual's ability to utilize his or her full social–cognitive capabilities. That class meetings resulted in the most depressed interpersonal reasoning scores suggests that their group context coupled with real-life interpersonal problems increased the size of the discrepancy with reflective thought. Discussions concerning only distant topics apparently did not present the specific performance constraints of real-life interpersonal problem-solving discussions, implying that a group context *alone* cannot be considered the major performance constraint on expression of reflective capabilities. Similarly, real-life topics in a reflective interview did not appear to constrain expression of understanding, implying that immediacy of content *alone* is also unlikely to account for the discrepancy between NIU and all other measures. The evidence suggests that (*a*) naturalistic real-life interpersonal understanding is lower than reflective hypothetical interpersonal understanding and (*b*) the cause of this drop in performance appears to be the combination of naturalistic context *with* real-life content, not simply naturalistic context *or* real-life content.

TIME–SERIES ANALYSES OF INTERPERSONAL FUNCTIONING

The most striking time-series pattern is the growth in interpersonal understanding expressed by the group during the first two-thirds of the school year followed by a distinctive termination-regression effect in the final third. The correlations of .81 for the progressive trend and .92 for the regressive trend demonstrate the strength of these patterns. The individual time-series patterns indicate that the growth and termination–regression curves are not simply the product of what the *group itself* did, but are also the product of how the individual group members functioned. Five of the eight cases demonstrated growth *and* regression and all eight cases showed growth during the first two-thirds of the school year. No case presented an overall regressive time-series pattern.

Empirical evidence documenting the termination-regression effect is particularly valuable to the analysis of interpersonal functioning of disturbed children. The impending loss of school supports can cause striking back in the form of regressive behavior and reasoning, a loosening in the children's impulse controls and a weakening in their organizational skills, and a straining of the cognitive organization which resulted in higher level functioning in the middle of the year such that more readily available low-level thinking is employed.

These are possible explanations for the termination–regression effect. As for the growth pattern in the first two-thirds of the year, one would expect a developmental construct with hierarchical stage properties to reflect a slow progress. Because of situational performance constraints, children's earliest expressions of naturalistic interpersonal understanding were at a lower level than that of which they were capable. As they became more familiar with the class meeting process and procedures, an increasing facility in reasoning appeared. It seems likely that the greater adequacy of higher stages was one natural impetus for growth, because higher-stage concepts provided better practical solutions to difficult interpersonal problems.

IMPLICATIONS FOR RESEARCH IN DEVELOPMENTAL PSYCHOLOGY

The present study stresses the observation and analysis of developmental functioning rather than the description of formal developmental sequences. That such a functional study of developmental processes should be naturalistic follows from the conviction that the "testing" procedures currently used in developmental research can have a powerful influence on the results themselves. Reflective interpersonal understanding may not possess the same functional properties as naturalistic interpersonal understanding. This finding should be taken as a precaution against too rapidly generalizing "testing" results to real-life conditions, but also as an invitation for more developmental research within the naturalistic environment. The class meeting procedures provide an opportunity to observe and code spontaneous expressions of social reasoning.

In addition to a specified natural social environment such as a class meeting, a naturalistic methodology requires a systematic method for assessing development within this environment. The scoring criteria and procedures for assessing naturalistic interpersonal understanding are an attempt to directly assess naturalistic real-life reasoning. Despite the indications of the potential for reliable measurement of natural social development, many procedural and theoretical questions remain. How does one decide how much of a speech act or speech interaction represents one score versus two or more scores? How can one reliably assign issue categories? Can stage criteria developed from hypothetical reflective interview methods using follow-up questions and counterprobes be used in scoring responses which do not permit follow-up clarification? How does one score judgments which are minimally characteristic of a stage, but which could also be expressed appropriately at higher levels?

A time-series design is particularly useful for a functional analysis of naturalistic development, providing what should be a major objective of developmental research, a way to characterize developmental transition. The time-series analysis may provide a much needed way to record the development of the same individuals or the same group over enough observations to observe the patterns of growth, stabilization, or regression.

IMPLICATIONS FOR STAGE THEORY

A sample of eight emotionally disturbed preadolescents does not necessarily constitute a representative sample from which to make generalizations about stage criteria. However, the findings from this case study probably do have relevance beyond this relatively narrow population if one views "disturbed" children's naturalistic interpersonal understanding as representing a more striking example of the same social thought processes found in normal children. Our observations in the past have been of slower development, greater intensity of expressiveness, and greater oscillation on the part of disturbed children.

A stage sequence may be generated which conforms to principles of invariant, hierarchical sequence. However, if children's interpersonal thinking in naturalistic situations is totally unlike that observed under interview conditions, this would call into question the relevance and validity of stages of interpersonal understanding in describing real-life insight. However, the results reported here do support the consistency between the kinds of concepts used in reflective interviews and the kinds of concepts used under real-life conditions and in the order of their emergence in both contexts. While a child may function at a different stage or develop slower, the concepts themselves are scorable at one or another of the interpersonal understanding levels and demonstrate overall forward developmental sequence.

This research also pertains to stage homogeneity, or structured wholeness. Comparisons of disturbed children's reflective reasoning with their naturalistic reasoning indicate that social cognition may fluctuate according to conditions. Further research is necessary to assess whether this stage oscillation is characteristic of only disturbed children or of a more general population. However, it is worth noting that the discrepancy between reflective and naturalistic understanding and the degree of stage oscillation within naturalistic conditions was no smaller for the three students returning to public schools. This may indicate that some stage oscillation may be common among all children.

The patterns of growth and regression revealed in the time series are particularly intriguing in light of the stage theory assumption of hierarchical stage progression. In a developmental system where higher stage concepts are thought to be naturally preferred over less adequate, lower stage concepts, a regression effect might be troubling. However, it should be stressed that in this study we observed natural functioning or application, *not basic competence*. Stage *theory* deals primarily with optimum competence, not with variations in functional application; therefore, a regression such as that found in this study does not necessarily call stage theory into question.

The time-series results demonstrate the need to study developmental patterns over short-term periods with frequent monitoring. It may be that the pattern of invariant progression found in reflective data on social cognition is a function of the intermittent testing approach. Temporary regressive phases within a general pattern of forward development may emerge as a more realistic social–cognitive picture when enough observations are gathered close enough together on the same individual.

Despite the stage oscillation, the lower average stage used, and the patterns of developmental regression, the present study clearly indicates that social–cognitive stages *are* a valid and reliable tool in the analysis of social development. If these results are found to be generalizable, two of the basic tenets of stage analyses of reflective thought are called into question in the case of naturalistic thought: the structured wholeness of the child's thought and the hierarchical invariance of the developmental sequence. More orthodox developmentalists find stage oscillation and developmental regression so troubling that they repudiate the notion of stages altogether. Rather than discarding the stage concept, these results can be seen to refine our understanding of social–cognitive stage in more than one context. Under stable conditions the homogeneity and invariant sequence doctrines do hold up. Even under less predictable real-life conditions, the occurrence of stage regression was even evaluated by the children themselves as regression (i.e., "she's acting like a baby"). The qualities of stage hierarchy and homogeneity exist in the child's basic mental capacities, but these stage-related qualities compete in a real world with other sources of variation. Stages do provide a logical system for characterizing outputs in which the adequacy of one response can be compared to the adequacy of others. However, the experience of observing children's problem-solving discussions provides the researcher with a more realistic picture of the complexities of social cognition and social development.

10

Application of a Formal Model to Functional Analysis: Case Studies in the Growth of Interpersonal Understanding

Psychological research often inquires into theoretical concerns or collects and organizes information about a general class of people, processes, or events. Another test of the utility and relevance of a model or approach is whether or how well it can be applied to a particular case. The preceding chapter reports in detail one such case study.[1] In it, a method for functional analysis of interpersonal understanding was tested, natural and reflective reasoning were compared, and a close-up look at functional development was taken using a time series. The study is a good illustration of several important facets of how we approach the third, or application, phase of our model.

First, it is exploratory. We regard the use of a formal analysis for functional analysis as a wide open field with a multitude of unanswered and even unposed questions about functioning social cognition. Second, it is a case study. At this point, as we begin work in this area, we feel individual or small group investigations can yield rich and provocative data which have both initial, innate, albeit limited, validity and tremen-

---

[1] Among other things, the Jaquette study demonstrates how beneficial prolonged, integrated access to a clinical–educational facility has been for our project and its members; these advantages will be abundantly clear in this chapter as well.

dous suggestive power for future work. Third, it has theoretical, clinical, and educational implications. A major conviction underlying our work is that in addition to providing information which can amplify and add a dimension to the academic–theoretical picture of social cognition, the application phase can generate information and tools with practical usefulness for the educator and the clinician.

The work reported in this chapter is anecdotal, observational, informal, formal, detailed, and sketchy all in turn. It deals with questions of theory, model validity in functional application, clinical and educational uses and implications, analysis of reasoning, analysis of behavior, and directions for future research. It is for the most part exploratory and individual, yet we would claim some generalizability of some of our findings. It is in essence a potpourri, a wide ranging sampling of our work to date which indicates its direction and style.

Cognitive and Affective Components of Development: Contrast and Complement

Because so much of our applied work deals with clinical issues and troubled children, in this section I discuss some differences between cognitive–developmental and clinical–affective approaches.

In an effort to describe the rich and changing interior of the child's world, much has been written about various intrapsychic processes in childhood ranging from mechanisms of defense to feelings of self-esteem. Perhaps some of the most intimate data can be found in the accounts of those who work with troubled youngsters in psychotherapy. Guided by clinical methods and precepts, these investigators have given us rare glimpses of the complex and often confusing interplay of inner thoughts and feelings that help shape the child's behavior, both adaptive and maladaptive.

Of particular interest to us in these reports are indications of the child's own growing capacity for *reflective awareness* of intrapsychic experiences. Until recently, this area had not received systematic attention, despite its clinical and developmental importance. According to Anna Freud:

> The ego of the young child has the developmental task to master on the one hand orientation in the external world and on the other hand the chaotic emotional states which exist within himself. It gains victories and advances whenever such impressions are grasped, put into thoughts or words, and submitted to the secondary process. For a variety of reasons, young children come into analytic treatment with this development delayed or uncompleted. With them, the process of interpretation proper goes in hand with verbalizing numerous strivings which as such are not incapable of consciousness (i.e., under primary repression) but have not yet succeeded in achieving ego status, consciousness, and secondary elaboration [1965, p.32].

Although we learn in this excerpt that children can reflectively know a great deal of their inner world, questions remain concerning just how much they are capable of understanding and what form such understanding takes at different ages. Unfortunately, whenever questions of this nature are addressed in the clinical literature, statements of what the young child comprehends often suffer from logical inconsistencies. As an example, several pages after cogently arguing that young children are incapable of grasping the inherent polarities of their own and/or another's character structure, Bettelheim (1976) claims:

> Just as important for the [young] child's well-being as feeling that his parents share his emotions . . . is the child's feeling that his inner thoughts are not known to his parent until he decides to reveal them. If the parent indicates that he knows them already, the child is prevented from making the most precious gift to his parent of sharing with him what until then was secret and private to the child [p. 11].

Are we to assume that the same child whose mind is dominated by concrete polarization is also capable of reflectively knowing that he or she has complex hidden inner thoughts, his or her parents may have them, too, and these thoughts can be hidden until the appropriate time? If so, Bettelheim seems to be asking us to regard early childhood as an unpredictable era characterized by both precious naivete and precocious conceptual insight.

Yet we recognize that empirical approaches to the problem of intrapsychic understanding in children are not without their inherent limitations as well. In trying to reach out to larger samples and to use standardized measures and procedures, developmental psychologists interested in normal development have generally failed to capture the richness potentially available. Children will simply not share easily the nature of their own understanding about experiences that they view as very private, personal, or difficult to articulate. What one gleans from these more cautious-qua-scientific studies is the somewhat general and pallid conclusion that children's thinking about the inner workings of the human mind grows more complex, psychological, systematized, and abstract with age, a conclusion that only begins to do justice to the phenomena under examination.

In the remainder of this section, I briefly illustrate some points of contention and agreement between affective and cognitive approaches to socialization and social development by means of describing differing conceptions of dreams.

At least as much as the broad differences in methods of observation, concern with changing structures of interpersonal thinking, rather than with the specific content acquired, characterizes the difference between affective–clinical and cognitive–developmental approaches. One illustration of this is the distinction between a Freudian–psychoanalytic and a Piagetian–developmental conceptual analysis of dreams as a psychic phenomenon. From a psychoanalytic perspective, what is most important about dreams is that the manifest or surface content masks remote or latent meanings related to such general emotional issues as separation, dependency, competition, or rivalry. If a 3-year-old is having recurrent nightmares about large, angry monsters chasing him or her out of the house, one possible interpretation might be that the monster–child relationship is a manifest symbol of a frightening, hence repressed or latent, conflict around feelings of competition in another relationship, perhaps with a father or authority figure. A 6-year-old having a similar dream might well be seen as dealing with the same underlying theme, since the latent content of conflicts which the dream process plays out are timeless and universal. Thus when looking at the latent content of children's dreams, the age of the youngster or the way he or she actually experiences the dream itself would not be of central importance.

However, for a developmentalist whose major focus is on the ontogenesis of children's conceptions of intrapsychic and interpersonal phenomena like dreams (or friends or feelings), of particular relevance would be how the 3- and 6-year-old, upon awakening, differ in their understanding of the dream experience. The expectation would be that the 6-year-old might more readily understand that "it was just a dream" and that "the monster was not real," whereas the 3-year-old might be afraid to look in the closet, where he or she may well assume the monster is still hiding. In other words, the Piagetian focuses on the development of the *conception* of dreams, beginning by defining the structures or intrinsic psychic qualities of a dream: its intangibility, its internal locus, its origin in intrapsychic experience and conflicts. The Piagetian then tries to discover the developmental sequence of dream concepts through which children progress in coming to understand each of these basic properties that adults usually take for granted in their own thinking about dreams.

The developmental claim is that there is a logic to the emerging sequence of conceptions of dreams, each step or stage of which depends on the discoveries or conceptual differentiations made at the prior stage. For example, the child must first differentiate between tangible and intangible experiences before he or she can understand that a dream is internally located. This sequence is logical and universal; not until the child "knows" that the two tangible bodies cannot be located in the same space at the same time can dreams be clearly seen as simultaneously intangible (psychological) and located within a tangible self. For the child who conceptualizes dreams as "real" or tangible, the locus must remain external.

Although the clinical focus on the symbolic meaning of the content of experience and the development focus on the structure[2] of understanding are not inherently contradictory, they can lead to different "explanations" of specific instances of behavior. For example, the 3-year-old might be scared at least as much because the monster was conceptualized as "real" as because it symbolized an important and frightening intrafamilial conflict. Consequently, both affective and cognitive factors are critical determinants of the psychological meaning of experience. Knowing the structures of the child's social understanding helps us, as adults, to understand why the content of a child's affective concerns is manifest in a particular way, that is, is given a particular form at a particular developmental level.

Child Psychotherapy as a Natural Setting for Developmental Research[3]

with Gregory Jurkovic
Georgia State University
Atlanta, Georgia

In this section we turn away from the theoretical, discuss some potential uses of the child psychotherapy session as a natural environment for understanding the mechanisms of social–cognitive development, and draw some implications from this source for psychotherapy and for further research at the border of clinical and developmental interests. Throughout this particular section, we rely heavily on our developmental analysis of the four issues in the individuals domain (subjectivity, self-awareness, personality, and personality change), for it is in the domain of intrapsychic experience that the greatest relevance and interest is found for professionals concerned with the practicalities of childhood development and psychopathology. In addition, we shall also spell out some implications of the social–cognitive–developmental approach and model for the diagnosis and treatment of emotionally troubled children.

To review briefly, the study of cognitive developmental aspects of social behavior under natural conditions requires at least two tools. The first is a social–cognitive map—with a developmental sequence of levels as "latitudes" and a set of comprehensive issues as "longitudes"—that

---

[2] Clinical theories also use the term *structure*, usually to refer to personality structures, for example, id, ego, superego. Here, however, we are using the term *structure* in the cognitive–developmental sense, the way conceptions are organized, in juxtaposition to the term *content*, or the "objects of thinking." For a detailed discussion of the relation between content and structure in cognitive–developmental theory, see Selman, 1976b.

[3] This section appears in a somewhat modified form in a paper by Gregory Jurkovic and Robert L. Selman, "A Cognitive-Developmental Analysis of Intrapsychic Understanding," and appears in a book edited by Robert L. Selman and Regina Yando, *New Directions in Clinical-Developmental Psychology*, published by Jossey Bass, San Francisco, California, 1980.

is both broad enough to capture the range of topics or themes likely to be discussed by those being observed and detailed enough to relatively, reliably, and validly specify the level of understanding upon which the actions or statements are based. The second is an environment or atmosphere that encourages or facilitates the expression of social reasoning in ways that are amenable to observation and categorization.

In the previous chapter, Jaquette identified one such natural setting for the study of issues in friendship and peer-group organization. While many thorny problems in method and theory remain, the results are encouraging, particularly with respect to advances in methodology. Still, a class meeting is not a natural or facilitating environment for the discussion of *all* the issues across the domains of interpersonal relations. In fact there are very few environments where the issues of the domain of intrapsychic or parent-child relations are both freely expressed and easily accessible to the eavesdropping of voyeuristic social scientists. One natural environment for the discussion of these issues that does come to mind, and that our project has had some access to, is the individual psychotherapy session.

In fact, like class meetings, psychotherapy, with its regularly scheduled weekly meetings often lasting over a period of several years, provides a unique "natural environment" that allows us to look at issues of individual and interpersonal relations in critical longitudinal perspective.

In this section, we shall describe a pilot investigation of dialogues between a therapist (Jurkovic) and several children in psychodynamically oriented child psychotherapy and report on one case. Although the treatment of these children was oriented to traditional dynamic considerations, there also was a strong social–cognitive–developmental component in the analysis of the therapy process, and particularly in the analysis of the discourse. The collaboration between Jurkovic and Selman was, in part, modelled after conventional clinical supervision, that is, the therapist and the developmental psychologist met once a week to review process notes of the psychotherapy sessions.[4] However, we both viewed our meetings *primarily* as a chance to search for evidence of social–cognitive–developmental trends and variations in the discourse and only secondarily as a time to plan treatment or arrive at traditional diagnoses. We hope that clinician and researcher alike will be struck, as we are, with how much closer than one might suspect at first glance are the processes of observation required by their two different and sometimes conflicting psychologies.

[4] For purposes of exposition we shall refer to Jurkovic as "therapist" and Selman as "developmental psychologist" where such distinctions are necessary.

METHODS

The first step in our preparation to look developmentally at the dialogues in child psychotherapy was for the therapist to get a working understanding of the issues and stages in the interpersonal understanding manuals. This led inevitably to some changes in the way therapy would be conducted. In particular it changed the therapist's approach from focusing only or predominantly on the child's identification (perception) of *feeling states* ("How did you feel when Billy snubbed you?") to focusing on what might be called the child's *understanding* of the function of social relations and interactions ("How would you go about changing that if you did not like it?"; "How would you go about resolving your fight with Billy?").

The major source of data on each child's conceptual ability in the social domain was a series of detailed process notes on discussion and interaction that evolved between child and therapist during twice weekly, 50-minute therapy sessions. These notes were then reviewed by the therapist and developmental psychologist in regular weekly meetings. Interpretation of these notes focused on (a) what issue the child and therapist were discussing; (b) what stage the child's conceptions represented; and (c) what *function* the reasoning appeared to serve for the child.

A primary source of additional information on each child's behavior and reasoning was discussion with each child's teacher. Biweekly meetings were held with the teacher at which time each child's general behavior and peer relations with others in the classroom were reviewed. Of particular concern in these meetings was evidence of the child's level of problem solving on a broad range of issues, nonsocial as well as social. Achievement and psychometric test scores were also available from this source.

Other sources of data were: twice-yearly case conferences attended by therapist, developmental psychologist, teacher, child care counselors, and supervisors; biweekly discussions with child care counselors of each child's peer relations and progress in activity groups and recess; direct observation event sampling of social behavior and reasoning by the developmental psychologist once a week for 30 minutes for each child during lunch time in the cafeteria[5]; midyear interpersonal reasoning interviews that tapped each child's perception of the function of the various adults in the school; midyear standard reflective interpersonal understanding interviews for each child; and detailed information about

---

[5] Because the developmental psychologist was perceived by most students as "the guy who ran the school" (or by younger children as "the man who owned the school"), his presence at lunch was not viewed as unusual.

the home environment and past history from clinical records and discussion with the social worker assigned to work with members of each child's family.

RESULTS

Listing the sources of information available to us is meant to demonstrate how the researcher and clinician are interested in some very similar sources, types, and categories of data. The differences usually lie in the way the data are collected. The clinician, both because of his circumstances and because he or she is dealing holistically with a child rather than with certain part processes of the child, usually cannot define the unit of analysis employed in as fine detail as the researcher, nor under the conditions required for validation of the information gained. Obviously the data we have collected fall into the category of clinical evidence and place the endeavor to be reported in a formative, clinical, or exploratory phase. Nevertheless, one can see the great potential for doing more formal research in a clinical setting where with the infusion of some degree of rigor and systematization, every professional is a potential researcher with an important perspective to add. To provide an example, we present the following case, which has been particularly challenging to us, as it has raised a number of important theoretical and practical issues.

Background

"Charlie" is a 14-year-old boy who was referred to the clinic by his mother in spring of 1974 following a period of disruptive behavior in public school. His difficulties had led to a number of suspensions. His mother also reported that her son was made a scapegoat of by other children in the neighborhood. Following an evaluation, Charlie was referred for individual psychotherapy which began in January, 1975. In November, 1975, Charlie was transferred to another therapist who saw him until he started treatment with one of us in September, 1977. Charlie attended camp in the summers of 1976 and 1977 and became a student at the clinic school in January, 1977.

Previous therapists, counselors, and evaluators had generally viewed Charlie's emotional adjustment as borderline psychotic. Prevalent in their reports are comments about his limited range of affect, proclivity to distort events and deny the reality of his actions, poor peer-group relationships, tendencies to victimize himself as well as being made a scapegoat by classmates, and need for structure and clearly defined goals.

September, 1977 to February, 1978: The Search
for Charlie's Social-Cognitive Capacity

Charlie, a nice-looking, sturdy, well-dressed adolescent, always appeared promptly for therapy sessions. Initially, he was quite shy, although by midyear he had relaxed considerably, maintaining eye contact and generally appearing to be invested in the therapeutic relationship. Yet, as noted by others, Charlie rarely reacted spontaneously or initiated conversation unless to make a request. Early in the course of therapy, Charlie decided to construct several car, van, and airplane models. He said he wanted to build models as a hobby, but felt a need for help, particularly since his previous efforts in this area had ended in failure. Thus the construction of models occupied a significant portion of his therapy sessions.

Early on, Charlie very quickly became confused and disoriented while working on models. He had obvious difficulty reflecting on his actions and displayed a kind of cognitive slippage or instability of classificatory functioning that did not appear to be within normal limits. In one session, for example, he decided to draw pictures of cars, classified according to manufacturer. After proceeding in a reasonably organized fashion, Charlie drew two cars within a category, but suddenly concluded that they could not belong to the same company because of their differences in shape. Further evidence of logical-causal difficulties emerged when Charlie, immediately after gluing the wheels on a model, placed it forcefully on the table, causing the wheels to buckle. He concluded the table was too hard, apparently ignoring the possible effect of his own action—pushing down on the weak model.

In another early session, Charlie discussed his belief that vans get better gas mileage than cars because they stop less often at the filling pump. When it was suggested that the gas tanks on vans might be bigger than those on cars and that could account for fewer fill-ups, Charlie's reaction was to stick defensively by his original claim. The puzzle for the clinician was whether Charlie's responses were actually a function of a specific defensive posture in the face of perceived criticism or indication of a general dysfunction in reasoning, for example, an inability to consider the effects of multiple variables (distance and size) at the same time. In either case, Charlie frequently appeared to be bound by perceptual or intuitive impressions which impaired not only his logical thinking but also his understanding of social situations.

With respect to social relations, Charlie's descriptions of conflicts with peers and adults in the school were often difficult to follow and reflected his tendencies to confuse as well as to be confused by interpersonal interactions. It appeared that he often allowed himself to be victimized by peers or antagonized them without recognition of his role in these conflicts. Early in therapy, he reported that he tried to avoid the "troublemakers" or to recognize when he was being "set up." Upon close scrutiny, however, his notions of being "set up" were revealed as simplistic, that is, probing indicated they represented merely the idea that he was being "picked on" by others rather than an insight that he was provocative in a way that was likely to elicit a particular response in others. When discussion was oriented toward the possibility that he, himself, might do things to set himself up to be the object of his peers' frustration, a Stage 2 conception, he appeared totally confused, retreating to an insistence that he was a better person this year because the troublemakers had left the school.

Although from a psychodynamic perspective, one can comment on Charlie's projective or externalizing style—"the table broke the van," "the other kids caused me to be bad"—these observations, not coincidentally, also fall into the lower stages of the social-reasoning model and show how a developmental model can be used to characterize reflections on social interaction. In another instance, early in the therapy process, while talking about the possibility that he might feel jealous of the attention being paid by the therapist to another child in the class, Charlie commented, "You like him because he has a better car model," equating imagined favoritism with a desire for material possessions (issue: jealousy—Stage 1). It became increasingly clear that Charlie's interpersonal and intrapsychic concepts appeared to be very immature for a 14-year-old boy, and that the meaning he attributed to words or phrases needed careful exploration. His usage frequently reflected a lower level of understanding than might ordinarily be assumed.

For example, in a subsequent hour Charlie shared that he had "accidentally smashed" a clay model that his classmate had constructed with the therapist. Questions probing for Stage 2 understanding, relating to the possibility that he may have fooled himself into believing that his action had been unintentional, were generally avoided or misconstrued. He appeared to have considerable trouble grasping the notion, which emerges at Stage 2, that surface actions may stem from inner attitudes, for example, rivalrous feelings (issue: self-awareness—Stage 2). Again, his response may be viewed as merely defensive; however, even if defensive, it is of interest developmentally that Charlie relied heavily on coping strategies that embodied central features of Stage 1 social cognition. After several months, we had a picture of Charlie's *functioning* at an abnormally low level of social cognition for a child of normal intelligence, but a less certain picture of his *potential reflective* level of social understanding.

February, 1978 to May, 1978: The Observing Ego Emerges

Up until January or February, repeated attempts to help Charlie clarify or reflect on his experience typically met with mild resistance in the form of denial, projection, or a smoke screen of confusing remarks only tangentially related to the issue under consideration. Serious questions were even raised in our minds as to whether he had the capacity to look reflectively at his own actions (Stage 1), let alone his feelings about these actions (Stage 2). In later sessions, however, he began to lower his guard and to acknowledge painful feelings about himself in a way that indicated a higher social–cognitive capacity.

One day, after his therapist made numerous suggestions to help Charlie correct mistakes in his assembly of a model, suggestions he had trouble hearing and generally ignored, Charlie was asked whether he felt that his therapist "thought he was doing poorly," that is, whether he felt his therapist "was putting him down." Charlie vigorously denied such feelings initially but then admitted that he in fact did feel that way. This incident and interpretation led to further discussion in subsequent sessions of Charlie's strong need to deny his errors and to deflect feedback about his performance to save face. That Charlie might use this same pattern with others, particularly in school, was explored as well. Although only a beginning for Charlie, this exchange demonstrated his growing *functional* capacity to think about his behavior reflectively, at least within the context of a supportive relationship. Whether Charlie had the social–cognitive capacity all along or whether it developed in the therapy and school milieu, the important practical issue at hand was the emergence of a *functioning,* Stage 2, self-reflective self-awareness.

Evidence for the continued functioning of this self-reflective process began to show up elsewhere. In the school lunchroom, for example, Charlie was able to tell his teacher that he did not want to sit at a certain table because he always got himself in trouble there. While this may not be an impressive remark for most 14-year-olds, for this one it marked the exercise of a reflective awareness hitherto unobservable in his day-to-day life in the school.

While the particular event in therapy emphasized above—asking Charlie if he felt criticized—may or may not have been itself the causal or interpretive "turning point," it serves nicely as a signpost of the period when a shift to being able to use the observing ego, that is, self-reflective awareness at a Stage 2 level, was observed. Furthermore, that his behavior was observable to us not only in the therapy session, but also periodically during the 6 hours a day he was in the school, allows us to claim, at least clinically, that the shift in orientation had some generalizability across situational contexts. By May, then, our picture of Charlie's social understanding had changed. His level of *functional* (i.e., practical) understanding had gone up and his *reflective* awareness, as expressed in therapy sessions, was at least at Stage 2.

Conclusion

Charlie's case illustrates how it is possible to code many aspects of children's spontaneous comments and social interactions during psychotherapy sessions in social–cognitive–developmental terms. Although only a beginning, these findings provide encouraging evidence for the external validity of the model. Because of its apparent utility for analyzing several domains as well as modes of reasoning, including both reflective reasoning and reasoning-in-action, we believe that the stage sequence described in this book represents a potentially powerful lens for observing the psychological growth and development of children in naturalistic contexts. We are particularly intrigued by what is implied for the investigation of psychotherapy with children. Systematic research in this area has been severely hampered by the lack of a reliable and valid means for describing the therapeutic process. Too often only global outcome measures are employed, and when the process per se is considered, the richness and complexity involved are typically lost. As exemplified in our discussion of Charlie, the stage descriptions can serve not only as valuable markers of the child's progress in therapy but also as a means for analyzing the complex interplay of patient–therapist transactions.

From the perspective of research there are of course difficulties, particularly with the issue of obtrusiveness. If a therapist (or a child) is aware of the process being observed, there are likely to be distortions in what otherwise would be a natural process. While one alternative is to attempt to be as unobtrusive as possible, this may not be the most useful strategy during the exploratory phase of model application. Another alternative is to include the practitioner–clinician in the research process from its inception. In this way one maximizes chances for understanding the strategies, thoughts, feelings, and ideas of the child in a process that by definition is subjective and deals with subjective material. Once some feeling for the process is obtained, perhaps it is time to turn to more unobtrusive applications and objective systems of behavioral observation and classification.

We have also found that the atmosphere of a research process is often conducive to the generation of practical or clinical suggestions. For instance, we discovered in our work with Charlie that this kind of analysis has surprising technical value and can be a rich source of hypotheses concerning possible areas of cognitive and affective interference in the child's functioning. It is this last point that we would like to consider now in more depth.

SOCIAL-COGNITIVE-DEVELOPMENTAL PERSPECTIVES ON CHILD PSYCHOTHERAPY

In view of growing evidence that environmental, affective, and cognitive variables combine to shape the individual's behavior, members of the therapeutic community turn increasingly to more "holistic" or "multimodal" treatment strategies (Dimond, Havens, & Jones, 1978; Schaefer & Millman, 1977). Although this is a healthy and long overdue trend, what appears to be missing, at least in the case of children, is clear acknowledgment of the important role of developmental level as a foundation for determining how variables interact and what path therapy might most productively follow. We would like to highlight ways that an appreciation of predictable sequences of social understanding can help child clinicians (a) grasp the developmental significance of their patients' and their own communications; (b) see how this understanding can enrich the therapeutic relationship they form with their patients; (c) form strategies for facilitating social–cognitive development of children as a natural part of the therapeutic process; and (d) understand the importance of distinguishing between the child's potential and applied levels of intrapsychic and interpersonal understanding. Our discussion of these issues is restricted primarily to the application of social–cognitive-developmental methods and models to dynamic therapies with children. However, to the extent that this perspective implies a naturalistic set of therapeutic goals and principles oriented to enhancing the development of social–cognitive structures necessary for long-term adaptation, we believe that it also has direct implications for a variety of other treatment modalities, including recent holistic approaches.

Patient-Therapist Communications: Toward a Developmental Hierarchy

Perhaps one of the most important contributions of a social–cognitive-developmental orientation is that it alerts us to how the meanings we attribute to interpersonal and intrapsychic concepts or statements can differ radically from those attributed by our young clients. When we work with children in psychotherapy, it is important to avoid assuming that their communications are readily decodable. For example, consider the following exchange between Charlie and his therapist:

CHARLIE: I've been thinking of going to live with my father again.
THERAPIST: I thought you said he drank a lot and sometimes hit you.
CHARLIE: Well, he's changed.

THERAPIST: Changed?
CHARLIE: Well, ya . . . he's moved to another apartment; he's changed apartments.

As another example, recall from the case presentation Charlie's ideas about "setting himself up." To him, this meant the other kids caused him to get into trouble. There are at least two alternative, but not contradictory, interpretations. First, it is possible that Charlie was responding defensively, that is, misperceiving the locus of the problem and unconsciously projecting angry feelings onto others. It is also possible that Charlie was conceiving the nature of "being set up" at a low social-cognitive stage, equivalent to one at which the child naturally believes or assumes that his or her manifest behavior is under the control of external agents rather than under self-control. Based on the first attribution, the course of the treatment with Charlie could have easily begun with a focus on his "need to be made the scapegoat" at some deep and unreflective motivational level. However, in the path taken here, the *initial* diagnostic concern was for ascertaining the developmental level at which Charlie was understanding his own actions and motives and then to proceed to focus on helping Charlie to clarify the meaning of "setting oneself up" at a higher level. This would seem, from a strategic perspective, to be a more logical first step.

Just as we cannot be sure that we understand our clients' communications, so can we not assume that they understand ours. For instance, whereas the child's lack of response to the therapist's inquiry "Do you think I don't like you because I'm criticizing your model-building?" may reflect a form of resistance, it may also be that from a social–cognitive–developmental perspective, the concepts are too complex or cognitively demanding to be understood at the level at which the therapist means them to be taken.[6]

Following Lewis (1974) and Sperry (1975), social–cognitive–developmental theory may represent a useful paradigm for ordering therapist communications into a developmental hierarchy. For example, *attention statements* (Lewis, 1974), designed to highlight certain feelings or actions accompanying the child's play, may vary in their impact depending upon the social–cognitive stage of the child and how such statements are structured. The youngster whose highest level of intrapsychic understanding is Stage 0 or 1 may not grasp reflective comments even about simple affective states, inasmuch as inner feelings are not well differentiated from actions at these levels. This may help explain why seasoned

---

[6] Very often difficulties of the kind referred to here are seen from a clinical perspective to be problems of word definition as if the therapist were using words unfamiliar to the child. However, whether an understanding can be achieved using more familiar words or simpler syntax is a different although related problem than whether the child has the *same* understanding of the meaning of those words as the adult.

play therapists intuitively frame their reflections about the preschooler's feelings in an action language. That is, rather than saying to a 3-year-old who is aggressively kicking a stuffed bear, "You seem angry or mad today," they might talk in terms of the child's "kicking feelings." Similarly, drawing the youngster's reflective attention to mixed or ambivalent affections prior to his or her development of Stage 3 concepts of intrapsychic processes will most likely be resisted or reinterpreted along more familiar but less mature lines. However, for children who are approaching some understanding of ambivalence and part–whole relations in the affective domain, techniques to concretize or graphically represent discordant feelings and parts of self as described recently by Harter (1977) may facilitate discussion in this area.

The Social–Cognitive Foundations of the Therapeutic Relationship

Stage models of social cognition can inform therapists of a hierarchical framework for understanding the conceptual level of their communications with their patients; such a model may also broaden the base of the therapeutic relationship (Sperry, 1975). Indeed, the rapport that supports and sustains successful therapeutic ventures has roots in the client's perception that his or her internal frame of reference is comprehensible and acceptable to the therapist. Although the ability of the clinician to empathize plays a major role in this process, an understanding of the ontogenesis of social understanding in various domains may be crucial, particularly in work with children. The tendency of grownups, including child therapists, toward "adultocentrism" is not easily checked by empathy alone. Nor can episodic memories from one's own childhood effectively bridge the psychological gap that separates the therapist from the children seen in therapy, as the therapist's recall of earlier forms or patterns of thinking and feeling remains at best incomplete. Familiarity with lines of development described here, however, may appreciably expand the therapist's capacity both to listen and to respond to how the child patient is structuring and interpreting his or her experience.

Beyond developing a mutual trusting relationship in the initial phase of treatment, the therapist attempts to encourage the child to understand why he or she is having problems. The extent to which this task can be accomplished, however, depends on the answers to at least two questions, both of which relate to the child's interpersonal understanding.

Can the child join the therapist in a "working therapeutic alliance"? According to Scharfman (1978):

> That capacity which in adults we call "the splitting of the ego," namely, the experience in which the ego is alternately able to experience certain aspects in the

treatment situation and then shift to being the observer of those experiences, is very difficult for children, often impossible. The self-observing function of the ego does not really appear much before late latency and it is, therefore, much more difficult for the child to join the analyst in understanding the nature and meaning of their interaction [p. 50].

In essence, we agree with this analysis. However, the developmental approach, using the five stages of interpersonal understanding, allows us to pinpoint more precisely the limits of the child's capacity to self-reflect or to develop a working alliance at *each* of the various stages in his development. It also demonstrates that there are several reorganizations, not just one, in the child's understanding of this phenomenon, some occurring prior to latency, some later, well into adolescence.

Can the child see some of his problems as intrinsic rather than as extrinsic? Scharfman (1978) observes:

The child tends to see problems as caused by the external world, whether by parents, school, friends, etc. Children are more likely to seek to change the external environment rather than to look inside themselves and understand their reaction to that environment. They can become intensely disappointed and frequently angry when the analyst expresses an unwillingness to interfere in changing the external environment in one way or another [p. 50].

This tendency on the part of children to externalize can again be seen as related to their social–conceptual capacity. This, in turn, helps determine the degree to which therapists can expect their child patients to tolerate or appreciate psychodynamic or intrapsychic interpretations of their behavior. However, as discussed above, the astute clinician, knowledgeable about developmental theory, can allude to inner determinants or processes, but in a way that respects and works with the child's level of understanding.

Facilitating Social Understanding in Children

Another implication of the developmental model is that it sheds light on the next step that the child needs to take in his or her journey to more complex levels of social understanding. Just how therapists can facilitate this next step represents a challenging area for study. Guidelines derived from the experimental investigation of social or moral reasoning in educational and correctional settings may be applicable in psychotherapeutic contexts as well (Sperry, 1975). Interpretations, clarifications, and queries that are appropriately "matched" to the child's developmental stage may not only insure greater comprehension and acceptance of their content but foster stage change in interpersonal and intrapsychic understanding. For example, clarifying for a guilt-ridden 6-year-old that *angry* feelings toward parents do not erase *affectionate* feelings for them may help to lead to the child's acceptance and consideration of previously unexpressed anger as well as to his or her conceptualization of the relation among feelings at a higher developmental level.

Indeed, child patients often present conflicts and dilemmas related to their lives both inside and outside the therapist's office that can be used as a springboard to developmentally provocative dialogues and interactions. By focusing on children's reasoning processes per se and by helping them consider alternate perspectives and roles, therapists may provide their patients an impetus for thinking at their optimal level of reflection, if not stimulate a higher level (Sperry, 1975). Let us return briefly to the exchange between Charlie and his therapist in which the therapist chose not to challenge or directly interpret his client's wish to live with his father. Rather, struck by Charlie's conviction that his father had "changed," the therapist focused on helping Charlie understand the broader issue of personality change. Questions of whether enduring shifts in personality functioning can be inferred from physical evidence (e.g., changing apartments) or whether there might be some other basis for determining personality change prompted Charlie to wrestle with an abstract, although highly personal, issue. That the discussion did stimulate conflict and further deliberation on his part became eminently clear in a subsequent session. No longer convinced that his father had changed, Charlie decided to defer his decision about living with him until he had more information. "I guess I hoped he'd gotten his act together by now," Charlie reflected.[7]

A Recurring Theme: Competence or Functional Ability?

While either natural, general limitations or specific deficits in social–cognitive development can create problems in the interpersonal and emotional sphere, it is important to remember that even once a child understands complex intrapsychic processes (i.e., for example, that evaluations of the self as a whole can be differentiated from evaluations of a specific aspect of one's functioning) an "affective confusion" about such issues may still be evidenced by the child. This is common not only in the neurotic conflicts of otherwise conceptually sophisticated adults but also in the conflicts of many children whose functional level is lower than their optimal level because of anxiety and associated defensive processes. (The research described in Chapter 9 has indeed suggested

---

[7] Of course, the therapist also could have initially addressed the wish underlying Charlie's comments, that is, that his father *had* changed. But as his reflections intimate, this motive did occur to Charlie in the course of his thinking about the constituent elements of personality change.

that reflective social–cognitive performance may functionally regress under a variety of stressful social and emotional conditions.) Thus developmentalists and clinicians alike must be careful to keep in mind the distinction between stage analyses of understanding as a *competence* that slowly develops over a number of years and social understanding as functional or usable ability once developed.

In Charlie's case, we would speculate that he probably had the basic social–cognitive competence necessary for at least Stage 2 self-reflection all along, that is, that the competence did not ontogenetically develop over a relatively short, 9-month course of therapy. The *application* of his higher-level abilities may have simply been too difficult for him to manage in the face of emotional stress in the beginning phase of treatment. Application of higher-level thinking also held some emotional threat for Charlie; by reflecting about himself at a Stage 2 level, he might have become acutely aware of what we later observed to be his extreme anger and depression about the seemingly insurmountable obstacles in his life. Charlie's defensive style severely constricted the range of what he could express, both affectively and cognitively. It can be surmised that within an environment of trust and safety, a therapeutic alliance developed that made it easier and less frightening to vent his anger and in turn opened up the possibility of his applying his dormant intrapsychic and interpersonal awareness capacity on a functional plane.

It also could be postulated that as a result of the therapist's efforts to help Charlie become aware of his thoughts and feelings while working on neutral cognitive tasks (e.g., building model cars) he developed an attitude or set that had correspondences in the affective domain. As noted in the case presentation, any direct attempt to break through Charlie's wall of denial and avoidance to address underlying affective concerns about charged relationships was patently unsuccessful. It has often been suggested that an alternate route to these issues, especially when working with rigidly defended people, is through the patient's associations to current cognitive activities. This technique may be particularly well suited for those children such as Charlie who come to therapy neither prepared nor inclined to reflect about their inner experiences.

SUMMARY

In this section we have taken a social–cognitive–developmental analysis into a psychotherapeutic context with an emphasis on the child's evolving conceptions of psychological functions which are viewed as uniquely critical from both developmental and psychodynamic perspectives. We have been particularly interested in the significance of our model for describing dialogues and processes in child psychotherapy. As indicated by our presentation of Charlie, the stage model appears not only to have validity in this setting but to add significantly to the conceptualization of a patient's functioning and the course of treatment. We are reminded that Anthony (1956) anticipated the clinical value of cognitive–developmental methods and models when he stated:

> It is not sufficient to understand the dynamics of feelings; we must also understand the genetics of thinking, after which we may claim with greater truth that we really understand our patients [p. 34].

Important questions remain, however, concerning the manner in which cognitive and affective processes interact at various points in the child's development. Previous discussions of this issue (e.g., Odier, 1956) have tended to focus on the disruptive influence of anxiety, whatever its source, on cognitive–developmental processes, although more recently the converse has received some deserved attention (e.g., Harter, 1977; Shantz, 1975). For example, our clinical evidence suggests that deficiencies or distortions in the child's thinking and behavior often reflect stage-specific limitations or lags in social–cognitive development rather than emotional conflict. Yet we are well aware that as appeared to be the case with Charlie, affective mechanisms can prevent application of reflective understanding and related social–cognitive functions in children who are normally capable of higher levels of conceptualization. Consequently, social–cognitive abilities, as defined in the developmental model, can be seen as either an independent or dependent variable, although even this may represent an oversimplification. That is, the direction of effects is most probably reciprocal, such that a lag in reflective understanding may be both antecedent and consequent to the child's difficulties in psychosocial functioning (cf. Sameroff & Chandler, 1975). It is plausible, then, that extreme defensiveness and ego constriction in a youngster can lead to deficiencies in understanding of intrapsychic and interpersonal experience, which in turn can increase defensive rigidity, and so on. Viewed in this way, intervening on either front would be predicted to have reverberations throughout the cognitive–affective system.

Although we have pointed out several potential techniques and guidelines for enhancing the reflective abilities of children that could be implemented with little modification of the conventional therapy format, some form of direct tuition or social–cognitive tutoring may be indicated for many troubled children to help remedy their "deficits" in social cognition and to encourage functional application of what reflective skills they do have. Depending on the needs of the child, such a "psychoeducational" supplement to the treatment plan might range from discussion of personal and hypothetical social dilemmas to the playing of social–cognitive games demanding advanced perspective taking. It is our working assumption that the "intellectually" stimulating nature of these tasks—when interwoven into the therapeutic process in a sensitive and timely fashion—is perforce "emotionally" stimulating and therefore can contribute substantially to the restructuring of both cognitive and affective schemes at higher developmental levels.

This concludes our somewhat detailed discussion of one case and of implications of our model for conventional child psychotherapy. In the next three sections, I present seven more examples or cases—three of "disturbed" children, three of "normal" children, and one of "disturbed" children from a different perspective—which illustrate various aspects of our explorations of application of our model. As in the case of Charlie, it should be noted in the following cases that use of a stage model of social reasoning is not viewed as an *alternative* to conventional clinical methods, but as an adjunct, an addition, and a complement.

Three Clinical Examples

BEN, STEVE, AND HANK: IMMEDIATE OR "CRISIS" THERAPEUTIC APPLICATIONS

In the last section, Jurkovic and I described an individual, intensive, short-term–longitudinal analysis of reasoning in a therapeutic setting. The analysis had particular implications for model validity and conduct of psychotherapy. The case I describe here is at the other end of the spectrum of therapeutic applications, dealing with a one-shot intervention into the behavior and reasoning of a small group of children in a clinic school as a result of a physical fight, a crisis. It serves as an anecdotal illustration of the interpretive and therapeutic use of understanding interpersonal understanding in such a crisis using the technique of a dyadic counseling session.

During recess, two 13-year-olds, "Ben" and "Steve," were playing catch on the sidelines while a more organized softball game was taking place nearby. "Hank," while waiting for his turn at bat, left the game, came over to Ben and Steve, and said, "Throw it here, throw it, throw it." Steve hesitated but Ben's response was "Get the [expletive deleted] out of here. There's not enough room for another guy in our catch." Hank persisted and the confrontation with Ben escalated until a physical fight ensued, requiring their counselor to separate them and bring them to a "time-out" room for a "crisis" dyadic counseling session with the counselor and the school principal.

The first and often most difficult phase of such a session is to gain some consensus on what happened. In this case, for 5 or 10 minutes Ben was in a rage, refusing to do anything but curse and threaten Hank, while Hank simply looked morose and sullen. However, over the course of the next 15 minutes, as they calmed down, both boys began to do some constructive work. Hank reported, "I asked him to throw me the ball, that's all." Ben's report was that, "Hank barged in and screwed up what we were already doing. I told him there was no room for a third guy and he was already playing in the softball game anyway." Hank's version continued that Ben tried to order him away, and "Nobody does that to me."

It is sometimes difficult for adults to realize that a particular social event may be perceived differently by different participants. It is even more difficult for troubled children to do so, especially under conditions of emotional stress and arousal. Nevertheless, once feelings have subsided a bit and various versions of the facts are on the table, the second phase of the crisis dyadic counseling session begins. Each child is asked to reflect upon his or her own feelings during the fracas and what other events may have contributed to the problem. In this particular session Ben was able to acknowledge he got angry and fought not only because there was no room in the catch for Hank but because he felt that he and Steve were special friends and friends need time without others bugging them, and he felt jealous when Hank "butted in" to this time. Ben's expression of this clearly Stage 3 *concept* of friendship, closeness, and jealousy was immediately useful as a partial explanation for his strong *feelings* to both himself and the counselor and principal. This conception also gave the adults a sense of what Ben's developmental capacity was and what they could expect him to be able to understand. Of course, other psychological knowledge is equally important. For example, that Hank was new in school and extremely sensitive to rejection is an important piece of information to add to knowledge of each child's capacity for reflective interpersonal understanding.

In the final phase of the session, each child is asked to look at the behavior and aims of each participant and asked (in more colloquial terms, of course) what social-influence strategies each might have used to achieve his or her respective aims more effectively. In this case, Hank was asked to reflect on the differences among ways of asking to be included in an ongoing dyad and what to do if rejected. It was suggested to Ben he think about how to communicate to a third party the importance of a special friendship in a way that would be neither embarrassing to himself nor insulting to the other child. In such a session, the adults try not to be unrealistic and not to tell children that everyone can or should be friends; we wouldn't want to be preached to like that ourselves. Yet learning how to be able to form and maintain friendships, one of the most difficult processes for these children, must be given some systematic attention. And in crisis counseling, as well as in coping with day-to-day situations, being armed with knowledge of the development of interpersonal conceptions can be a very useful conceptual tool for adults helping children to sort out their relationships. When Hank and Ben could finally *understand* the various aspects of this painful altercation, their *feelings* were also easier to deal with.

TOMMY: CODING AND COMPARING BEHAVIOR AND SOCIAL-INFLUENCE STRATEGIES

In the last anecdote, we focused on naturally occurring reasoning and related behavior and using knowledge of that reasoning in a crisis intervention. We have also found our map of interpersonal understanding can be directly applied to the observed social behavior of children—their interaction strategies for making friends, solving conflicts among themselves, etc. This procedure has had some clinical utility in our work with children with a history of poor social relationships. As an example, I will draw from our experience with "Tommy," a boy referred to the clinic school.

When first admitted to the school at age 14, Tommy, who had a history of severe social deprivation and abuse, frequently hid under his desk out of fear of teachers and peers. Gradually, however, he began to form a close tie to his teacher; this tie was almost entirely a one-sided "you give, I take" affair, characteristic of a Stage 1 friendship understanding. By the end of his second year, Tommy had formed his first real peer relationship. Rather than being based on what is usually the source of an adolescent friendship—Stage 3 style sharing of feelings and establishing a common bond of trust—Tommy's relationship was based on playing and sharing toy trucks with a younger child in his class. This relationship, like the relation with his teacher, exemplified a Stage 1, one-way notion of friendship, both a "do what I want" orientation and a reciprocity limited to a give and take of activities and possessions. In his occasional attempts to make new friends, Tommy would approach a child with a toy to share or go up to other children and try arbitrarily to join in their play. If the others did not respond in kind, Tommy would become upset and leave, unaware of the inadequacy of his social strategies. Further, the occasional child who attempted to form and maintain a friendship with Tommy in a more age-appropriate way—by mutual sharing of ideas or feelings along with activities, for example—was not responded to and would give up the effort.

The anecdote illustrates how it is possible to code some aspects of social interaction strategies in structural developmental terms and demonstrates some functions of the similarities and differences that emerge within and across individuals when this comparative analysis is done. Tommy's behavior, for example, is fairly consistently illustrative of one-way, Stage 1 notions of friendship concepts, formation, and maintenance. When other children appearing to demonstrate a higher-level understanding of making friends approached him, Tommy was not able to respond in kind. And his low-level social approaches were rejected by same-age peers. Hence no relationships were formed. The exception was his friendship with a younger, less socially–developmentally mature child who interacted in a way characteristic of Stage 1 reasoning. Our stage-by-issue map appears able to help us not only to understand developmental patterns in reflective reasoning, but to help place Tommy's *behavior* along a developmental continuum. Rather than leading us to focus on his "rebuff" of the other children, it leads us to look at Tommy's social-interaction *strategies* and to see him not necessarily as hostile or *un*friendly, but as a child whose *way of making friends* is developmentally lagging far behind that of his peers. And for Tommy's teachers and therapists this social–cognitive perspective helped to make sense of Tommy's behavior and suggested ways of approaching him and his development.

DENNIS: REASONING IN ACTION AND OSCILLATION

Our third example from a clinical setting of applying a formal model in a functional context comes from a series of class discussion meetings, similar to those described by Jaquette in Chapter 9, in which five to eight children assessed their group interactions and planned various activities weekly from November to April. Reasoning in this naturalistic context about real-life content was found by both Jaquette and, in this case, Lavin (1979) to fluctuate in stage more than did reasoning in the hypothetical reflective interview. Here, I report on "Dennis," a particularly interesting case of a child manifesting an extreme degree of "interpersonal oscillation," which term has been used primarily to refer to the degree to which fluctuation in reasoning stage can be observed under either hypothetical or natural conditions. The following report draws, in part, on an analysis presented in a paper by Selman, Lavin, and Brion-Meisels (1979).

Dennis was initially admitted to the school at the age of 8 with a diagnosis of borderline schizoid personality development, with autistic symptoms. During his 4 years at the school, he made slow but steady progress. For instance, when first admitted, Dennis acted as if he believed he was really a robot and not a boy, but by the age of 11 or 12 he had apparently abandoned this fantasy. Over the 4 years, he also moved from being interested only in powerful machines to beginning, during the year he was observed, to make and maintain a friendship with a child 2 years younger than he in the same class.

Although Dennis made gains over the 4 years he was at the school, these gains still left him relatively far behind age-mates with respect to his overall social development. Furthermore, replacing his initial identification as a robot, Dennis adapted a reverse negative ethical and interpersonal philosophy. For instance, Dennis would assert that it was fun to make younger children cry, that he enjoyed seeing other persons embarrassed, that he took pride in being the school's most proficient curser, and that he had no fears or anxieties.

As noted above, Dennis, when 12, was a participant in a year-long class meeting study. In September, 1977, before the start of the class meetings, Dennis was administered a reflective interpersonal understanding interview; his IMS score was 1.56. However, this mean score hides the extreme oscillation evident when stage scores across all the interpersonal issues are examined, as in Table 10.1.

Dennis's therapist reported to us the following typical dialogue from one session:

DENNIS: I went up to the top of the John Hancock Building and looked over the ledge. Everybody else was scared, but I wasn't scared.
THERAPIST: Gee, well, I would be kind of frightened looking down from way up there, wouldn't you?
DENNIS: Well ... If I were a therapist and I was trying to get a kid to see that it was all right to admit that he feels frightened about some things, I might say that I would feel afraid to show him that it was okay to show that you were scared ... But I'm not a therapist and I'm also not afraid of anything.

TABLE 10.1
Profile of "Dennis's" Stage Scores across Interpersonal Understanding Issues in a Reflective Interview (September, 1977, Before Class Meetings)

Issue	Stage
Subjectivity	X
Self-awareness	2
Personality	2
Personality change	0(1)
Friendship–group formation	1(2)
Closeness and intimacy	2
Trust and reciprocity	2(1)
Jealousy–exclusion	2
Conflict resolution	0
Group cohesion	1(2)
Conformity	2
Role orientations	1
Decision-making and group organization	X
Leadership	1
Friendship–group termination	X

As the excerpt indicates, in a calm, supportive atmosphere some very troubled children, like Dennis, can exhibit a highly sophisticated understanding of the reciprocal coordination of their own and others' perceptions of social events and psychological reactions, even when, as in this excerpt, the function of the expressed attitude appears to be hostile or defensive.

Just as Dennis showed extreme oscillation in his conceptions-in-theory reflective interview scores [he is the only child in the study to have interview responses coded at three levels (0, 1, and 2)], this same pattern of oscillation, characteristic of what we call the *disequilibrated child,* that is, one with a high-level social–cognitive capacity but variable functioning, is evident in the class meetings as well, as seen in Table 10.2. His *average* NIU scores for 12 meetings range from .56 to 1.56. The difference between highest and lowest individual scores within all 12 meetings was 2.33 stages or NIU points.

Following is an example of Dennis's reasoning in action during a midyear meeting:

1. CARL: [As class leader, reading suggestion] "What should we do about swearing in the classroom?" Who wrote that?
2. TEACHER: I did.
3. CARL: I knew you did. All right, [to Alice] go ahead.

TABLE 10.2
Profile of "Dennis's" Mean NIU[a] Scores for Twelve Class Meetings, November, 1977 to April, 1978[b]

Class meeting number	Mean NIU score
1	1.20
2	1.38
3	.81
4	.92
5	.56
6	1.00
7	1.33
8	1.23
9	1.48
10	1.10
11	.67
12	1.56
	Mean = 1.23

[a] Naturalistic Interpersonal Understanding: see Chapter 9.

[b] Overall NIU mean calculated from all responses in all 12 meetings = 1.10.

4. ALICE:	We should make them put their hands in the cage and let the gerbil bite their fingers.
5. GEORGE:	He doesn't bite.
6. CARL:	Three warnings and you're out [the present rule].
7. LEADER-RESEARCHER:	Before you go to that, let me make a suggestion. How about cutting down to a two-warning rule? Could kids handle that, do you think?
8. BILL:	No!
9. DENNIS:	I wouldn't want that. I think a three-warning rule would be better. Three in the morning, three in the afternoon.
10. TEACHER:	Frank's got something to say.
11. FRANK:	You might break my head for saying this, but the person who gets three warnings in the morning and three in the afternoon should be kept after school.
12. DENNIS:	Frank—that's a dumb thought, mentally retarded you know!
13. FRANK:	That's how you are! [General confusion ensues with lots of insults and name calling within the group.]
14. TEACHER:	You don't have to call names, you just say you disagree.
15. CARL:	(to Leader–Researcher who had hand raised) Go ahead.
16. LEADER-RESEARCHER:	How do people feel when someone says something like that about them?
17. CARL:	Frank, you made some stupid ones, too, and I made some, too.
18. FRANK:	But I didn't say things like cutting their throats off or stuff. [Dennis often describes gory actions such as the one Frank notes.]
19. DENNIS:	Yeh, well people say my ideas are stupid so if they say my ideas are stupid, I can say their ideas are stupid.
20. CARL:	Okay, [Teacher's Name]. [The teacher has raised his hand.]
21. TEACHER:	I have a suggestion. How about if an idea comes up that you think is wrong, instead of saying it is a stupid idea, say that you disagree.
22. CARL:	Yeah, that sounds good.
23. DENNIS:	Or you can say, well, that idea really ain't the *smartest* idea.

Dennis's statement 19 is coded as Level 1, for although Dennis is talking about "ideas," he does not deal with them psychologically; he is referring only to a "reciprocity of *actions*," that is, the reciprocity of insults, rather than to two or more individuals actually evaluating each other's intentions and expectations. This is in marked contrast to the developmental capacity he demonstrates by his remarks in therapy. Although Dennis generated a solid number of lower-level responses, particularly when he felt attacked or challenged, he also provided the greatest number of Level 2 communications. In addition, Dennis sometimes used higher-level social–cognitive abilities in a defensive or hostile way a significant portion of the time.

The functions of Dennis's natural communications varied. Some served a prosocial or "collaborative" goal, such as giving support to a peer through recognizing the peer's feelings or guiding decision-making by predicting responses of peers to possible actions. However, many of Dennis's natural statements served a negative function, showing defen-

that much of adult psychotherapy, a process that is particularly concerned with social relations and interaction, is spent in reflection. In addition to reflective thought being a useful tool of social discourse that appears to develop and be used more extensively with age, self-reflection in social behavior is also thought to be a mark of mental health as opposed to pathology. For instance, troubled children are often characterized as having extraordinary difficulty looking "inside" themselves and understanding relationships among their own feelings and motivations. Their problems are said to increase when they are expected to understand the further relationships between their feelings and motivations and their actions. From one clinical perspective these difficulties interfere with the child's ability to self-regulate or control the active expression of internal experiences, impulses, and reactions, making necessary an increase in external controls or structure.

Natural progressions in children's understanding of self and social relations have important implications for understanding when and how a child looks at his own behavior and its consequences. When working with any child it helps to know to what extent difficulty in looking at his or her own behavior (if there is such difficulty) is a function of the natural level of social understanding common to all children at the given age-period or to what extent there are specific pathological processes involved. Furthermore, if disturbances in inward-looking abilities do exist, it helps to know the extent to which they may be a function of developmental *lags* in social–cognitive capacity and to what extent they may represent defensive *distortions* of otherwise age-appropriate *concepts*. It is all too easy to say that reflective thought is *not* related to social behavior, when in fact *reflective* thought in many instances is a major component of social behavior.

Finally, the distinction we have made between self-reflection, as a key achievement of Stage 2, and the increasingly reflective general style or nature of normally developing thought is a minor one, because these "reflectivenesses" are, of course, closely interrelated.

THE DEVELOPMENT OF INTERPERSONAL
UNDERSTANDING AND OF THE EGO:
A BETWEEN-MODEL CONSIDERATION OF SOCIAL
COGNITION AND PERSONALITY

What is the relation between a developmental analysis of interpersonal understanding and findings and theory on the growth of personality? This area is quite open to empirical study, although related research has been undertaken in the past, using developmental social–cognitive variables (e.g., moral judgment stages) as *independent* variables or personality determinants, and has attempted to look at how

TABLE 11.2
Some Milestones in Loevinger's Model of Ego Development[a]

Roughly corresponding stage of interpersonal understanding	Stage	Code	Impulse control, character development	Interpersonal style	Conscious preoccupations	Cognitive style
	Presocial			Autistic		
	Symbiotic	I-1		Symbiotic	Self versus non-self	
0	Impulsive	I-2	Impulsive, fear of retaliation	Receiving, dependent, exploitative	Bodily feelings, especially sexual and aggressive	Stereotyping, conceptual confusion
1/2	Self-protective	△	Fear of being caught, externalizing blame, opportunistic	Wary, manipulative, exploitative	Self-protection, trouble, wishes, things, advantage, control	
2/3	Conformist	I-3	Conformity to external rules, shame, guilt for breaking rules	Belonging, superficial niceness	Appearance, social acceptability, banal feelings, behavior	Conceptual simplicity, stereotypes, cliches
3/2	Conscientious-conformist	I-3/4	Differentiation of norms, goals	Aware of self in relation to group, helping	Adjustment, problems, reasons, opportunities (vague)	Multiplicity
3	Conscientious	I-4	Self-evaluated standards, self-criticism, guilt for consequences, long-term goals and ideals	Intensive, responsible, mutual, concern for communication	Differentiated feelings, motives for behavior, self-respect, achievements, traits, expression	Conceptual complexity, idea of patterning

3/4	Individualistic	I-4/5	*Add:* Respect for individuality	*Add:* Dependence as an emotional problem	*Add:* Development, social problems, differentiation of inner life from outer	*Add:* Distinction of process and outcome
4	Autonomous	I-5	*Add:* Coping with conflicting inner needs, toleration	*Add:* Respect for autonomy, interdependence	Vividly conveyed feelings, integration of physiological and psychological, psychological causation of behavior, role conception, self-fulfillment, self in social context	Increased conceptual complexity, complex patterns, toleration for ambiguity, broad scope, objectivity
	Integrated	I-6	*Add:* Reconciling inner conflicts, renunciation of unattainable	*Add:* Cherishing of individuality	*Add:* Identity	

Note: "*Add*" means in addition to the description applying to the previous level.
[a] Table reprinted from Loevinger, 1976, by permission of Jossey Bass.

variation along developmental lines *predicts* variation in social actions or personality dimensions. I would suggest instead that research be undertaken in which level of social–interpersonal understanding be considered a *dependent* variable to see what effect variation in personality factors has on level of expressed reasoning or on the relation between reasoning expressed in different modes. While the personality–social-cognition relation is surely more interactive than a consideration of interpersonal understanding as either a dependent or an independent variable alone implies, some starting point is needed. To continue to explore this subject requires two further important considerations be kept in mind. First, because a structural–developmental analysis focuses on hierarchical changes or reorganizations rather than on stability, it makes sense to attempt to relate ontogenetic models of social cognition to models of personality *development* and reorganization rather than to models of personality change, adjustment, or dynamics. Second, to understand how developmental aspects of interpersonal understanding and personality correspond, one place to start is with an examination of how psychologists have decided to assess each.

I have chosen the contemporary work of Jane Loevinger (1976) and her colleagues studying ego development as providing the most fertile grounds for a comparison of similarities and of differences between social–cognitive development and personality development. Table 11.2 is a synopsis of Loevinger's model of ego development.

The most obvious first place to look for similarities between developmental models is in the stage descriptions of each. To do so, however, requires a good working understanding of both the practical and theoretical aspects of each descriptive system, an understanding that will allow one to be able to look through brief verbal synopses to the heart of the stage characterizations in each system without distorting the underlying meanings of either. If this can be accomplished without too much assimilation of one model to the other some interesting relations can be elaborated.

Both Loevinger's Impulsive stage (I-2) and our own egocentric, undifferentiated Stage 0 contain remnants of earlier fusions of self and other, but now these fusions are taking place on a mental plane rather than on the nonsymbolic physical level of kinesthetic interactions. The fusions are represented by a lack of a clear understanding of differences between self's wants and other's ability to provide, of differences between thoughts and actions, and of differences between physical and psychological causations.

The behavior that characterizes Loevinger's Self-protective (Delta) stage, that is, receiving, dependent, and exploitative, bears a resemblance to the reasoning strategies we observe and interpret in the young child as being one-way (Stage 1). Here both behavior and understanding can be characterized as imbalanced, either too demanding for the self or too intrusive or coercive toward others. (It must be remembered this is a natural form of interaction for a 5- to 7-year-old, and terms like *dependent* and *exploitative* have fairly benign meanings when they describe the natural self-centeredness of young children. When these terms describe styles maintained into later life they take on more pathological implications.) There also appears to be some overlap between characteristics of Loevinger's Delta stage and our Stage 2 reasoning and understanding, a stage characterized by a certain delight in exercising the newfound understanding of psychological deception and manipulation.

Both Loevinger's Conformist stage (I-3) and her Conscientious-conformist stage (I-3/4) appear to require the third-person perspective taking that underlies our Stage 3. But the parallels are not exact. For example, we stress that one ramification of this third-person perspective is the idea or conception of persons in terms of traits. (At Stage 2 traits are not understood as enduring but as momentary.) Loevinger does not assign the understanding of traits until the Conscientious stage (I-4). She notes one typically finds a kind of pseudo-trait conception in the transitional Conscientious-conformist stage (I-3/4) which is in a way more similar to our Stage 2: "Pseudo-traits partake of the nature of moods, norms, or virtues, such as those mentioned in the Boy Scout oath [1976, p. 20]."

We can see that although the general flow of the two streams matches fairly closely, the assignment to particular stages of particular ideas and conceptions does not always perfectly correspond. For another instance, our Stage 3 appears to have certain aspects in common with three of Loevinger's ego stages (I-3, I-3/4, I-4), with her I-4 appearing to represent a highly consolidated form of our Stage 3 understanding.

In addition, there appears to be a striking resemblance between an understanding that Loevinger codes at the Individualistic stage (I-4/5) and what we have noted as a transitional form of understanding between Stages 3 and 4. This is the belief expressed by many adolescent subjects that closeness must give way to autonomy. Rejecting the mutuality of Stage 3 and opting for a complete independence appears to be a conscious attempt to avoid the pain of losing what is recognized to be hard-won: another's commitment. Loevinger notes at Stage I-4/5 a similar heightened sense of individuality and concern for *emotional* independence: "What characterizes this stage is the awareness that it is an emotional rather than a purely pragmatic problem that one can remain emotionally dependent on another even when no longer physically or financially dependent [1976, p. 22]." Finally, the Autonomous stage (I-5) appears highly concordant with our Stage 4, autonomous interdependence, at which stage the problems of overdependence and counterdependence, if not resolved, are at least acknowledged.

On the surface, then, although stage-to-stage isomorphism across systems is lacking, that such similar overall systems were constructed using different methods and assumptions generates strong evidence for the construct validity of developmental characteristics of interpersonal growth, a point to which Loevinger has devoted a great deal of scholarship (1976). Of course, in this respect, it is not coincidental that both systems have an intellectual heritage in the thinking and writing of Baldwin, Mead, Piaget, and Sullivan.

If these are the perceived similarities, what then are the critical differences? This aspect of the inquiry must begin with an examination of methods of data collection and analysis. Here Loevinger has made use of a projective method for collecting data and a strict psychometric set of algorithms for coding the data so obtained. Subjects are traditionally asked to complete a set of 36 sentence stems (Loevinger, Wessler, & Redmore, 1970) and scoring of the completed thoughts is done in conjunction with a detailed manual. The manual itself has gone through several revisions and there are different stems for different populations, for example, males and females.

Although Loevinger does not deny the importance of the theoretical model for arriving at a scoring system, once it is derived, she does advocate an empirical measurement approach to "Phase-2" validation, one that does *not* rely upon each interviewer or scorer having an intimate knowledge of that theory. (In fact, in her approach an interviewer is not really needed and a scorer often tends to be a technician.) These strategies reflect Loevinger's belief that psychometrically sound measurement is not simply a necessary part of research on ego development but in fact the cutting edge of any scientifically based psychological discipline as well as the best way to feed back revisions into theory. Inferences about the relation between general theoretical models and specific data coding analyses are worked out preceding (and after) the Phase-2 data collection–construct validation process, and are in fact largely independent of it, at least for that interim period during which the theoretical model is being "tested" through the collection of additional data. Thus, whereas Loevinger gains a certain actuarial or nomothetic validity by eliminating potential sources of bias that are inevitably incurred with reliance on well-trained interviewers, she loses the clinical or idiographic validity that is gained through the use of an in-depth and well-probed interview. Thus researchers involved in large-scale correlational studies requiring the objective assessment of a relatively large number of subjects might be advised to choose the Loevinger approach over one like our own. On the other hand, small-scale clinical studies which are focused on an explication of the meaning each subject gives to interpersonal events and interactions, such as those described in Chapters 9 and 10, may require the kind of clinical and interpretive analysis that our method more readily provides.

Referring back to an earlier distinction, Loevinger's projective technique is more closely aligned to what I have characterized as a mode of spontaneous orientation rather than reflective understanding. In this sense, the ego development assessment can be thought of as a test of "performance" rather than of "competence." In other words, if theoretically parallel descriptions could be drawn across developmental points in the two respective systems, I suspect that using an in-depth, well-probed interview would on the average elicit higher levels or stages from a subject than would the unprobed, sentence completion technique.

It is here that the relation of theoretical models and measurement techniques can be better understood. While stages of ego development, as conceptualized by Loevinger, appear to have close parallels to our own model of interpersonal understanding, they are not thought of as stages of reasoning or understanding. Interpersonal reasoning or understanding is just one part or process in the ego-stage construct. In this sense, ego stages reflect a greater level of theoretical abstraction than do interpersonal understanding stages. Ego stages do not describe a formal or structural cognitive function, but a further abstraction, one which nevertheless is dependent on the level of competence that each social-cognitive structure provides. In other words, developmental ego stages are an inferential step further removed from observed action than reasoning stage; inferences about ego stages must rely in part on inferences about social–cognitive stages. Relatively speaking, social-cognitive stages are probably more directly in correspondence with social interactions. I think this might explain Loevinger's emphasis on a method, a projective technique, that plays down social context, and itself is not adaptable to direct use in the observation of interpersonal interaction over time in natural settings. Since relative to cognitive structure the degree of inference and interpretation is necessarily greater, it may usefully be called a "second-degree-of-inference" construct when compared to phenomena we examine under the rubric of interpersonal understanding.

Furthermore, in comparing these two systems, I suggest that Loevinger's emphasis on a method that deemphasizes context and is not readily amenable to use in natural settings also reflects her strong working hypothesis that ego stages reside within an individual as a process, and are relatively generalizable and stable (although obviously developmentally alterable as well as open to some degree of fluctuation and oscillation). In comparison, while our own evidence suggests that under calm conditions there is a developmental coherence to interpersonal understanding, our naturalistic research is a constant contextual reminder that interpersonal understanding is *not* located solely in the individual, and that there is no such thing as interpersonal understanding alone. It is always an interpersonal understanding of something, of *some* problem or conflict or idea in *some* context, even if only hypothetical. Interpersonal understanding therefore is not as abstract (second-degree) a construct as ego development nor one that is quite so impervious to context. To the extent that we have already noted the difficulty in making "first-degree" inferences from action to underlying social–cognitive structures, either in interview or natural settings, the "naturalistic" study of ego development would be that much more difficult and interpretive.

There is a final distinction between these two models worth consideration. Our model's primary focus has been on ontogenetic aspects of development, and Loevinger's model's primary focus is on developmental aspects of individual differences in adulthood. While I believe the former approach can lead into the latter, that is, one can work from the bottom up, there are greater difficulties working from the top down, that is, trying to construct a descriptive model that can capture both similar (same-stage) processes in individuals at widely disparate ages *and* different processes in individuals of roughly the same age. For example, Loevinger notes that at the Self-protective (Delta) stage of development, the individual is characterized by a fear of being caught for misdeeds, by an externalizing of blame, by opportunism, and by a manipulative and exploitative orientation toward interpersonal relations. Now this set of orientations provides a partially valid but one-sided assessment, as Loevinger recognizes, of the young child who "naturally" goes through this stage. It certainly seems to paint a negative picture of childhood, and while it is true that children do externalize, etc., surely children passing through this stage are more gratifying, giving, or at least fun to be with than these descriptions would imply. The problem is that to the extent that the descriptive terms represent personality characteristics and not formal social–cognitive structures, the ego stage descriptions, of necessity, must be value oriented and to a certain extent content bound. Otherwise they would not be able to capture the subtleties of developmental differences in adult personality and interaction. In being so, they use terms which paint a vivid behavioral picture of the adult who functions at a low stage, but an overly biased and unforgiving picture of the normal child functioning at the same level. While the adult cynic (Delta) may indeed have the mind of a child, the child does not necessarily have the mind of a cynic. It must be made clear that words like "manipulative" and "exploitative" are not context-free. They take on very different meanings depending on the age, level of understanding, and interactional context of the particular individual being described.

It is for this reason that a formal model, such as that of perspective-taking levels, is of value in helping to distinguish when the individual has the social–cognitive capacity for higher-level understanding but does not use it, as say in the case of most adults functioning at the Delta stage, versus the child (or adult) whose social–cognitive capacity does not *permit* functioning at a higher level. This would imply that in the assessment of an individual's stage of ego development as a mode of interpersonal functioning, it would also be important to have some idea of that individual's social–cognitive capacity. *Reflective* "tests" of interpersonal understanding capacity would to an extent supply or closely approximate such information. Thus in comparing ego stages and social–cognitive stages we are led to the same conclusion as before: to focus on both formal and functional aspects of behavior at one and the same time.

A Final Word on the Validity of Research Using a Stage Model of Interpersonal Understanding

The state of the art of research based on social–cognitive stage approaches can be compared to the state of the art of the field of photography before the availability of the motion picture camera. The static stage descriptions, still pictures, are orderly and meaningful, providing a sense of the stability of the child, just as the family portraits of the early twentieth century gave us some feel for the order of a group or the basics of a character. But just as this level of technology lacked the flexibility to capture motion, social–cognitive stage analyses and assessment through reflective interviews cannot capture children in the real world, who are fast-moving creatures in every sense and who seldom display the order that the old-fashioned pictures represented or stage analyses imply. Like a contemporary photographer learning to exploit a new adjustable lens, the developmental researcher is still learning how to understand the range of behaviors and the level of their analysis he or she can speak to, how fast (or slow) his or her subject, the child, can move in real-life conditions and still be described with some validity from a developmental perspective.

Guided in part by the descriptive work of the developmental interview, our research suggests a critical area in great need of study: the longitudinal day-to-day and week-to-week socialization process in children, especially under structured conditions or planned intervention. Two types of research tools in combination are needed: first, a way to structure the environment so that the child's developing understanding of the child's own and other's social behavior can be stimulated and observed, and second, a developmental model that can focus more precisely on particular social relationships and strategies, both *behavioral* and *conceptual*, from a developmental point of view.

For example, in research currently in progress, we have observed that fifth-grade children who demonstrate on a reflective interview the capacity for Stage 2 form of interpersonal understanding are more likely to use certain kinds of sarcastic verbal behavior in their daily natural interactions with peers than are fifth-grade children who do not demonstrate this level of understanding. They also demonstrate a different type of sense of humor, often either more self-deprecatory or self-congratulatory. It is this kind of search for behavioral concomitants of underlying social–cognitive capacity that is the direction of our research, less tied to demonstrating the validity of stages, and more tied to using the developmental model to provide a framework for understanding the growth and maturity of observable social behavior.

My outlook for the study of social behavior within a developmental framework is optimistic. Our experience with the children at the clinic school has shown that theory can be served if it is used retrospectively to order the data observed during the natural implementation of practice, as well as to structure or preplan programs to enrich the likelihood of eliciting the phenomenon that one seeks to observe, for example, social reasoning behavior. This experience has convinced me that better understanding of children's developing relationships depends on their being given the chance both to *express* these values and to *act* upon them, to test their orientations for themselves. Longitudinal observation of children can be accomplished over time in all manner of natural and educationally structured social interactions with each other and with adults: in play groups, in Cub Scouts and Brownies, in community center activity groups, at summer camp, as well as in school-based programs. Any one of these can provide a wealth of knowledge about the social life of the child for the researcher committed to integrating developmental, educational, clinical, social–psychological, and anthropological techniques to working with and learning from children.

Finally, the stage approach to understanding the developmental aspects of interpersonal understanding must employ a wide-angle lens as it surveys the span of human development. Its strength lies less in being able to specify, predict, or account for each child's particular set of social attitudes than in providing a model for understanding the organizing principles that underlie these strategies and changes in them. Work in this area has already begun to provide tentative understanding of how these underlying social–cognitive processes work in the day-to-day interaction of the child. Certainly stage orientations (or processes) are not conscious preoccupations; they are not usually understood or reflected upon by the child in making specific social decisions or making specific actions in relation to others. It also is misleading to state, "This child *first thinks* at Stage x and *then acts* according to this stage about this event." It may be more reasonable to state, "This child has *acted* in certain consistent (or inconsistent) ways across a number of observed social interactions; from these we can infer that he or she is *capable* of structuring his or her social relations in ways best characterized by Stage x."

While stage analyses have provided useful insights into formal development, the functional question boils down to this: is it valid to think of an individual's interpersonal cognition-in-action as relatively stable (at a particular stage), or is there so much oscillation due to situational factors that the stage construct is rendered psychologically impotent?

Our own research suggests three major themes to guide future research on the question of the developmental integrity and stability of interpersonal understanding.

1. The development of the organizing capacity for interpersonal understanding proceeds under natural conditions in an orderly and sequential fashion, that is to say, the development of social–cognitive capacity or maturity can, with some validity, be represented as stages in the child's continuing attempt to organize and give a sense of order to social interactions.

2. One way to conceptualize interpersonal functioning from a developmental perspective is as an interaction of the relative (or age-related) maturity of the individual's cognitive capability for interpersonal understanding and the individual's ability to function at his or her most competent level under a range of circumstances. This theme is qualified by the next.

3. An individual's functioning at stages lower than the highest he or she is capable of is in itself not necessarily an indication of individual immaturity, pathology, or immorality, but must be looked at in relation to the demands of the social situation, the interpersonal context or atmosphere, a topic critically in need of further study.

As Heinz Werner (1948) specified years ago, developmental maturity is not necessarily to be thought of as simply being capable of functioning at one's *highest* level, but may also be the ability to choose (although not necessarily in a conscious way) among a more differentiated developmental hierarchy of responses to meet the needs of a particularly and situationally structured social problem. A hierarchical model of social–cognitive development implies that the definition of a socially mature individual would be one with a relatively more differentiated set of qualitatively and hierarchically ordered social concepts *potentially* available for adaptation to various social contexts, *and* one who generally is capable of consistently being able to function at a higher level even when the social milieu does not lend itself to eliciting high-level functioning. As the saying goes, "A wise man can act the fool, but a fool cannot act the wise man." If the saying is correct, then we have no choice but to try to learn how our children become socially wise, to provide opportunities for them to do so, and to try to understand through both "educational" and "naturalistic" research how this ethical and interpersonal wisdom can best be put into practice.

Illustrations of Suggested Methods for Interpersonal Understanding Interview [1]

The interviewer may interview the child on questionnaires covering any one of four domains: individuals, friendships, peer-group relations, or parent–child relations. Regardless of the particular questionnaire used, certain general guidelines for interviewing ought to be kept in mind.

1. The interviewer's task is to bring out the child's own naive theory of interpersonal relations through his understanding of *issues* specifically related to each of the domains. These issues are the basic organizing system and the interviewer should always ask questions that seek to help the child articulate his thoughts about one of these issues.

Issues Related to Concepts of Individuals

I. *Subjectivity*—Covert properties of persons—thoughts, feelings, motives. Conflicts between thoughts or feelings within the person.

II. *Self-Awareness*—Awareness of the self's ability to observe his/her own thoughts and actions.

III. *Personality*—Stable or predictive character traits—a shy person, etc.

IV. *Personality Change*—How and why people change—growing up, etc.

---

[1] This material is drawn in large part from the 1977 version of our manual.

Issues Related to Concepts of Friendship

I. *Formation*—How and why friendships are made; the ideal friend. A. why = motives; B. how = mechanisms; C. ideal friend.

II. *Intimacy*—Types of friendship; the ideal friendship; intimacy.

III. *Trust and Reciprocity*—Doing things for friends; trust in friends.

IV. *Jealousy*—Feelings toward an intrusion into a formative or established friendship.

V. *Resolving Conflicts*—How problems are resolved between friends.

VI. *Termination*—Why friendships break up.

Issues Related to Concepts of Peer-Group Relations

I. *Formation*—How and why groups are formed; the ideal group member. A. why = motives; B. how = mechanisms; C. ideal member.

II. *Cohesion*—Unity within the group.

III. *Conformity*—Reasons for and types of conformity.

IV. *Rules*—The types of rules and reasons for them.

V. *Decision-making and Organization*—How groups decide on goals, resolve problems, and work together.

VI. *Leadership*—Qualities of the position and its function to the group.

VII. *Termination*—Why groups break up; why a member may be excluded.

Issues Related to Concepts of Parent–Child Relations

I. *Formation*—Adults' motives for having children; why children need parents; what are the ideal qualities of parents.

II. *Emotional Ties*—Why is there love between parents and children; factors which help parents and children get along.

III. *Obedience*—Why and when children should do what parents ask them to; limits of parental control.

IV. *Punishment*—Causes and purposes of punishment.

V. *Conflict Resolution*—Strategies that parents and children have and use to resolve differences.

The interviewer should constantly ask himself or herself: About what issue is the child thinking and at what stage?

2. Two general requirements ought to be filled by the interviewer. First, interviewing requires a nonthreatening or clinical approach to the subject as having natural abilities to make sense of these sometimes complex concepts. We do not seek to test by an absolute criterion, but rather to provide an atmosphere wherein a child can perform at his or her highest level of competence. The child should be made to feel at ease in the interview, that his or her thinking makes a great deal of sense and that the interviewer is personally interested in the child's ideas. Second, the interviewer ought to have a good knowledge of the stages. By knowing the kinds of responses made at the different stages, the interviewer is more likely to pick up and clarify ambiguous responses. Without both of these requirements the interviewer may never obtain the child's confidence enough to promote insights into interpersonal relations or adequately probe vague responses necessary to elucidating the child's level of interpersonal understanding.

3. Given the basic requirements of interviewing, the initial task is to move from surface opinions or choices ("I think Jerry should be with his friend") to underlying cognitive structures, concepts, or *reasons* ("because without friendship you would be pretty lonely"). To this end each of the numbered questions can be seen to have two parts. First, there are the standardized questions as written in the interviews. These standardized questions and their answers by the child are called the *structured phase* of interviewing. Often this structured phase of interviewing will produce scorable cognitive structures (concepts or reasons), but frequently the interviewer must resort to the *open-ended phase*. The open-ended phase represents the questions which the interviewer must create in the course of the interview to clarify reasons or move the child from opinions to underlying reasons. Usually the difference between an adequate interview and an excellent one is based on the interviewer's ability to think on his or her feet and come up with probes that both interest the child and serve to produce or clarify important conceptions. While the open-ended phase remains primarily an art form, two general open-ended probe approaches should be kept in mind. First, there are probe questions aimed at why a particular quality in persons, friends, peer groups, or parent–child relations is important or necessary (e.g., "How come it's important to take votes in a group?"). This *relevance probe* challenges the child to provide justifications for a particular idea. Second, there are probes that seek to uncover the specific stage-related nature or characteristic of a given concept. For example, children often say you have to *know* a friend before you can be really good friends. Using what we call the *meaning probe*, the interviewer might say: "What kind of things do you have to know about someone before you become good friends?" The child who responds "names" or "what they look like" would then be giving a different stage of interpretation to the word *know* than the child who says, "what kind of personality they have." We find these *relevance* and *meaning* probes to be the most obvious of the many different tactics to use in interviewing. Of course, the interviewer will and should come up with his or her own that work even better.

4. Related to the problem of confusing surface opinion with reasoning or conceptions, sometimes the subject's initial reactions may be mechanistic, dealing only with physical or overt behaviors. Sometimes these mechanistic explanations are indicative of a lower stage but often individuals capable of higher stages will initially give only mechanistic answers. They may be thinking at higher levels, but only giving the interviewer a chance to hear responses which are simpler. For example, any subject may respond to the question, "What would it take to get a team going?," with the idea of "practice" characteristic of at least Stage 1 thinking. However, further probing may reveal practice as a means for instilling coordinated "teamwork" (Stage 2) or "getting the team to

work as a unit" (Stage 3). Therefore, even when reasons sound like they are at a particular stage of development, the interviewer should always explore the possibility of higher stages of understanding by using the relevance or meaning probes. Continuing with the example of practice, the interviewer might ask, "Why do you think practice might help them out?" or "What kind of things will practice do for a team?"

5. Our interviews initially use a hypothetical context for discussion (e.g., "In the story you have just seen, what kind of person is Jerry?"). However, we often find the hypothetical modality too limited and move to other social contexts. Three contexts are present in the interpersonal relations interviews: (a) the *hypothetical* ("Was Jerry a good friend in that story? Why?"); (b) the *general* ("What kind of person do you think makes a good friend?"); and (c) the context of *personal experience* ("What kind of person is your best friend, Charlie?") To improve the quality of the subject's insights, the interviewer may wish to change contexts of the questions. For example, a child unmotivated to discuss social–psychological issues in a hypothetical story may become more verbal and insightful when the discussion is shifted to issues of conformity, cohesion, or leadership in his own peer group. On the other hand, children who become too involved in the mechanistic details of their own clubs or gangs may improve the quality of their reasoning by getting away from their personal experience through a hypothetical or general context of discussion. We do not seek to "test" the child but constantly to adjust our interview to *observe* the conditions which bring out the *highest* level of competence of which the child is capable, as well as those conditions under which the child functions at a lower level.

6. Some of our questions use words (team spirit, loyalty, personality, jealousy) which the younger children or those from different cultural backgrounds may not be familiar with. This, of course, creates a serious problem when interviewing. Two methods are used to reduce this problem. First each issue in which difficult vocabulary is used also contains questions in which only a basic vocabulary is required. For example, in the peer-group issue of "Cohesion" there are questions of both loyalty, an obviously difficult word, and "what keeps a group together," which requires no special vocabulary. If the child does not know the meaning of a certain word, the interviewer need only find a more comprehensible or idiomatic question within the same issue. Since subjects are not scored for what they cannot answer, the limited vocabulary theoretically has less direct effect on the measurement of stage.

Second, following each of the most difficult concepts is a brief explanation in simpler terms. The interviewer may even supply his or her own definition. If a child does not appear to understand a given concept, the interviewer provides the definition and continues with the questioning. It has been our experience that such definitions organized at the child's own level of reasoning do not appear to bias the interview. Observe the following:

DO YOU THINK TEAM SPIRIT IS IMPORTANT IN YOUR GANG?
What's team spirit?
IT'S WHEN EVERYONE LIKES EACH OTHER. DOES YOUR GANG HAVE THAT?
Yah, we all say "hi" to each other.
WHY IS TEAM SPIRIT IMPORTANT?
Cuz if you don't, you'll get in a fight.

The interviewer supplies a definition at least of Stage 2 ("spirit is liking each other"). However, the child orients to "each other" only in terms of surface behaviors (Stage 1) ("we say hi to each other"), not to the inner feelings of reciprocated affection.

7. For younger children, ages 3 to 6, we often find it necessary to bend our interviewing procedures. For example, when showing a film-strip, the interviewer may stop the projector during the story and ask one or more questions which might be appropriate at that time. In this way the child need only hold his attention on the questions for a few minutes before returning to the more enjoyable filmstrips. Another approach used by Brion-Meisels (1977) has been the creation of cartoon pictures which recreate some of the interpersonal dilemmas. Questions may be built in after short episodes in the dilemma so that the interview is a series of episodes and questions. Often, very casual questioning about the young child's own friendships, at a moment that may not be thought of as part of a standard interview, has proven effective.

8. Enjoy yourself! Interviewing children on their conceptions of interpersonal relations is a creative challenge for even the "experts" on developmental stages. We often find interviewing techniques used by the "newcomer" which surpass the ideas we have come up with. Just remember to always ask yourself, in what way am I adding to my understanding of how this child defines this issue in interpersonal relations (jealousy, leadership, etc.). Try to listen to your first few interviews, perhaps with others, and think of ways to improve your clinical approach and open-ended probes. Try not to lead the child too strongly with your own assumptions, but don't be afraid to try new ideas.

Following are two sample dilemmas from the individuals domain, for younger and older children, followed by sample interview questions.

Individuals Domain Interview

For interviewing younger children on concepts of individuals, we have found the *Puppy Story* preferable, while for older children, adolescents, and adults, the *Ping-Pong Story* is better. These same stories are available in filmstrip form published by Guidance Associates.[2] For the *Puppy Story,* show *First Things: How Would You Feel? Part I* and for the *Ping-Pong Story,* show *First Things: How Do You Know What's Fair? Part I.*

THE PUPPY STORY (FOR CHILDREN BELOW THE AGE OF 9 OR 10)

Tom has just saved some money to buy Mike Hunter a birthday present. He and his friend Greg go downtown to try to decide what Mike will like. Tom tells Greg that Mike is sad these days because Mike's dog Pepper ran away. They see Mike and decide to try to find out what Mike wants without asking him right off. After talking to Mike for a while the kids realize that Mike is really sad because of his lost dog. When Greg suggests he get a new dog, Mike says *he can't just get a new dog and have things be the same.* Then Mike leaves to run some errands. As Mike's friends shop some more they see a puppy for sale in the pet store. It is the last one left. The owner says that the puppy will probably be sold by tomorrow. Tom and Greg discuss whether to get Mike the puppy. Tom has to decide right away. What do you think Tom will do?

(An asterisk indicates an especially important question.)

Open-ended Probes
1. What do you think Tom, the boy who is buying the birthday present, should do? Why? Have you ever known a boy like Mike; what was he like?

I. *Subjectivity*
1. How do you think Mike might have felt if Tom gave him the new puppy?
*2. If Mike is smiling could he still be sad, how is that possible? Could someone look happy on the outside, but be sad on the inside? How is that possible?
3. Could he feel happy and sad at the same time? Have you ever been in a situation where you felt happy and sad at the same time?
4. Could he feel *both* happy and sad about the new puppy? Could he have mixed feelings? How can feelings be mixed, like happy and sad?
5. Can you ever know another's feelings? When?

II. *Self-Awareness*
1. Mike said he never wants to see another puppy again. Why did he say that?
*2. Did he mean what he said? Can someone say something and not mean it? How?
3. Do you think Mike would change his mind later? Why? Is it possible that he doesn't know his own mind?
4. Might Mike feel guilty about losing his dog? Why? What is guilt, anyway?
5. Is it possible that Mike doesn't know how he feels? How is that possible?
6. Is it possible to not know your own feelings, even if you think about them?
*7. Did you ever think you'd feel one way and then find out you felt another? How could that happen? Can you ever fool yourself? How? What's the difference between fooling yourself and fooling somebody else?

[2] Guidance Associates, Communications Park, Box 300, White Plains, New York.

III. *Personality*

  *1. What kind of person do you think Tom is, the boy who had to decide whether or not to get Mike the puppy?
  *2. Was he a thoughtful (kind) person? What makes a person thoughtful (kind)? How can you tell if a person is thoughtful (kind)? What do you think makes someone become a thoughtful (kind) person?
  *3. What kind of person is Mike if he doesn't care if the dog is lost? Can you tell what kind of person someone is from a situation like this? How does one get to know someone else's personality? What is a "personality"? Can someone have more than one personality?
  4. Do you think Tom will lose self-esteem if he gets Mike a puppy and he doesn't like it? Why? Does one's self-esteem have anything to do with what kind of person you are?

IV. *Personality Change*

  *1. What do you think it will take to change the way Mike feels about losing his old dog Pepper? How long will it take him to get over it? Why? What will it take to make him happy again?
  2. If Mike had been older, say 18, do you think he would have acted the same way about losing his dog? Why? How does being older change the way a person acts?
  *3. If Mike is usually an unhappy kid now, what will he be like when he grows up? Do you think he will change or stay the same? How do people usually change as they get older?
  *4. If you were Mike's friend, what would you do to help him get over his lost dog? Anything besides buying him another dog? What might you say to him?

THE PING-PONG STORY (FOR CHILDREN 9 OR OVER)

Keith, 10, and Jerry, 8, live across the street from each other and are good friends, even though Keith is older. They have a lot in common, but Keith especially likes playing Ping-Pong at Jerry's house. However, Keith always wins, and finally one day when he beats Jerry 21–10, Jerry throws down his paddle and says that's it. There's no sense in his playing Ping-Pong anymore because he always loses.

He and Keith argue, Keith saying he should keep trying, Jerry saying you don't know what it feels like to lose all the time. Keith says, "You don't want me to think you're a poor sport, do you?" Jerry says it's not being a poor sport, it's just no fun for him when he never wins. Keith says, "Think about me. If you won't play with me, where am I going to play? No one else has a Ping-Pong table." They argue louder and louder, and Jerry's 11- or 12-year-old sister, Jean, and her friends, Lisa and Ellen, come in to see what's the matter. When the boys tell Jean, she says she can see that they both have a point. Why don't they not play Ping-Pong with each other for a while, and she will let Jerry practice with her. Then maybe when he gets better, he could try playing with Keith again. At first Jerry says that wouldn't do any good. Finally, Jean suggests that maybe it's time to try playing with Keith again. Jerry says he doesn't think he's good enough, and he doesn't want to lose. Jean says he'll never know if he doesn't try. So they play.

At the beginning of the game, Jerry says that if he loses this time, he'll give up Ping-Pong for good. Keith claims he's out of practice, says Jerry really has gotten a lot better. Jerry wins and is all excited, but Lisa says, "Boy, Keith, you sure didn't do very well." Jerry stops leaping around and says, "You *were* just out of practice, right? You didn't let me win, did you?"

Open-ended Probes
1. What do you think is the problem in this story?
2. What do you think the older boy, Keith, did? Do you think he let Jerry win? Why would he do that? Why might he not let Jerry win?
3. Have you ever known a kid (person) like Jerry? What was he like? What do you think made him that way?

I. *Subjectivity*
1. If Jerry wins, but finds out that Keith let him win, how will Jerry feel? Why? Could he feel more than just___about winning? Could he feel both happy and upset? Happy that he won, but upset that Keith let him win? How could that be? How can you feel two ways about something?
*2. If Jerry is happy about finally winning, but sad that Keith let him win, how would he feel overall? Could he have "mixed feelings"? What would that mean? Have you ever had mixed feelings about something? Tell me about it. How can feelings be mixed, like happy and sad?
*3. If Jerry is smiling even after he finds out that Keith let him win, does that mean he is happy? Is a person always happy when you see that person smiling? Could a person look happy on the outside, but be sad on the inside? How is that possible?

II. *Self-Awareness*
1. Suppose Jerry finds out that Keith let him win and he says to Keith, "I never cared about Ping-Pong anyway." Why might he say something like that? Why might he say something he didn't mean?
*2. Could Jerry fool himself into thinking he didn't care about the game? How could he do that? (Why couldn't he do that?) Is it ever possible to really fool yourself?
3. Is there a difference between fooling yourself and fooling another person? What is it?
*4. If Jerry tells himself he is going to lose, will that affect the way he plays the game? Why would that be?
5. Would it help Jerry if he had confidence? Why might confidence help? What is confidence, anyway? (If Subject says he or she doesn't know, say, a feeling a person can do a good job.) How does a person gain confidence? Can you have confidence even if you lose? How?
6. If Keith lets Jerry win, but then Jerry finds out, what will happen to Jerry's confidence? Do you think Jerry might be embarrassed if he finds out that Keith let him win? Why? What does it mean when someone is embarrassed?

III. *Personality*
1. What kind of person do you think Jerry is? Does watching how he plays Ping-Pong with Keith tell you what kind of person he might be? From seeing the way he plays Ping-Pong, what kind of person do you think he would be in school?
*2. Do you think Jerry is a poor sport (or sore loser, stubborn, thin-skinned, overly competitive)? What would that tell you about him? What does it mean when you say a person is a poor sport? What makes a person become a poor sport?

*3. Is there a difference between being a poor sport and just being tired of losing? What is the difference?
4. Can Jerry be a poor sport sometimes but other times not make a big deal if he wins or loses? How is that possible?
5. Can there be a different side to Jerry, other than just being a poor sport? Can there be different parts to a person?
*6. What kind of personality do you think Jerry has? What does it mean when you say that you know what kind of personality someone has? Can a person have more than one personality? How is that possible?

IV. *Personality Change*
*1. If Jerry is a poor sport now, what will he be like when he grows up? Do you think he will change or will he stay the same? What might make him change? How do people change as they get older?
2. If Jerry was older, do you think he would act the same when he lost at Ping-Pong? How does being older change the way a person acts?
*3. If Jerry knows he is a poor sport, do you think there is any way he can change the way he is? How can persons change themselves?
*4. If you were Jerry's friend, how might you help him change from being a poor sport? Anything besides letting him win? What might you say to him to help him change? Why that?

Following are two sample dilemmas from the friendship domain for younger and older children, followed by sample interview questions.

Friendship Domain Interview

For interviewing younger children on concepts of friendship, we have found the first version below to be preferable, while for adolescents and adults the second version is more appropriate. These same stories are available in filmstrip form published by Guidance Associates. For the children's version, show *First Things: Elementary Sound Filmstrips: How Would You Feel? Part II*. For adolescent–adult version, *Relationships and Values: Friendship—Caught in the Middle, Part I*. One set of questions is used to interview after either story. However, the names for the childhood version (Kathy, Becky, and Jeanette) differ from those of the adolescent version (Charlene, Joanne, and Tina).

THE FRIENDS' DILEMMA (CHILDREN'S VERSION)

Kathy and Becky have been best friends since they were 5 years old. They went to the same kindergarten and have been in the same class ever since. Every Saturday they would try to do something special together, go to the park or the store, or play something special at home. They always had a good time with each other.
One day a new girl, Jeanette, moved into their neighborhood and soon in-

troduced herself to Kathy and Becky. Right away Jeanette and Kathy seemed to hit it off very well. They talked about where Jeanette was from and the things she could be doing in her new town. Becky, on the other hand, didn't seem to like Jeanette very well. She thought Jeanette was a showoff, but was also jealous of all the attention Kathy was giving Jeanette.

When Jeanette left the other two alone, Becky told Kathy how she felt about Jeanette. "What did you think of her, Kathy? I thought she was kind of pushy, butting in on us like that."

"Come on, Becky. She's new in town and just trying to make friends. The least we can do is to be nice to her."

"Yeah, but that doesn't mean we have to be friends with her," replied Becky. "Anyway, what would you like to do this Saturday? You know those old puppets of mine, I thought we could fix them up and make our own puppet show."

"Sure, Becky, that sounds great," said Kathy. "I'll be over after lunch. I better go home now. See you tomorrow."

Later that evening Jeanette called Kathy and surprised her with an invitation to the circus, the last show before it left town. The only problem was that the circus happened to be at the same time that Kathy had promised to go to Becky's. Kathy didn't know what to do, go to the circus and leave her best friend alone, or stick with her best friend and miss a good time.

THE FRIENDS' DILEMMA (ADOLESCENT AND ADULT VERSION)

Charlene and Joanne have been good friends since they were five. Now they were in high school and Joanne was trying out for the school play. As usual she was nervous about how she had done, but Charlene was there to tell her she was very good and give her moral support. Still Joanne was worried that a newcomer in school would get the part. The new girl, Tina, came over to congratulate Joanne on her performance and then asked if she could join the girls for a snack. Right away Charlene and Tina seemed to hit it off very well. They talked about where Tina was from and the kinds of things she could do in her new school. Joanne, on the other hand, didn't seem to like Tina very well. She thought Tina was a little pushy, and maybe she was a bit jealous over all the attention Charlene was giving Tina.

When Tina left the other two alone, Joanne and Charlene arranged to get together on Saturday, because Joanne had a problem that she would like to talk over with Charlene. But later that day, Tina called Charlene and asked her to go to Washington to see a play on Saturday.

Charlene had a dilemma. She would have jumped at the chance to go with Tina, but she had already promised to see Joanne. Joanne might have understood and been happy that Charlene had the chance to go, or she might feel like she was losing her best friend when she really needed her.

Open-ended Probes

1. What do you think the problem is in this story?
2. What do you think Kathy/Charlene will do, choose to be with her old friend, Becky/Joanne, or go with the new girl, Jeannette/Tina? Why? Which do you think is more important: to be with an old friend or make new friends? Why?
3. Do you have a best friend? What kind of friendship do you have with that person? What makes that person your best friend? (Use this information for probing personal knowledge of remaining friendship issues.)

I. *Formation*
   A. *Motives—Why friends are important.*
      1. Jeannette/Tina is a new girl in town and is trying to make friends. Why do you think making friends is important to her?
      *2. Why are friends important? Why does a person need a good friend?
   B. *Mechanisms—How one goes about making friends.*
      1. How should Jeannette/Tina go about making new friends? What are some things she should keep in mind?
      *2. Is it easy or hard to make a good friend? Why? Why is it sometimes_____(the opposite)?
   C. *Ideal friend—Qualities of persons who make a good friend.*
      *1. What kind of person makes a good friend?
      2. What kind of person would you not want as a friend?

II. *Closeness–Intimacy—*Different types of friendships and factors which make for close and affectionate friendships.
    *1. What kind of friendship do you think Kathy/Charlene and Becky/Joanne have? (Do you think it is a good or close friendship?) What is a really good close friendship? Does it take something special to have a very good friendship? What kinds of things do good friends know about each other?
    2. What does being friends for a long time, like Kathy/Charlene and Becky/Joanne have, do for a friendship?
    3. What makes close good friendships last?
    *4. What kinds of things can good friends talk about that other friends sometimes can't? What kinds of problems can they talk over?
    5. What makes two friends feel really close to each other?
    *6. What's the difference between the kind of friendship Becky/Joanne and Kathy/Charlene have and Kathy/Charlene's and Jeannette/Tina's friendship? Are there different kinds of friendship? What's the difference between "regular" and "best" friendship?
    7. Is it better when close friends are like each other or different from each other? Why? In what way should good friends be the same? In what way should they be different?
    *8. Which is better to have (be with)—one close friend or a group of regular friends? Why?

III. *Trust and Reciprocity—*The value and nature of trust and reciprocity in a close friendship.
     *1. What kinds of things do good friends, like Becky/Joanne and Kathy/Charlene, do for each other? Is it important to do things for each other for a good friendship? Why?
     2. Do you think it is important for Becky/Joanne and Kathy/Charlene to trust each other in order to stay good friends? Why?
     *3. Do you think trust is important for a good friendship? Why?
     *4. What is trust anyway? Is it something more than just keeping secrets and paying back? Is there something more, something deeper to trust?
     5. Is there a difference between the trust someone has in a best friend and the trust you have in someone you just know from school or something?

IV. *Jealousy—*The nature of jealousy and its effects on friendship.
    1. If Kathy/Charlene and Jeannette/Tina (the new girl) become good friends, what will that do to Kathy/Charlene's and Becky/Joanne's friendship?

*2. How do you think Becky/Joanne feels about the new friendship? Do you think she might get jealous? What do you think she is jealous of?
*3. What does it mean to be jealous in a friendship? What does jealousy do to a friendship? How can jealousy hurt a friendship?

V. *Conflict Resolution*—How arguments or conflicts are settled between good friends and the effect of arguments on friendships.
   1. If Becky/Joanne and Kathy/Charlene have a big argument over this problem, how could they work things out so they stay good friends?
   2. Could their friendship actually become better from having this argument? Can arguments ever help a friendship?
   *3. Can people be friends even if they are having arguments? How is that possible?
   *4. How should arguments be settled between good friends?
   *5. What kinds of things do good friends sometimes fight or argue about?

VI. *Termination*—How and why close friendships break up.
   1. If Kathy/Charlene and Jeanette/Tina become good friends, what do you think will happen to Becky/Joanne's and Kathy/Charlene's friendship? Do you think it might break up because of it?
   *2. What makes friendships break up?
   3. Why is it that these little things can sometimes become arguments big enough to ruin a friendship? How do little things sometimes get blown up between friends?
   *4. What does a person lose when they lose a good friend?
   *5. Why is it that good friends sometimes grow apart? What does it mean to grow apart from a good friend?

References

Anthony, E. J. The significance of Jean Piaget for child psychiatry. *British Journal of Medical Psychology*, 1956, *29*, 20-34.

Baldwin, J. M. *Social and ethical interpretations in mental development.* New York: Macmillan, 1906.

Bettelheim, B. *The uses of enchantment: The meaning and importance of fairy tales.* New York: Knopf, 1976.

Blatt, M., & Kohlberg, L. The effects of classroom moral discussion upon children's moral development. *Journal of Moral Education*, 1975, *4*(2), 129-161.

Blumer, H. *Symbolic interaction.* Englewood Cliffs, N.J.: Prentice-Hall, 1969.

Blurton-Jones, N. (Ed.) *Ethological studies of child behavior.* Cambridge, England: Cambridge University Press, 1972.

Box, G. E. P., & Jenkins, G. M. *Time-series analysis forecasting and control.* San Francisco: Holden-Day, 1979.

Brion-Meisels, S. Helping, sharing, and cooperation: An intervention study of middle childhood. Unpublished doctoral dissertation, University of Utah, 1977.

Brion-Meisels, S. Applications of social-cognitive research in practical settings. Unpublished paper, Judge Baker Guidance Center, Boston, 1979.

Bronfenbrenner, U. *Two worlds of childhood: U.S. and U.S.S.R.* New York: Russell Sage Foundation, 1970.

Bronfenbrenner, U. Toward an experimental ecology of human development. *American Psychologist*, 1977, *32*, 513-531.

Bronfenbrenner, U. *The ecology of human development.* Cambridge, Mass.: Harvard University Press, 1979.

Broughton, J. The development of concepts of self, mind, reality, and knowledge. In W. Damon (Ed.), *Social cognition: New directions for child development (No. 1)*. San Francisco: Jossey Bass, 1978.

Brown, R. Moral reasoning and conduct. In R. Brown & R. Hernstein (Eds.), *Psychology*. New York: Harcourt, Brace, Jovanovich, 1975.

Bruss-Saunders, E. Children's thought about parents: A developmental study. Unpublished doctoral dissertation, Harvard Graduate School of Education, 1979.

Byrne, D. F. The development of role taking in adolescence. Unpublished doctoral dissertation, Harvard Graduate School of Education, 1973.

Campbell, D. T. From description to experimentation: Interpreting trends in quasi-experiments. In C. W. Harris (Ed.), *Problems in measuring change*. Madison, Wis.: University of Wisconsin Press, 1963.

Campbell, D. T. Reforms as experiments. *American Psychologist*, 1969, *24*, 409–429.

Campbell, D. T., & Stanley, J. C. *Experimental and quasi-experimental designs for research*. Chicago: Rand McNally, 1963.

Chandler, M. J. Egocentrism and antisocial behavior: The assessment and training of social perspective-taking skills. *Developmental Psychology*, 1973, *9*, 326–332.

Chandler, M. J. Social cognition: A selective review of current research. In W. F. Overton & J. M. Gallagher (Eds.), *Knowledge and development (Vol. 1): Advances in research and theory*. New York: Plenum Press, 1976.

Chandler, M., Paget, K., & Koch, D. The child's demystification of psychological defense mechanisms: A structural and developmental analysis. *Developmental Psychology*, 1978, *14*(3), 197–206.

Chassan, J. B. Intensive design in clinical research. *Psychosomatics*, 1965, *6*, 289–294.

Chassan, J. B. *Research designs in clinical psychology and psychiatry*. New York: Appleton-Century-Crofts, 1967.

Chassan, J. B., & Bellak, L. An introduction to intensive design. In L. Gottschalk & A. Auerbach (Eds.), *Methods of research in psychotherapy*. New York: Appleton-Century-Crofts, 1965.

Clarfield, S. P. The development of a teacher referral form for identifying early school maladaptation. *American Journal of Community Psychology*, 1974, *2*(2), 199–210.

Cole, M., Gay, J., Glick, J. A., & Sharp, D. W. *The cultural context of learning and thinking: An exploration in experimental anthropology*. New York: Basic Books, 1971.

Cole, M., Hood, L., & McDermott, R. Ecological niche picking: Ecological invalidity as an axiom of experimental cognitive psychology. Unpublished paper, Rockefeller University, 1979.

Cole, M., & Scribner, S. *Culture and thought: A psychological introduction*. New York: Wiley, 1974.

Cooney, E. W. Social-cognitive development: Applications to intervention and evaluation in the elementary grades. *The Counseling Psychologist*, 1977, *6*(4), 6–9.

Cooney, E. W. Social-cognitive development: An experimental intervention in the elementary grades. Unpublished doctoral dissertation, Harvard Graduate School of Education, 1978.

Cowan, P. A. *Piaget with feeling: Cognitive, social, and emotional dimensions*. New York: Holt, Rinehart & Winston, 1978.

Cronbach, L. J., Gleser, G. C., Nanda, H., & Rajaratnam, N. *The dependability of behavioral measurements: Theory of generalizability for scores and profiles*. New York: Wiley, 1972.

Damon, W. *The social world of the child*. San Francisco: Jossey-Bass, 1977.

Damon, W., & Gerson, R. Hypothetical and "real-life" moral judgment. Paper presented at the 1975 meeting of the Eastern Psychological Association, New York.

Dimond, R., Havens, R., & Jones, A. A conceptual framework for the practice of prescriptive eclecticism in psychology. *American Psychologist*, 1978, *33*, 239–248.

Enright, R. D. An experimental analysis of a social-cognitive model through a cross-age training program. Unpublished doctoral dissertation, University of Minnesota, 1977.

Erwin, J., & Kuhn, D. Development of children's understanding of the multiple determination underlying human behavior. *Developmental Psychology*, 1979, *15*(3), 352–353.

Feffer, M. H. The cognitive implications of role-taking behavior. *Journal of Personality*, 1959, *27*, 152–168.

Feffer, M. J., & Gourevitch, V. Cognitive aspects of role taking in children. *Journal of Personality*, 1960, *28*, 383–396.

Flavell, J. H. The development of inferences about others. In T. Mischel (Ed.), *Understanding other persons*. Oxford, England: Blackwell, Basil & Mott, 1974.

Flavell, J. H. *Cognitive development*. Englewood Cliffs, N.J.: Prentice-Hall, 1977.

Flavell, J. H., Fry, C., Wright, J., & Jarvis, P. *The development of role-taking and communication skills in children*. New York: John Wiley, 1968.

Flavell, J. H., & Wohlwill, J. F. Formal and functional aspects of cognitive development. In D. Elkind & J. H. Flavell (Eds.), *Studies in cognitive development: Essays in honor of Jean Piaget*. New York: Oxford University Press, 1969.

Forbes, D., & Selman, R. L. Symbolic logic assessment battery. Harvard—Judge Baker Social Reasoning Project, Cambridge, Mass., 1974.

Freud, A. *Normality and pathology in childhood*. New York: International Universities Press, 1965.

Gesten, E. A health resources inventory: The development of a measure of the personal and social competence of elementary school age children. Unpublished doctoral dissertation, University of Rochester, 1974.

Gibbs, J. C. The meaning of ecologically oriented inquiry in contemporary psychology. *American Psychologist*, 1979, *34*(2), 127–140.

Gilligan, C. In another voice. *Harvard Educational Review*, 1977, *47*(4), 481–517.

Glass, G. V., Willson, V. L., & Gottman, J. M. *Design and analysis of time-series experiments*. Boulder, Colo.: Laboratory of Educational Research Reports, University of Colorado, 1972.

Gottman, J. M. "N" of one and "N" of two research in psychotherapy. *Psychological Bulletin*, 1973, *20*, 93–106.

Gottman, J. M., & McFall, R. M. Self-monitoring effects in a program for potential high-school dropouts: A time-series analysis. *Journal of Consulting and Clinical Psychology*, 1972, *39*, 273–281.

Gottman, J. M., McFall, R. M., & Barnett, J. T. Design and analysis of research using time series. *Psychological Bulletin*, 1969, *72*, 299–306.

Gottman, J., & Parkhurst, J. A developmental theory of friendship and acquaintance-ship process. In A. W. Collins (Ed.), *Thirteenth Minnesota symposium on child psychology*. Hillsdale, N.J.: Lawrence Erlbaum Associates, 1980.

Harter, S. A cognitive-developmental approach to children's expression of conflicting feelings and a technique to facilitate such expression in play therapy. *Journal of Consulting and Clinical Psychology*, 1977, *45*, 417–432.

Heider, F. *The psychology of interpersonal relations*. New York: Wiley, 1958.

Hill, J. P., & Palmquist, W. J. Social cognition and social relations in early adolescence. *International Journal of Behavioral Development*, 1978, *1*, 1–36.

Hoffman, M., & Saltztein, H. Parent discipline and the child's moral development. *Journal of Personality and Social Psychology*, 1967, *5*, 45–57.

Hollingshead, A. *Two-factor index of social position*. New Haven: Yale University Press, 1965.

Hollos, M., & Cowan, P. Social isolation and cognitive development: Logical operations and role-taking abilities in three Norwegian social settings. *Child Development*, 1973, *44*, 630–641.

Holstein, C. Development of moral judgment: A longitudinal study of males and females. *Child Development*, 1976, *47*, 51–61.

Holtzman, W. Statistical models for the study of change in the single case. In C. W. Harris (Ed.), *Problems in measuring change*. Madison, Wis.: University of Wisconsin Press, 1963.

Inhelder, B., & Piaget, J. *The growth of logical thinking: From childhood to adolescence*. New York: Basic Books, 1958.

Inhelder, B., & Sinclair, H. Learning cognitive structures. In P. H. Mussen, J. Langer, & M. Covington (Eds.), *Trends and issues in developmental psychology*. New York: Holt, Rinehart & Winston, 1969.

Inhelder, B., Sinclair, H., & Bovet, M. *Learning and the development of cognition*. Cambridge, Mass.: Harvard University Press, 1974.

Jaquette, D. Developing conceptions of peer-group relations from childhood through adolescence: A developmental social psychological approach. Paper presented at the 1976 Eastern Psychological Association, New York City.

Jaquette, D. S. A longitudinal analysis of interpersonal awareness and real-life problem solving in a group of disturbed preadolescents: A clinical-developmental approach. Unpublished doctoral dissertation, Harvard Graduate School of Education, 1979.

Jones, M., Bayley, N., MacFarlane, J., & Honzick, M. (Eds.) *The course of human development*. Waltham, Mass.: Xerox College Publishing, 1971.

Kohlberg, L. Stage and sequence: The cognitive-developmental approach to socialization. In D. Goslin (Ed.), *Handbook of socialization theory and research*. Chicago: Rand McNally, 1969.

Kohlberg, L., Sharf, P., & Hickey, J. The justice structure of the prison—theory and an intervention. *The Prison Journal*, 1972, *51*(2), 3–14.

Kuhn, D. Inducing development experimentally: Comments on a research program. *Developmental Psychology*, 1974, *10*(5), 590–600.

Kuhn, D. Short-term longitudinal evidence of the sequentiality of Kohlberg's early stages of moral judgment. *Developmental Psychology*, 1976, *12*(2), 162–166.

Kuhn, D., & Angelev, J. An experimental study of the development of formal operational thought. *Child Development*, 1976, *47*, 897–906.

Kuhn, D., & Brannock, J. The development of the isolation of variables scheme in experimental and "natural experiment" contexts. *Developmental Psychology*, 1977, *13*(1), 9–14.

Kurdek, L. A. Perspective taking as the cognitive basis of children's moral development: A review of the literature. *Merrill-Palmer Quarterly*, 1978, *24*(1), 3–28.

Lavin, D. R. A study of the patterns of social reasoning in emotionally disturbed children under varying contexts. Unpublished doctoral dissertation, Harvard Graduate School of Education, 1979.

Lewis, M. Interpretation in child analysis: Developmental considerations. *Journal of Child Analysis*, 1974, *13*, 32–53.

Lieberman, M. Evaluation of a social intervention. Paper presented at the 1979 Society for Research in Child Development, San Francisco.

Livesley, W. J., & Bromley, D. B. *Person perception in childhood and adolescence*. New York: Wiley, 1973.

Loevinger, J. *Ego development*. San Francisco: Jossey-Bass, 1976.

Loevinger, J., Wessler, R., & Redmore, C. *Measuring ego development, Vols. 1 and 2*. San Francisco: Jossey-Bass, 1970.

Lorion, R., Cowen, E., & Caldwell, R. Problem types of children referred to a school based mental health program. *Journal of Consulting and Clinical Psychology*, 1974, *42*(4), 491–496.

McCall, R. B. Challenges to a science of developmental psychology. *Child Development*, 1977, *48*, 333–344.

Mead, G. H. *Mind, self and society.* Chicago: University of Chicago Press, 1934.

Miller, P. H., Kessel, F. S., & Flavell, J. H. Thinking about people thinking about people thinking about . . . : A study of social-cognitive development. *Child Development,* 1970, *41,* 613–623.

Moir, D. J. Egocentrism and the emergence of conventional morality in preadolescent girls. *Child Development,* 1974, *45,* 299–304.

Mueller, E., & Brenner, J. The origins of social skills and interaction among playgroup toddlers. *Child Development,* 1977, *48,* 854–861.

Nesselroade, R. J. Application of multivariate strategies to problems of measuring and structuring long-term change. In L. R. Goulet & P. B. Baltes (Eds.), *Life-span developmental psychology: Research and theory.* New York: Academic Press, 1970.

Odier, C. *Anxiety and magic thinking.* New York: International Universities Press, 1956.

Parke, R. Issues in child development: On the myth of the field-lab distinction. *Newsletter of the Society for Research in Child Development,* Winter, 1976.

Piaget, J. *The language and thought of the child.* London: Routledge & Kegan Paul, 1952. (Originally published in 1926.)

Piaget, J. *The moral judgment of the child.* New York: Free Press, 1965. (Originally published in 1932.)

Piaget, J., & Inhelder, B. *The growth of logical thinking from childhood to adolescence.* New York: Basic Books, 1958.

Piaget, J., & Inhelder, B. *The early growth of logic in the child: Classification and seriation.* London: Routledge & Kegan Paul, 1964.

Porges, S. W. Ontogenetic comparisons. *International Journal of Psychology,* 1976, *11*(3), 203–214.

Redl, F. *When we deal with children.* New York: Free Press, 1956.

Redl, F., & Wineman, D. *Children who hate: The disorganization and breakdown of behavior controls.* New York: Free Press, 1951.

Redl, F., & Wineman, D. *Controls from within: Treatment of the aggressive child.* New York: Free Press, 1952.

Rest, J. Developmental psychology as a guide to values education: A review of "Kohlbergian" programs. *Review of Educational Research,* 1974, *44,* 241–259.

Rest, J. Longitudinal study of the Defining Issues Test of moral judgment: A strategy for analyzing developmental change. *Developmental Psychology,* 1975, *11*(6), 738–748.

Rest, J. *The D.I.T.* Minneapolis: University of Minnesota Press, 1979.

Sameroff, A., & Chandler, M. Perinatal risk and the continuum of care-taking casualty. In F. Horowitz, M. Hetherington, S. Scarr, & G. Siegel (Eds.), *Review of child development research, Vol. 4.* Chicago: University of Chicago Press, 1975.

Santostefano, S. *A biodevelopmental approach to clinical child psychology: Cognitive controls and cognitive control therapy.* New York: Wiley, 1979.

Schaefer, C. E., & Millman, H. L. *Therapies for children.* San Francisco: Jossey-Bass, 1977.

Scharfman, M. The psychoanalytic approach. In B. Wolman, J. Egan, & A. Ross (Eds.), *Handbook of treatment of mental disorders in childhood and adolescence.* Englewood Cliffs, N.J.: Prentice-Hall, 1978.

Selman, R. L. The relation of role taking to the development of moral judgment in children. *Child Development,* 1971, *42*(1), 79–91. (a)

Selman, R. L. Taking another's perspective: Role-taking development in early childhood. *Child Development,* 1971, *42*(6), 1721–1734. (b)

Selman, R. L. Social-cognitive understanding: A guide to educational and clinical practice. In T. Lickona (Ed.), *Moral development and behavior.* New York: Holt, Rinehart & Winston, 1976. (a)

Selman, R. L. Toward a structural-developmental analysis of interpersonal relationship concepts: Research with normal and disturbed preadolescent boys. In A. Pick (Ed.), *Tenth annual Minnesota symposium on child psychology*. Minneapolis: University of Minnesota Press, 1976. (b)

Selman, R. L., & Byrne, D. F. A structural-developmental analysis of levels of role taking in middle childhood. *Child Development*, 1974, *45*(2), 803–806.

Selman, R., & Damon, W. The necessity (but insufficiency) of social perspective taking for conceptions of justice at three early levels. In D. DePalma & J. Foley (Eds.), *Contemporary issues in moral development*. Hillsdale, N.J.: Lawrence Erlbaum Associates, 1975.

Selman, R., & Jaquette, D. Stability and oscillation in interpersonal awareness: A clinical developmental approach. In C. B. Keasy (Ed.), *Twenty-fifth Nebraska symposium on motivation*. Lincoln: University of Nebraska Press, 1978.

Selman, R. L., Jaquette, D., & Bruss-Saunders, E. Assessing interpersonal understanding: An interview and scoring manual. Harvard—Judge Baker Social Reasoning Project, Cambridge, Mass., 1979.

Selman, R., Jaquette, D., & Lavin, D. Interpersonal awareness in children: Toward an integration of developmental and clinical child psychology. *American Journal of Orthopsychiatry*, 1977, *47*(1), 264–274.

Selman, R. L., Lavin, D., & Brion-Meisels, S. Developing the capacity for self-reflection: A look at troubled children's conceptions-in-theory and conceptions-in-use. Unpublished manuscript, Harvard University, 1979.

Selman, R. L., & Stone, C. The self and social relations. Unpublished manuscript, Harvard University, 1979.

Selman, R. L., & Yando, R. (Eds.) *Clinical-developmental psychology: New directions for child development (No. 7)*. San Francisco: Jossey Bass, 1980.

Shantz, C. U. The development of social cognition. In E. M. Hetherington (Ed.), *Review of child development research, Vol. 5*. Chicago: University of Chicago Press, 1975.

Siegel, L. S., & Brainerd, C. J. (Eds.) *Alternatives to Piaget: Critical essays on the theory*. New York: Academic Press, 1978.

Sperry, L. A hierarchy for clinical interpretation. *Individual Psychologist*, 1975, *12*, 19–24.

Stein, N. How children understand stories: A developmental analysis. In S. Asher & J. Gottman (Eds.), *The development of friendship*. New York: Cambridge University Press, 1980.

Sullivan, H. S. *The interpersonal theory of psychiatry*. New York: W. W. Norton, 1953.

Templeton, R. G., Sperry, B., & Prentice, N. M. Theoretical and technical considerations in therapeutic tutoring of children with psychogenic learning problems. *Journal of the American Academy of Child Psychiatry*, 1967, *6*, 464–477.

Turiel, E. Developmental processes in the child's moral thinking. In P. Mussen, J. Langer, & M. Covington (Eds.), *Trends and issues in developmental psychology*. New York: Holt, Rinehart & Winston, 1969.

Turiel, E. The development of social concepts: Mores, customs and conventions. In D. DePalma & J. Foley (Eds.), *Moral development: Current theory and research*. Hillsdale, N.J.: Lawrence Erlbaum Associates, 1975.

Turiel, E. Morality and social convention: Two separate and distinct systems. In C. B. Keasey (Ed.), *Twenty-fifth Nebraska symposium on motivation*. Lincoln, Nebraska: University of Nebraska Press, 1978.

Turner, R. H. *Family interaction*. New York: Wiley, 1970.

Weiner, M. L. *The cognitive unconscious: Piagetian approach to psychotherapy*. Davis, Calif.: International Psychological Press, 1975.

Wellman, H. M., & Lempers, J. D. The naturalistic communicative abilities of two-year-olds. *Child Development*, 1977, *48*, 1052–1057.

Werner, H. The concept of development from a comparative and organismic point of view. In D. Harris (Ed.), *The concept of development.* Minneapolis: University of Minnesota Press, 1957.

Werner, H. *Comparative psychology of mental development.* New York: International Universities Press, 1964. (Originally published in 1948.)

Willems, E. P. Behavioral ecology and experimental analysis: Courtship is not enough. In J. R. Nesselroade & H. W. Reese (Eds.), *Life-span developmental psychology: Methodological issues.* New York: Academic Press, 1973.

Wohlwill, J. F. The age variable in psychological research. *Psychological Review,* 1970, *77,* 49–64. (a)

Wohlwill, J. F. Methodology and research strategy in the study of developmental change. In L. R. Goulet & P. B. Baltes (Eds.), *Life-span developmental psychology: Research and theory.* New York: Academic Press, 1970. (b)

Wohlwill, J. F. *The study of behavioral development.* New York: Academic Press, 1973.

Zigler, E., Levine, J., & Gould, L. Cognitive processes in the development of children in appreciation of humor. *Child Development,* 1966, *37,* 507–518.

Subject Index

Training issues, 282–288
  practioner training, 285–288
  researcher training, 283–285
Transition, developmental stage, *see* Stage
  transition, developmental
Trust, 84, *see also* Friendship domain of interpersonal understanding
Two-person strategy games, 6, 26, 51–55, *see
  also* Flavell's 5¢/10¢ game; Social
  perspectve taking, pure perspective
  taking
  levels of, 58–61
  skills of
    nonsocial logical, 52–55
    nonsocial perceptual, 52–55
    social logical, 52–55
    social perceptual, 52–55
Two-way relations, *see* Interpersonal understanding, stages of, stage 2

U

Unconscious, 105, 135, *see also* Mind
Understanding, interpersonal, *see* Interpersonal understanding
Unilateral relations, *see* Interpersonal understanding, stages of, stage 1

V

Validity, 6, *see also* Research, phases of,
  phase 2, validation; Reliability; Stage
  developmental theory
  of levels of social perspective taking,
    40–46, *see also* Coding; Demographic
    variables; Social perspective taking
  of measures, 5
  of stages of interpersonal understanding,
    159–162, 171–174, 175–211, *see also*
    Coding; Demographic variables; In-
    terpersonal understanding; Sample
    characteristics
  behavioral correspondences, 200–204,
    see also Behavior; Teacher ratings
  clinical-comparative analysis, 193–199
  demographic data, 183–189
  longitudinal sequential analysis, 189-
    193
  measures used, 171–174
  structured wholeness and variability,
    175–182

W

Werner, Heinz, 206, 283, 298, 311